OMAN

COMPARATIVE POLITICS
AND INTERNATIONAL STUDIES SERIES

Series editors, Christophe Jaffrelot and Alain Dieckhoff
Series managing editor, Miriam Perier

The series consists of original manuscripts and translations of noteworthy manuscripts and publications in the social sciences emanating from the foremost French researchers.

The focus of the series is the transformation of politics and society by transnational and domestic factors—globalisation, migration and religion. States are more permeable to external influence than ever before and this phenomenon is accelerating processes of social and political change the world over. In seeking to understand and interpret these transformations, this series gives priority to social trends from below as much as to the interventions of state and non-state actors.

MARC VALERI

Oman

Politics and Society in the Qaboos State

HURST & COMPANY, LONDON

First published in the United Kingdom by
C. Hurst & Co. (Publishers) Ltd, 2009.
This revised and updated paperback edition published 2017.
41 Great Russell Street, London, WC1B 3PL
© Marc Valeri, 2017
All rights reserved.
Printed in India

A catalogue data record for this volume is available from the British Library.

ISBN: 9781849044851

This book is printed using paper from registered sustainable and managed sources.

www.hurstpublishers.com

This volume has been published and translated with the financial support of the Centre National du Livre.

CONTENTS

CONTENTS

ACKNOWLEDGEMENTS

The book is based on a doctoral dissertation supervised by Olivier Roy at the Institut d'Etudes Politiques in Paris. I am deeply grateful to him for his unfailing help, trust and support all along the work. I also benefited substantially from all my professors and colleagues whose criticism and comments were of essential help in giving this work its final form; first of all, the dissertation's examiners: Gilles Kepel, who made me the honour to chair the *viva voce* and who supported me since my Master's academic year; Henry Laurens, Elizabeth Picard and Ghassan Salame, whose inputs and experience considerably sharpened my own thinking; François Bafoil, who introduced me to scientific research and never saved his encouragement; Jean-François Bayart, for his constant interest in my research and without whom this book would not have been possible; Laurence Louër and Dale F. Eickelman, for their helpful comments. I will always be grateful to the staff of the Institute of Arab and Islamic Studies of Exeter, where I prepared the manuscript of this book, for their support and encouragement; I would like to express my special gratitude to Tim Niblock, Gerd Nonneman and James Onley, for their invaluable interest and enthusiasm for my research and for their constant support. I don't forget Claire Beaudevin, for the time she took to read and to comment on this study, and from her knowledge of the Omani society I have learnt so much. I must also pay tribute to Michael Dwyer, who gave me the great opportunity to publish this book, and to Jonathan Derrick and Maria Petalidou, who made a considerable job of editing throughout the different versions of the manuscript. May all find here a modest testimony of the debt of gratitude I owe them.

I would like to thank the staff of Sultan Qaboos University, who took me under their wings for one year, as well as the French Embassy in Muscat, for the financial help they provided to me and their continuous interest in my work. My

ACKNOWLEDGEMENTS

stays in Oman were possible thanks to the UK Economic and Social Research Council [grant number ES/J012696/1] and a "Lavoisier" research fellowship from the French Ministry of Foreign Affairs, and thanks also to the assistance I received from the University of La Rochelle and the University of Exeter.

Moreover, I would like to express my gratitude to all those who facilitated my research and who became my friends in Oman. It is not excessive to consider that nothing would have been possible without the confidence Dr Ahmad, Aiman, Humaid, Jamil and Jihad placed in me, for which I will always be grateful. I would like to thank all those who contributed directly or indirectly, by their personal involvement, their enthusiasm or their support, to the progress of my research in Oman, especially Abdallah, Abdelmalik, Agnès and Nasser, Ahmed, al-Mu'tasim, Amer, Anshan, Arshad, Habib, Haitham and his family, Hamud, Hassan, Hassina, Ishaq, Jangbahadur, Khalid, Lindbergh, Muhammad, Muhammad Redha, Murtadha, Musalam, Raid, Said, Saif, Salim, Sameer, Sami, Samira, Shabib, Shadya, Shoaib, Sylvie and Philippe, Vimal, Yahia... and the others.

Finally, I can not find the words to thank my family for their countless support and encouragement; a very special thank to Chérine, who may not realise how much her indispensable presence has helped me, during all these years devoted to Oman.

INTRODUCTION

On 28 April 2004, at the Muscat Intercontinental Hotel, a five-day symposium about the Magan civilisation, organised under the patronage of Oman's Minister of Heritage and Culture Haitham bin Tariq Al Saʻid, Sultan Qaboos' cousin on the paternal side, came to an end. The purpose of this conference, bringing together the world's most famous experts, was to summarise knowledge about this region, which is mentioned as far back as the third millennium BC in Sumerian tablets, because of its contacts with Mesopotamia. But in a more prosaic way, it was an occasion for the Omani authorities to reassert the longevity of human settlement on the modern Sultanate's territory, and to place Magan in the ancestry of the Omani nation.

That same evening, at the Sultan Qaboos Sports Complex in the Muscat suburb of Bawshar, more than 30,000 Omanis, mostly young, sporting the Omani colours, packed the stadium to attend the national team's football match against Iraq. After a good record in its qualifying group for the Athens Olympic Games, the Omani team was in good position to get one of the three positions reserved to Asia in the final tournament, and then participate for the first time in its history in a major competition. Never before had such great expectations crystallised around the team.

Even if it seems odd to link these events, doing so provides a striking snapshot of the identity preoccupations which are affecting the whole of Omani society at the beginning of the twenty-first century. The Sultanate, whose socio-political stability since the accession of the present ruler in 1970 contrasts with the recurrent convulsions in the region, is commonly presented as "the exception which proves the rule",[1] like an island of cautious development in a Persian Gulf disrupted by the great powers' greed. While this perception should not be rejected *a priori*, such a convenient short cut must not lead one

1

to forget the extent of the upheavals occurring in one of the less reported Muslim states, whose rich historical legacy contributes directly to the twists and turns of the contemporary political system.

Presentation of the Sultanate of Oman

The Sultanate of Oman lies in the south-eastern part of the Arabian Peninsula, astride the Tropic of Cancer; it is bordered on the west by the United Arab Emirates (UAE) and Saudi Arabia, on the south by Yemen and on the east by the Indian Ocean. Its area is just below that of Great Britain and Ireland combined. Oman enjoys a hot climate throughout the year over the major part of its territory, with peaks of temperature reaching 50°C in June and July. The heat is all the more stifling on the northern coast because the ocean humidity, blocked by the mountains, attains a 90% rate between May and July.

Very young in its contemporary shape, the country is split into five geographical sections. The Hajar range represents the backbone of the north of the country and stretches from the UAE to the Indian Ocean; these mountains, which reach 3,000 metres in height in their western part (Jabal Shams) and enjoy better rainfall (300 millimetres per year), are divided in the middle by the Wadi Sama'il, a natural gap connecting the Gulf of Oman coast and Muscat with the interior. North of the mountains stretches the Batina, a coastal plain which is only 30 kilometres wide. Greater Muscat lies at the eastern end of this plain. Because of its agricultural potential (palm groves, fruit, vegetables, cereals) the Batina is the most populated region of the country.

South of Hajar, a vast infertile region covers two-thirds of Omani territory, including the famous Rub' al-Khali described by Wilfred Thesiger[2] and populated by scattered nomadic pastoral groups. The most important oil and gas fields (Fahud, Ghaba, Jibal in the north; Nimr, Rima, Marmul in the south) are found in this desert area.[3] In the far north of the country the Musandam Peninsula, divided from the rest of Oman by the Ra's al-Khayma and Fujayra emirates, shuts off the Persian Gulf by projecting into the Strait of Ormuz.

Lastly, in the south, the Dhofar region, on the border with Saudi Arabia and the Yemeni Hadramaut, is organised around a triple mountain chain which forms a tight arc around the narrow coastal plain of Salalah, the second most important Omani town, and which leads in the north to the Rub' al-Khali. The summer monsoon ends its course on the Dhofar range between July and September; this phenomenon allows temperatures to fall to 25°C, so that the landscape looks a bit like a tropical Scotland.

INTRODUCTION

Stability in question

When Sultan Qaboos overthrew his father in July 1970 and assumed the title of Sultan, about fifteen years of civil war had been highlighting the social and political divisions of a territory officially known as the "Sultanate of Muscat and Oman" and marked by extreme international isolation. While the country was far behind its neighbours of the north of the Persian Gulf in oil production—which had started in Oman only in 1967—and there were huge problems in Dhofar, where two-thirds of the province was out of control, the new ruler possessed no legitimacy at all to rule. Neither his father nor he had seized independence from a colonising power; on the contrary Sultan Qaboos, who was not yet thirty, acceded to the throne, and was granted the official independence of the Sultanate, thanks to the British.

Against this background, and given the sensitivity of its geostrategic position, the sociopolitical stability that has characterised the Sultanate for almost forty years now stands out even more. Almost never before 2011 had the banning of parties or other means of public expression generated organised protests in this monarchy where the ruler holds concurrently the positions of Head of State, commander in chief of the armed forces, Prime Minister, Minister of Defence and Minister of Foreign Affairs. The fact that the current authority gives the impression of being perpetual, almost "natural" to observers suggests more than an explanation based on pure and simple coercion, even though that dimension should not be neglected. As Max Weber explained, "every genuine form of domination implies a minimum of voluntary compliance", which can be either by "custom, by affectual ties, by a purely material complex of interests or by ideal motives";[4] but all these elements were marginal or lacking in 1970 in Oman.

Before getting to the heart of the matter, it is necessary to put Sultan Qaboos' reign into the context of modern and contemporary Omani history, so as to understand better how far he is the natural or the arranged heir of his predecessors. While everything seems to indicate that the period after 1970 has radically broken with the previous socio-political arrangements, it is because this seems so obvious that one should be cautious. From the eighteenth century specific aspects of the Oman case appear, especially the unmatched importance attached by Britain to the administration of a region considered early on as highly strategic. The 1920 Seeb Treaty was the outcome of this effort to establish control. It established conditions for peaceful coexistence which was to last for 35 years between two powers each in quest of legitimacy (the Imamate and the Sultanate), but each too weak to overthrow the other and manage to do without the British tutelage over this balance. The discovery of oil came as a late cause of upheaval and can be seen as the root of three different conflicts (the Buraimi dispute in the 1950s, the Jabal Akhdar war in the late 1950s and the Dhofar war), all contributory explanations of the overthrow in 1970 of Sultan Sa'id, who was unable to extend the pact that had granted the political stability.

This historical background will allow us to move on to the study of Oman proper as it has been shaped under the authority of Sultan Qaboos for more than three decades. The ruler inherited a territory without a state in 1970 and immediately faced the need to assert the legitimacy of his accession to the throne, by defining a "new order" for which he alone would have the keys. For the American scholar Adam Przeworski, "What matters for the stability of any regime is not the legitimacy of this particular system of domination, but the presence or absence of preferable alternatives."[5] This assertion fits the Omani case well; Qaboos' idea has been to break with a model in which the temporal Sultanistic legitimacy was only perceived as one among other legitimacies (tribal, Ibadite, etc.), and impose it as the legitimacy above the others, acknowledged as the arbiter of all the others. He had to set himself up as the only worthwhile candidate for power, like a "natural" sovereign; this was to be achieved with the definition of a new collective identity, able to gather together all the ethno-linguistic groups present on Omani territory.

In an important paper on the stability of Middle East monarchies, Lisa Anderson emphasised what she calls the "affinity between monarchy as a regime type and the projects of nation building and state formation".[6] Similarly to what happened in European monarchies in the nineteenth century, these regimes are better equipped than their republican counterparts in the region to develop a centralised policy and appeal to traditions and historical legacies they can model with the aim of dynastic legitimisation. The formation of national identities is a highly political process, which springs up when a group of individuals decides to demonstrate the existence of a nation, with two objectives: first, to discredit the desires of another actor (usually a larger political entity, like a colonial power) to assert its control; secondly, to create and spread allegiance to the nation.

In the Oman case, this strategy was based on previously unknown economic and social development, involving exploitation of a newly significant oil rent, at the same time as full-scale expansion of the state over the territory and the upheaval of traditional socio-political structures. This process made easier the promotion of an Omani national identity, which reframed the references of identity by being centred on the person of Qaboos, who is identified in historiography with the state and, therefore, with contemporary Oman as a whole.

Paradoxically, this process of substitution of identity allegiances, the local giving way to the national, was not to lead to the extinction of "group feelings" (*'asabiyya*, pl. *'asabiyyat*). These became involved in political strategies aimed at the capture of resources granted by the state; thus there was encapsulation of traditional legitimacies, which had operated until recently, into the state apparatus.

At the same time, the ruler endeavoured to inscribe his regime within the framework of a "sultanistic" reinvented tradition, which was a mask for the arbitrariness of his decision making. The appeal to tradition is aimed at toning down population's feelings about the situation of encapsulation imposed by the nation-state. While this "reinvented tradition" has taken concrete form through the pre-eminent position given to "heritage" (*turath*) in a national culture whose "authenticity" is constantly emphasised by the authorities, it has also developed into the political sphere. Thus political practices presented as old and inherited from an Omani consensual and official "political tradition" were adapted to the contemporary context.

Logically, we will be led later to question the viability of such a model. Will it be possible, for Qaboos himself but above all for his successor, to carry on the same policy which is so connected to the current ruler and his close allies? In other words, is "Omanity" firmly rooted enough in mentalities to resist the new social and economic challenges faced by the Sultanate, and potentially adjust while transforming itself to adapt to change? With prospects of diminution of the oil rent, Omani society has to deal with the arrival on the job market of a plethoric youth, torn between the difficulty of separation from traditional structures and the appeal of globalisation that the young appropriate in their own way. These dynamics make the promotion of nationals on the job market a particularly sensitive matter, and exacerbate the frustrations of many sectors of the population. This results in a resurgence of polarisations in society, with new *'asabiyyat* emerging according to lines of cleavage never seen before. Are socio-economic demands likely to call into question the coherence of the model, or will there be adaptation of actors' strategies to the formation of a substitution model? That is what we will try to determine.

1

FOUNDATIONS OF THE MODERN STATE

Very early in history the strategic significance of this peninsula between Mesopotamia and the Indus led the neighbouring empires to take interest in it. Its inhabitants, settled at the confluence of sea routes connecting Egypt, Gulf and India, developed as early as the Magan era a powerful tradition of trading from the ports of Sohar and Qalhat, which is believed to have gone as far as China. Extraction of copper and production of frankincense were the spearhead of this intense trade. At the beginning of the Christian era, colonies of Persian-origin peoples were settled in the Batina and the interior. But it was only after the bursting of Ma'rib dam, in Yemen, in 120 AD that the biggest Arab migrations occurred, in two waves: one through central Arabia and the Persian Gulf coast, the other in the south, by land (Hadramaut) and sea. These two migration waves are at the origin of the tribal affiliations that emerged in Oman, in the form of two alliances—the "Nizarite" tribes, derived from migrants coming by the north, and "Yemenite" ones, from migrants who came by the south. Among the "Yemenites", legend describes the Azd, led by Malik bin Fahm, as the first group to challenge the supremacy of the Persians, to the point of ousting them from the territory at the beginning of the fourth century. The word "*Uman*" seems to have emerged at that time. The scholar 'Abd Allah al-Salimi (1869–1914) explains that this name was that of the *wadi* near Ma'rib where the Azd came from.[1]

The Persians did not take long to return to Oman, so that at the birth of Islam, the territory was divided between a coastal region under direct Sassanid rule and semi-autonomous Arab tribes in the interior, ruled for the Persians by the Julanda dynasty, of Azd origin. Organised in villages in the Jabal Akhdar foothills, the Omani population was composed of sedentary farmers whose cultivation depended on irrigation channels (*falaj*, pl. *aflaj*); these make it possible to get the best return from palm groves, ensure self-sufficiency and thus limit contacts with the outside world.[2]

Table 1: Rulers of Oman since the middle of the 17th century

Dates	*Imam*	*Sultan*
al-Ya'arubi dynasty (1624–1737)		
1624–1649	Nasir bin Murshid	–
1649–1688	Sultan I bin Saif	–
1688–1692	Bal'arab bin Sultan	–
1692–1711	Saif I bin Sultan	–
1711–1719	Sultan II bin Saif	–
1719–1721	Muhanna bin Sultan	–
1721–1737	Sultan bin Murshid	–
Civil War (1737–1730)		
1750–1783	Ahmad bin Sa'id	–
1783–1784	Sa'id bin Ahmad	–
1784–1792	Hamad bin Sa'id	–
1792–1804	Sultan bin Ahmad	–
1804–1806	Badr bin Saif	–
1806–1856	–	Sa'id bin Sultan
1856–1866	–	Thuwaini bin Sa'id
1866–1868	–	Salim bin Thuwaini
1868–1871	'Azzan bin Qais	–
1871–1888	–	Turki bin Sa'id
1888–1913	–	Faisal bin Turki
1913	Imamate renaissance	–
1913–1920	Salim bin Rashid al-Kharusi	Taimur bin Faisal
1920–1932	Muhammad bin 'Abd Allah al-Khalili	–
1932–1954		–
1954–1955	Ghalib bin 'Abd al-Hina'	Sa'id bin Taimur
1955–1970	–	–
1970–...	–	Qaboos bin Sa'id

As early as Year 6 after the Hijra, some Oman inhabitants converted to Islam, and the first mosque of the territory was erected at Sama'il. Afterwards the Prophet's emissary 'Amr bin al-'As persuaded the Julanda to convert also. Islam soon became a political flag for rallying support, which made possible the expulsion of the Persians from the territory and the temporary strengthening of the established dynasty. But paradoxically, it was abroad that Oman's history was to take a different turn, with the birth of the Ibadi sect in Basra.

The primary political role of Ibadism

When 'Ali, Muhammad's son-in-law, was about to win the battle of Siffin in 657 against Mu'awiya, he agreed to the principle of "arbitration" for succession to the Caliphate—i.e. complying with a decision of two scholars on the basis of the Koran. Some of his supporters, shocked by this procedure which, according to them, contravened the principle that "there is no judgement other than God's", left 'Ali's camp in Kufa. This earned them the name of "Kharijite".[3] As their radical ideas attracted more and more sympathy, 'Ali decimated them at the battle of al-Nahrawan in 658. During the twenty following years, the Kharijites remained underground in the Basra region and only sporadically rose up against the town's governor. But their capacity of nuisance to the empire was not so negligible, as it is said to have been a Kharijite who assassinated 'Ali in 661.

In 682 the death of Abu Bilal Mirdas, who had succeeded in gathering around him the different Kharijite trends, hastened the break-up of the sect. Two of his companions took the leadership of the moderate tendency: 'Abd Allah bin Ibad al-Tamimi, who gave his name to the doctrine which would become Ibadism and was the first head of the higher council of Ibadi *'ulama'*, and Jabir bin Zaid al-Azdi. The latter, from Nizwa, is considered as the effective organiser of the sect, both politically and doctrinally. The Ibadi historical sources present him as "the origin of the faith" (*asl al-madhhab*) and name him as the first to hold the title of "Imam of the Muslims".[4] Most of his action consisted in promoting Ibadism to the Caliphs, but he also favoured expansion of his doctrine among many Omanis in Basra and in Oman itself.

The Ibadi doctrine. Ibadism is the moderate version of Kharijism. Ibadi initially differed from the most radical of the Kharijite sect by their refusal to consider non-Kharijite Muslims as apostates. The Caliphate issue was common to all the Kharijites: they rejected the principle of heredity which privileged the Prophet Muhammad's descendants and focused on the election of

9

the Imam. This position, they believed, could be entrusted to any believer, whatever his social class or his tribe, provided that he was morally and religiously irreproachable (both *mujahid* and *mujtahid*). The election must take place under the aegis of a council composed of religious scholars (*'ulama'*) and notables (*a'yan*); the result had to be proclaimed publicly, for popular acclaim. This principle explains why Ibadis call themselves the "people of consultation" (*ahl al-shura*). If the Imam does not respect religious requirements, for health or political reasons, the believers have to declare him illegitimate and dismiss him. Generally the Ibadi doctrine, which is based on a literal interpretation of the texts, is not very different from the Sunni one. The Ibadi believe in perpetual damnation and endorse corporal punishments, especially for murder and adultery, but reject saint worship.

Theoretically, the ultimate goal of the Ibadi is a return to an *umma* unified around an Imam who applies the precepts of the first Caliphs Abu Bakr and 'Umar. Nevertheless, in practice, the Imamate is not absolutely required in two situations: under a fair ruler, even if he is not an elected Imam; and, on the contrary, if the proclamation of the Imamate could endanger the community, when it lives for instance under a despotic regime. In that case, the community is in the state called *al-kitman* (concealment), which can last as long as is required by the political conditions: the *'ulama'* keep in touch in order to provide protection for the community and the transition to the state of *al-dhuhur* (proclamation of the Imamate). An Imam who is elected is not only a religious chief, who is helped in his tasks as judge and theologian by the *'ulama'* council and the *qadis* (judges), but also a head of state, assisted by a consultative council and the *walis* (governors) he appoints in the different towns. Besides, the Imam is a war chief when the community is in danger. Lastly, he is custodian of the public finances[5] and enjoys full power over the state (*dawla*) apparatus, which has always been very limited.

Thus, the confusion of spiritual and temporal powers in the same hands sanctions the perfect expression of the Imamate as the Ibadi *'ulama'* forged it over the centuries. It does not necessarily mean that the Imam was absolutely powerful, for his actions could not contradict the principle that "there is no other judgement than God's", as he could be dismissed by the *'ulama'*. Furthermore, the excommunication, exile or death of a member of the community could be proclaimed only by the *'ulama'* council. As John Wilkinson rightly explains, the Imam is not a legislator, but an executor of the laws, since the "creation of the law is from God and his Prophet; interpretation is the role of the ulama".[6]

Oman as the spiritual centre of Ibadism. When Caliph 'Abd-al-Malik died in 706, relations between Jabir bin Zaid and Basra's governor al-Hajjaj, who had succeeded in bringing Oman back into the Umayyad empire, worsened dramatically: most of the Ibadi chiefs were exiled, including Jabir, in Oman province, or jailed, like Abu 'Ubaida al-Tamimi, Jabir's successor as head of Basra's Ibadis. In 714 al-Hajjaj died and the Ibadis of the town were freed. Nevertheless the pressure on them remained strong at the beginning of the second century after the Hijra; Abu 'Ubaida decided to create a missionary corps, the "bearers of knowledge" (*hamalat al-'ilm*), whose goal was to promote the Ibadi doctrine. This move soon brought success, in the Maghreb[7] and also in Oman, where most of the Ibadi *'ulama'* originated and where a revolt broke out, led by a member of the former dynasty, Julanda bin Mas'ud, who was elected Imam in 750. This experiment lasted only two years, until the new Abbasid Empire reconquered the southern coast of the Gulf. Despite its brief duration, in this campaign for autonomy Ibadism was already a standard bearer for an Omani political demand. The Abbasids certainly never lost the control of the Batina trade ports, but for more than a century the Imam's rule prevailed in the interior of Omani territory. This explains why the region attracted the last Ibadi *sheikh*s of Basra, and replaced the latter town for good as the spiritual centre of the movement. Indeed, an Ibadi dictum says that "knowledge was laid in Madina, hatched out in Basra and took off to Oman".

At that time Ibadism became truly the cement of the emerging Omani identity, strengthened in the building of a political and geographical entity identifiable from abroad, *al-misr al-'umaniyya* ("the Omani country"). This "provisionally limited centre of true Islam"[8] was destined to spread its territorial but also its spiritual suzerainty, thanks to the conversion of peripheral populations to Ibadism. This notion of an Ibadi heartland, depositary of the original pure Omani features, has lived on until now.[9]

The Abbasid armies conquered Oman again in 893. In fact, the growing grip of the Yemeni-origin tribes of Rustaq town on the administration of the Imamate in the ninth century led to the revolt of some Nizarite clans living in Nizwa, who may have been at the origin of the Abbasid interference. Then a doctrinal quarrel between two trends began, surrounding the imposition of an Imamate historiography which could boost the legitimacy of one side's claim to embody the legacy of the Founding Fathers and thus gain the supreme office of Imam. The Nizwa school was considered as pragmatic and recommended forgetting the past to reunify the Imamate and concentrate on fighting against the foreigners, while the Rustaq school refused any compromise regarding interpretation of the facts. The eleventh and twelfth centuries, during which two Imams were elected concurrently in Nizwa and Rustaq, experienced a flourishing of historical and theological writings, the doctrinal basis for the political quarrels over legitimacy and succession.[10] This intellectually productive era illustrated the importance of the Ibadi history building process, and already then of its rationalisation, its rewriting in order to establish a historical identity within the quest for temporal power.

In 1052 the Imam of Rustaq proclaimed the excommunication of the Nizwa school's disciples. This decision led to the rejection of Ibadism by many Nizarite tribes in northern Oman (in contemporary UAE territory), who turned to Shaf'i Sunnism. Until then, the Imamate had ruled over a much wider territory than the one actually inhabited by Ibadi populations; after that date there began what the historians called the "dark age". The five following centuries are not well known, in view of the Imamate's hibernation and the accompanying decline of the historicist tradition. The Persian occupation on the coast is known to have been almost continuous, as attested by the wealth of the town of Qalhat which Ibn Battuta visited in 1331.[11] Portuguese expansion led to the conquest of Omani coastal towns by Afonso de Albuquerque in 1507.

Until the beginning of the seventeenth century, then, Oman's territory was characterised by fragmentation of suzerainties and a very unstable political situation. British interference in the regional game from the seventeenth century, aimed at protection of British interests in India, weakened the Portuguese positions on the Oman coast. In 1624 the 'ulama' of the rival schools of Rustaq and Nizwa, aware of the opportunity, reached an agreement on the election of an Imam, Nasir bin Murshid al-Ya'arubi, whose main task was to reunify the country politically. Under his rule, and that of Sultan bin Saif (1649–88), the Ibadis pacified the interior of the territory, supplanted the Portuguese on the coast in 1650 and took the towns of Mombasa and Zanzibar, as well as Baluchistan and Bahrain. This period can be considered as the beginning of modern Omani history.

Tribes and tribal confederations

In building a national identity and a stable political authority, Sultan Qaboos has had to work with Oman's rich but bulky social and historical legacy, and first of all with the diverse local solidarities (tribes, ethno-linguistic communities, etc.) which are usually considered as the basic structure of society in the

Arabian Peninsula. Nevertheless, an interpretation which portrays an "essence" of Omani politics surviving through the centuries is either speculation or idealisation and historical reinvention, by local actors or scholars, and loses sight of the continuous adaptation of social forces to the evolution of their environment. A study of the Omani tribal structure will clarify this point.

In Oman, the notion of "tribe" is conveyed by the term *qabila*, or sometimes *ta'ifa* (community) or *'ashira* (especially in Dhofar). The group's cohesion is supposed to rely on a common genealogy (*nasab*); the tribe, headed by a *sheikh*,[12] is thus a "group of parents who claim their ascendancy to a common ancestor according to a rule of unilinear filiation".[13] In Oman, this group of agnates is known as "*abna' 'amuma*" ("sons of paternal uncles" or "patrilinear cousins"). The eponymous ancestor is the *jadd* (grandfather). At lower levels, the tribe is organised in branches or sections (*far* or *fakhdh*), each one having its *sheikh rashid*, and subdivides into larger families (*batn*) and then into "houses" (*bayt*). The noble branches' *sheikh*s of the most powerful and numerous tribes are given the title of *sheikh tamima*. Moreover, in Oman, kinship with the Prophet is a minor socio-political factor as no tribe, except some Dhofari groups and a few Shi'a personalities in Muscat, invokes his lineage.

Within the tribe the *sheikh* derives his position from his genealogy and succeeds his father, his brother or his uncle, after consultation with the group's notables, but also and especially on the basis of his personal skills as a political chief. While his decisions must take the notables' opinion into account, he has the power to solve disputes or to approve marriages.

Internal hierarchisation. Every Omani, whatever his group or his native region, can be integrated in a three-level vertical classification within this tribe. At the top, the "nobles" (*qabili, nubala'* or *'arab*;[14] sometimes *asli*) are regarded as the descendants of the original heart of the Arab tribe and then of the eponymous ancestor. The *sheikh* belongs to one of these lineages. At an intermediate level are two categories: the *bayassara* (sing. *bayssar*, or "mixed-race"), descendants of Arabs and slaves, and *zuti* ("gipsies"). The latter are probably descendants of the tribe's prisoners of war, members of another tribe who sought asylum for economic reasons and became integrated, or the first settlers before the arrival of Arab tribes; they often are regarded as the tribe's clients (*mawala*) or its tributaries. Many professional activities remain the *zuti*'s prerogative. Outside Muscat (in the Batina, Dakhliyya, Sharqiyya), manual know-how related to work with raw materials like metal (blacksmiths, jewellers), leather (tanners, shoe-makers), stone (masons) or animals (fishermen, butchers) is still nowadays transmitted within the local *zuti* groups. *Zuti* women are the only ones, in some rural areas, to take care of excision, and *zuti* men of circumcision.

Lastly, the lower level is occupied by the descendants of slaves brought from Africa—*khadam* or *akhdam* ("servants"), also called *'abid* ("slaves") or *zunuj* (sing. *zinj*, "Black") in Sur and the Dhofar region. *Khadam* and *mawala* are considered as belonging to the solidarity group of the masters they depended on historically. All tribesmen, whatever their class, bear the group's name. In Dhofar alone, lower groups bear distinct surnames, which are nevertheless perfectly "situable" in the tribal landscape, in particular for connecting them to a noble group. Some districts remain almost exclusively populated by former slaves, like sea front areas of Salalah, Suwayq, Sur and Sohar. This geographical separation allows a symbolic distinction between the different social groups to continue, and vice versa.

These tribal classes do not determine automatically an individual's socio-professional rank, even if they strongly did in the past. For thirty years, unprecedented rural migration combined with the new state's official discourse preaching equality of rights and conditions for all Omanis slowed down the pre-eminence of this classification in daily social relations. Nevertheless some former client groups, either for lack of alternative or out of habit, remain connected to their former masters. A young Omani expressed the surprise he had when visiting a *sheikh* in the Batina region: "I needed a handkerchief and I started to get up to go to take it. But the *sheikh* put his hand on my shoulder to make me sit and said: 'In this house, nobody gets up for a handkerchief. The handkerchief comes to you': the *khadim* must anticipate your desires to bring it to you, even before you request it!"[15]

The tribe then appears at first sight as a coherent group, socially structured, in which matrimonial practices are directed towards the daughter of the paternal uncle. But this determinism, suggesting that individuals and clans are elements linked to the tribe by a supposed moral obligation, is not obvious from the anthropological point of view. In his pioneering study on the Nuer in Sudan, E.E. Evans-Pritchard admitted: "A tribe very rarely engages in corporate activities. The tribal value determines behaviour in a definite and restricted field of social relations, and is only one of a series of political values, some of which are in conflict with it."[16] Dale Eickelman shows that "there is no natural tie of obligation between men and groups, but that these must be maintained [...] The obligations that derive from identity are not necessarily binding in and of themselves."[17]

Tribalism is a process of culture and identity rather than a given structure.[18] John Wilkinson explains for instance that one of the most important contemporary Batina tribes, the Hawasina, appeared as such in the seventeenth century through a gathering of different clans, who "uncovered" an eponymous ancestor in order to resist the claims of neighbouring groups on their land.[19] It matters little if the common ancestor is actually a myth and if the tribe, genealogically speaking, is the result of the fusion of groups originating from different lineages and regions, even a reconstruction of genealogies *a posteriori*: the essence lies in the perception the individual or the group has, or wishes to give, of himself and of his socio-political history. A group is a "tribe" if it perceives itself as such. Thus, even if the tribal variable gives effective keys to understanding of some Omani social phenomenon, this paradigm is only part of an ensemble of strategies built up by the actors. To emphasise the role played by the actors in the formation of solidarity groups is crucial, while it is also necessary to reduce emphasis on their being a given social object. In particular, political instrumentalising of the tribal structure, consciously or not, is the cause of constant changes as this structure endeavours to adapt under the influence of the strategies and practices of social forces.

This observation can be extended to the other *'asabiyyat* we can find on the Omani territory. The word *'asabiyya* was introduced by Ibn Khaldun[20] and is translated as "group feeling"; an *'asabiyya* can be defined as a solidarity which is based on personal relations (genealogical, matrimonial, nepotistic, etc.) and acts as a group or thinks of itself as such, usually—but not necessarily—in order to pursue common goals (for instance, taking positions of power). In Oman as elsewhere, the *sheikh* makes the *'asabiyya*, and not the contrary: "the cohesiveness of all these groupings stems from a mixture of clan honour, economic interests and territorial ambitions; each element has a degree of potential for autonomous resolution of conflict and for alliance building. But the realisation of this potential is the work of a leader. *'Asabiyya* is potential tribal energy: it takes a *sheikh* to realize it."[21]

The political and social existence of a solidarity group does not ensue from anything substantial, but first and foremost from the political acts of human beings who know how to use this potential for determined purposes. The best illustration appears in the mid-eighteenth century, during the reign of Imam Sultan bin Saif (1711–19).

The Ghafiri and Hinawi confederations. The Ya'arubi State (1624–1737), initially guided by Ibadi doctrine, changed slowly into a maritime empire devoted to overseas trade, in which the Imam and his Rustaq allies were the main beneficiaries. The *'ulama'* gradually lost control over the process of choosing the Imam.

When Sultan II bin Saif died, he was the father of a ten-year-old boy, Saif. The Rustaq tribes wished to elect Saif as Imam, in order to maintain the established order, but came up against the majority of the *ulama'*, especially in Nizwa, who considered that a minor could not lead Friday prayers or administer the finances of the community. A twenty-year civil war started. As a *sheikh* explained later, "this war did not bring into conflict two religious groups or two ideas of the Imamate, but two political parties".[22] Indeed, as soon as one of the most important tribes, the Bani Ghafir, intervened directly in the election, its rivals, gathered around the Bani Hina, got into position to counterbalance what they considered as an excessive influence. All the tribes in Oman's territory and in what is now the territory of the UAE were ordered to rally to one or the other side, if they did not want to be marginalised. While the criteria of support for the confederations were initially linked to genealogy, geography and religious allegiance, the choice was very much determined by a survival strategy; the conflict allowed the small tribes to protect themselves against the ambitions of the most powerful ones, by making use of the threat of a stronger ally against a neighbour.

This factional division follows the lines of the former divisions of Omani society into two blocs, like Nizarite/Yemenite and Rustaq/Nizwa. That dichotomy has provided a considerable degree of political balance throughout history, ensured a counter-power against the dynasties and ruling elites, and usually prevented a small group obtaining an excessive grip on the levers of political and religious power. So this dichotomy contributes to one of the most common historiographic traditions: the mythical picture of an Imamate, presented as an example of democratic government based on basic Muslim principles[23] and on a balance reached through consensus among the different sides.

The golden age. The civil war took on a new dimension in 1737, when Saif II bin Sultan, entrenched in Muscat, asked for Persian help in regaining the position of Imam. In November 1742 the Persians clashed, near Barka', with forces grouped around Ahmad al-Busa'idi, governor of Sohar. Benefiting from the disturbances during the end of the Safavid dynasty in the Persian empire, Ahmad had the upper hand in 1745. He proclaimed himself Imam in 1750, after the death of the Ya'arubi pretenders, and got himself elected by the *ulama'* in 1753. The al-Busa'idi dynasty, in which Qaboos is the fourteenth ruler, was born.

In 1806 Ahmad's grandson, Sa'id bin Sultan, who was more interested in business than in theological debate, became aware of the strategic decline of the Gulf and the increasingly tough British commercial and military competition in the Indian Ocean. He decided to extend the overseas Omani possessions in order to consolidate trade relations with the various trading posts under his control. Sa'id made Zanzibar his capital in 1832, then conquered Mombasa in 1837.[24] During the 1840s, Sa'id's commercial and military fleet controlled the north of the Indian Ocean, making use of the monsoon winds to develop a commanding triangular commercial network between Africa (source of spices, slaves, precious stones, ivory, plantation products), India (manufactured articles and textiles) and Oman (dates and frankincense). The actual autonomy he enjoyed was nevertheless illusory, given the growing British military influence. On Sa'id's death, he bequeathed his two sons an empire whose formal sovereignty covered the whole north-western edge of the Indian Ocean, from northern Mozambique to Cape Guardafui, including ports of access to central Africa, from Dhofar to the Trucial Coast, and from Bandar Abbas to Baluchistan.

This temporary regional supremacy explains the demographic features of Oman. Indeed, the modern history of Oman is punctuated by numerous successive migration waves from and to Oman for three centuries. The point here is not to define homogeneous identity categories which could be thought to have a political relevance by themselves, as they usually overlap in practice, but to give an impressionist picture of different "touches of colour" which are responsible of the amazing contemporaneous diversity of the Omani painting. This prerequisite will allow us to analyse further the socio-political ins and outs of today's national identity.

The demographic legacy of the Omani maritime empire

The Swahili-speaking Omanis. Contacts between south-eastern Arabia and the Swahili coast go back at least to the first centuries of the Islamic era. At the beginning of the eighth century, when the Umayyads came to Oman, the Julanda rulers are said to have sought shelter in Africa. But the trade relations and migration waves were given a new shape under the al-Ya'arubi dynasty,[25] while a second huge wave followed Sa'id bin Sultan's move to Zanzibar in 1832. Under his rule, Sa'id firmly encouraged the settlement of Omani people on the eastern African coast. This political configuration soon allowed many of the immigrants to reach top political positions and to build economic supremacy on the Swahili coast. A new aristocracy appeared, based on the protection of and close relationships with the authorities and on recent

Omani lineage, and replaced the former Swahili elite. Despite the political decline of the Sultanate from the 1860s and the establishment of a British protectorate in Zanzibar in 1890, the waves of Omani migration to Africa did not dry up until the mid-twentieth century. Yet the most recent Omani-native settlers never enjoyed the same possibilities of enhancing their social and economic positions as their predecessors had encountered.[26]

The return to Oman of these various Swahili-speaking groups happened through several waves.[27] The first followed the decolonisation process and especially the revolution in 1964 in Zanzibar, which put an end to the local al-Busaʻidi dynasty. This event remained tragic in the Swahili-speaking Omanis' memory, as it is alleged that around 17,000 Arabs died. No collective repatriation process was organised by the Sultan of Muscat. Oman received 3,700 refugees only[28] and many other families were forced to settle in Dubai, Kuwait or Cairo. A second wave of return followed the call made in 1970 by Sultan Qaboos to the Omani elite abroad, inviting them to contribute to the "awakening" of the country. As many of them spoke English fluently and had been trained in technical fields in Europe, East Africa or other Gulf countries, the Omanis back from Africa provided a precious workforce for the ruler's planned modernisation.

Today, the "back-from-Africa" Omani people are locally called "Swahili" (referring to their vernacular language) or "Zanzibari". They are the descendants of the Omanis who emigrated to the eastern African coast, for political and commercial reasons, such as the Zanzibar settlement from the seventeenth century, or because of socio-economic factors from the end of the nineteenth century. This population is thought to number between 100,000 and 200,000.[29] Most of the tribes and ethno-linguistic groups contain within them so-called "Swahili" individuals or clans—including the royal tribe, the Shiʻa communities and the Omani groups native to Baluchistan—but in varying proportions. The greatest numbers are found within tribes from Inner Oman, like the Habus, Hirth, Bani Kharus, Kinud, Mahariq, Masakira, Mazariʻ (who ruled Mombasa until 1839), Bani Riyam and Bani Ruwaha.[30]

The "Swahili" are thus a highly heterogeneous group, which cannot be defined solely according to genealogical or geographical criteria. Families, or even individuals, descended from the same clan can be considered "Swahili" (or not) whether they have ties (or not) to Africa. The African place of settlement established a major dividing line, between the English-speaking Swahili-speaking Omanis who had lived in Zanzibar, Kenya or the former Tanganyika, on the one hand, and the French-speakers who had travelled to Central Africa

(Rwanda, Burundi and eastern Congo) on the other. The latter, who are estimated to be about 10% of the whole Swahili-speaking Omani population,
only came back to Oman at the beginning of the 1990s, when Rwanda and
Burundi exploded into crisis. But the most important dividing line is the one
inherited from hierarchisation in East Africa. The standard of living of the
twentieth-century Omani migrants to Africa, who sought to escape the dreadful living conditions in unproductive Inner Oman and who could not aspire
to much more than low level economic positions—small farmers, plantation
overseers, caravan managers or small traders—was never similar to that of the
Arab aristocracy there. This combination of social, cultural and economic
divides was a determining factor in the positions these returnees assumed back
in Oman (see chapter 8).

Finally one must keep in mind that a strict and well-known distinction is
established between the back-from-Africa Omanis who can lay claim to a
patriarchal genealogy in southeast Arabia and the Omani citizens who are
descended from slaves brought forcibly from Africa (*khadim*) and who are
considered not to be of Arab blood. As Mandana Limbert has put it,
"Through the paternalizing [...] care of the Arab-Omanis, the [*khadim*] could
become brothers, brothers, however, who would never be allowed to forget
that they had been slaves, that they had known nothing and that they had had
to be cultured."[31] Hence, to personally feel or be perceived as "Swahili" in
Oman nowadays has no link with having Black features. Many families with
noble (*qabili*) Arab lineages, who lived in Africa and are nowadays viewed as
"Swahili" in Oman, have always taken care to keep their Arab lineage "pure".
Marriages between "Arab" women and "African" men almost never occurred
because of the rule prohibiting female hypogamy.

People of Baluchistan origin. As the most recent works of archaeologists show,
the history of the two shores of the Gulf of Oman saw population movements
at an early stage. But the contemporary presence in Oman of the people native
to Baluchistan comes from the need for the Omani rulers, as early as the
Ya'arubi period, to raise a mercenary army so as not to be dependent on the
internal tribal forces. Such a practice has lasted until now. The contacts intensified following the occupation of the northern shore of the Gulf of Oman by
the Sultans of Muscat in 1794 (Gwadar was sold to Pakistan only in 1958).
Throughout the nineteenth century, Sultan Sa'id chose Baluchi contingents
to constitute the backbone of his army and assert his control on the East
African coast. Similarly in 1920, so as to face the challenges from Inner Oman

tribes and replace the British Indian Army which ensured his security, the Sultan of Muscat chose to enlist soldiers from Iranian Sistan and Baluchistan.

In Omani territory, the Baluchi-origin populations are Sunni and are the most numerous Omani non-Ibadi group. They are settled especially in the old towns of Muscat and Muttrah, and in the coastal Batina plain. Since 2000 a major urban renewal plan has forced the resettlement of many Baluchis in the western suburbs of Muscat, like al-Khud. Other old centres of Baluchi-origin people are located near 'Ibri (Dhahira) and Quriyat (south of Muscat). The total number of Omanis of Baluchi origin is estimated between 200,000 and 300,000, equally spread between the capital and the Batina. Family connections with Baluchistan vary; many people, who hold dual nationality, still possess lands in Pakistan and go back for major events.

Connections with the Indian subcontinent. The Omani population of Indian origin has historically been concentrated in Muscat and Muttrah, owing to their long involvement in maritime trade. They are divided into two major groups, the Shi'i Lawatiyya (sing. Lawati) and the Banyan, who belong to the Hindu faith.

The settlement of the first Hindus in Oman, who came from Sind and the Kutch Peninsula in Gujarat, is very old, as the ruins of a temple in the historic town of Qalhat are mentioned in the fifteenth century.[32] At the end of the eighteenth century the Danish traveller Carsten Niebuhr counted 1,200 Banyan in Muscat.[33] A century later, the trade network spread from Zanzibar, where the Banyan and the Lawatiyya acted as bankers for Sa'id bin Sultan, to Bombay via Muscat, where they used four temples at that time. The economic influence of those who were called at that time "Indians" (Banyan and Lawatiyya) in the Omani expansion to Africa was considerable. A gradual division of labour seems to have been established in the nineteenth century between the "Arabs", who dominated the trade and the transport of goods centred on the Muscat-Zanzibar-Central Africa axis (slaves, arms, etc.), and the "Indians", who managed the financial activities and the trade involving the Indian subcontinent (rice, sugar).

At the moment there must be 500 to 1,000 Banyan settled in Oman; they live in Muscat, Muttrah and Salalah and on the Batina coast (Sohar, Shinas, Suwayq, etc.). Most families have been established for six or seven generations. They nevertheless retain profound links with the town of Mandvi, where many Banyan of Muscat have their roots, and with Bombay, where the Banyan who returned to India settled. They usually invest their resources in these towns in real estate, and come back regularly to maintain the matrimonial connections. Few of these Hindus have Omani nationality today, so that they remain a very interdependent community, a bit on the fringe of society as a whole. Their isolation is enhanced by their difficulty with the Arabic language; their vernacular tongue is Kutchi, which is related to Lawati, Sindi and Gujarati. The community's centre of gravity is the Hindu Association, whose duty is to run the two temples (in Muscat and Darsayt), the four crematoria (Sohar, Sur, Salalah and 'Ibri) and the religious feasts.

Known also as "Khodja" or "Hyderabadi" (from the name of the Pakistani town in Sind), the Lawatiyya claim a presence in Oman that goes back four centuries, according to the date recorded in one of their Muttrah districts. While their origins are still the subject of divergent interpretations (see chapter 8), most of the Lawatiyya families appear to have settled in Oman in several migration waves from Sind between 1780 and 1850.[34] At that time, the Lawatiyya enjoyed the status of British subjects and therefore the protection of extra-territoriality. Initially disciples of the Aga Khan (Isma'ili Shi'a), the Lawatiyya were excommunicated after a quarrel over the legitimacy of the succession in 1862. This is the origin of the allegiance of the Lawatiyya, those of Oman but also those settled in Zanzibar, to the Twelver Shi'a, mostly linked to the *marja'iyya* of Najaf.

The Lawatiyya were for long separated from the rest of Omani society as they spoke Khodjki (or Lawati), which is close to Sindi and Gujarati, and lived in a closed district on the seashore of Muttrah, the *sur al-lawatiyya* ("Lawatiyya's enclosure"). Closed to non-Lawati individuals until the 1970s, this area, which is still inaccessible to outsiders not accompanied by a member of the community, is only inhabited by a hundred people, and only comes to life on religious occasions. The Lawati language is still spoken, but unlike the Banyan, the Lawatiyya have for long worn the Omani *dishdasha*, and speak Arabic as their vehicular language. They are estimated to be between 20,000 and 30,000 and live exclusively in the capital (Muttrah, Ruwi, Seeb districts) and in the Batina (al-Masna'a, al-Khabura, Sohar). Despite their small number, the Lawatiyya have a large economic influence, on which we will focus later.

Two other Omani Twelver Shi'a groups must be mentioned. The 'Ajam are said to originate from various Southern Iran regions (Lar, Bandar Abbas)[35] and live today in the Batina (Sohar, al-Khabura), where they represent the largest Shi'a group, and in the capital. Established in Oman for centuries, thanks to the immemorial relations between the two shores of the Gulf of Oman, they are thought to number no more than 20,000 today. The

'Ajam, who only rarely speak Persian, are today over-represented in the police and the army.

The Baharina (sing. Bahrani) are even fewer, thought to number between a thousand and two thousand. Related to various Arab Shi'a communities of the northern Gulf area (Bahrain, Kuwait, Southern Iraq), with whom they maintain sustained contacts,[36] they have been settled in the Muscat area for a century at least. Because of their economic and political position under the rule of Qaboos they are major actors in the contemporary political game.

The 'pax Britannica'

Imam and Sultan: two political legitimacies at the disposal of private interests. The title of "Sultan" appeared only in the second half of the nineteenth century, when the empire started to decline. In 1806, disputes over attribution of the title of Imam led Sa'id bin Sultan to renounce it and take the one of Sayyid ("highness"), in order to draw a distinction between the ruler and the other members of the al-Busa'idi tribe. This decision took on its full dimension in the troubled context of the struggle for power and legitimacy among the al-Busa'idi tribe, a struggle with several permanent traits that can be listed, lasting through the nineteenth century.

First, there was a change from selection by merit for the supreme position to a hereditary principle. Going back to the al-Ya'arubi Imams only, the succession has been handed down from father to son since the second ruler, Sultan I bin Saif, and from brother to brother on one occasion. This process lasted for all the nineteenth century and generated a tradition of parricide and fratricide which runs through the whole of modern and contemporary Omani political history (see figure 1). In 1806 Sa'id bin Sultan, who was seventeen, took power, murdering his cousin Badr, and pacified the territory, exiling some of the family members or operating vendettas, as against his cousin 'Azzan's sons, Qais and Hamud. In 1850, Hamud was murdered by Sa'id's son Thuwaini. In 1856 both sons of Sa'id, Majid and Thuwaini, fought each other over the imperial legacy. And ten years later, Thuwaini, who was Sultan of Muscat, died at the hands of his own son Salim.

Another constant trait was that these personal quarrels, among Imam Ahmad's descendants, acted as rallying points for tribal polarisation. One century earlier, the al-Busa'idi tribe belonged to the Hinawi coalition. Both the Hinawi and Ghafiri confederations constantly supported pretenders to the throne in order to impose their respective interests. Sa'id bin Sultan, like his

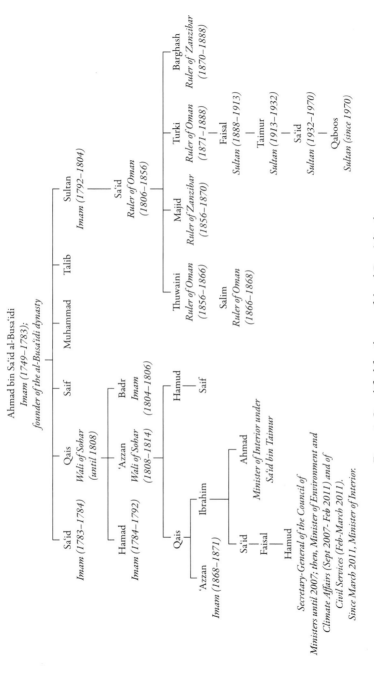

Figure 1: Simplified family tree of the al-Busaʿidi tribe

father, enjoyed Ghafiri support for most of his reign, while the Hinawi, who tried unsuccessfully to overthrow Sa'id's son Thuwaini in Zanzibar, helped 'Azzan to proclaim himself Imam in Muscat in 1868.[37] Three years later Sa'id's lineage, supported by the Ghafiri and the British, overthrew the new Imam and installed Sa'id's other son, Turki, on the throne.

The year 1868 signalled the official renaissance (*nahda*) of the Imamate. This revivalism was within a framework of confrontation between the various factions for supremacy over the territory; indeed, the religious reference (Imam) was used to promote the political interests of a group evicted from the positions of power ('Azzan bin Qais's lineage) and to re-position this clan as a legitimate competitor with the dominant lineage, Sa'id bin Sultan's one. What is striking is the actors' skill in exploiting to their own profit, whenever necessary, the legacy of a century-old conflict, and in encapsulating their interests into this double framework of historical references: Imam/Sultan and Ghafiri/Hinawi. Until 1913 the offices of Imam and Sultan were never merged, as the one's existence led inevitably to the extinction of the other, and the confrontation of these forces prevented reunification of the titles. From 1890, 'Azzan bin Qais's lineage never played a political role any more; it remained entrenched in the Rustaq area, and Ahmad bin Ibrahim, 'Azzan's nephew, made this town his fiefdom until the 1920s, when he declared support for Sultan Sa'id.

In this contention between Imams and Sultans, the British, via their Government of India which was in charge of Persian Gulf affairs from 1873, slowly imposed themselves as the necessary intermediaries between the Omani political forces.

Organisation of political life by the British India government. The first British-Omani "assistance" treaty was signed in 1798, with the declared goal of protecting the ruler of Oman from foreign attacks, especially by the Wahhabis. But it symbolised above all the first official compromise by the Omanis with the powerful East India Company, whose economic pre-eminence kept on strengthening well into the nineteenth century; this led in return to weakening of the Sultan's sources of revenue, and then of his social control over the territory. The British pressure was to be exerted more and more strictly on the Omani rulers.

First, British influence was decisive in the categorisation and hierarchisation of the Omani groups. Identity, whether ethnic, tribal or local, is the result of political and social interactions of forces which contribute to model it, deliberately or not. Within the context of various colonial empires, the authorities sought to classify local populations into bureaucratic categories which excluded multiple identities and strengthened the established order—creating what Linda Layne called a "pigeonhole model of collective identity".[38] The purpose was to change previously non-rigid, flexible and overlapping affiliations and identities into coherent structures, easily identifiable, conceived to be the continuation of quasi-primordial communities.

While colonial ethnography in Oman did not have such a profound importance as in other regions, like Morocco or Iraq, the knowledge of the social structure which was authoritative until 1970 originated in demographic inventories drawn up as early as the mid-nineteenth century by the few British travellers, usually government officials or soldiers, who ventured outside Muscat.[39] These accounts, which mixed travel narratives and sociological investigations, contributed to a congealed and timeless perception of these social groups and their mutual relations. Tribes were usually described with tables, which mentioned their factional connections (Ghafiri or Hinawi) and their estimated population. A paragraph went with these data for the most important ones, in which their branches, the *sheikh* lineages and links with neighbouring tribes were detailed. In addition, lists of tribal *sheikh*s in each region made it possible to officialise the favoured interlocutors of the Sultan and the British, and then to institutionalise local chiefs and major lineages. Far from confirming a pre-existing situation only, this policy allowed the *sheikh*s concerned to acquire an unprecedented visibility. From the 1860s the Sultan granted these notables regular allowances and gifts in order to ensure their loyalty; it gave these "approved" *sheikh*s the opportunity to consolidate locally the pre-eminence of their own family and clientelist networks, because they concentrated in their hands both material capital (ownership of the better lands) and symbolic capital (arbitration of conflicts).

These classifications have had a major impact on the picture of society that Omani historiography presents. The nineteenth-century Omani historians[40] developed a linear and usually event-based vision of their territory's history: individuals as political actors, like the rulers (Imam and Sultan) and their close supporters, on the one hand, and larger groups like peoples (the Portuguese, the British, etc.) or tribal confederations (Ghafiri, Hinawi), on the other, were emphasised. References to tribes and religious sects (Shiism, Ibadism, Sunnism), as political variables, were almost absent. It is symptomatic that the contemporaneous reading of Omani history presented by the country's scholars has adopted a different perspective; while not losing the event-based dimension, it grants tribes, but also ethnic and confessional groups, a prominent position.[41] A significant part is devoted to the description, one after the other, of the diverse demographic components (tribes, ethnic groups) as the British popularised them, with their supposed genealogical origins and eponymous ancestors, their religious affiliations, their geographical fiefdoms and the major events in their history.

The political and economic decline of Oman found expression in the 1861 Canning Award. This treaty took advantage of the inability of the Muscat and Zanzibar governors, Thuwaini and Majid, to settle peacefully their father's succession: it formalised the division of the empire into two distinct sovereignties and imposed use of the title of Sultan. Given the huge difference in sources of revenue, it planned moreover that Zanzibar should pay an annual subsidy to Muscat, which was to be stopped under Imam 'Azzan's rule (1868–71). After Zanzibar was made a protectorate in 1890, Britain paid this subsidy until 1967, when oil exploitation started.

The Canning Award announced a major orientation of British policy towards Oman, and more generally in the Persian Gulf: the wish to isolate the region and its political actors from the outside world, and make them tributary to Britain alone. The Gulf had to become a place "where time had stood still [...] frozen into the requirements of the *pax Britannica*".[42] These political entities were neither protectorates nor colonies, but only "in relation of treaty" with Britain; so, for instance, they could only establish diplomatic contacts under London's supervision. For a long time, the southern shore of the Gulf remained cut off from political convulsions. Except in Bahrain and Oman, this policy allowed the British authorities in India to maintain a very weak presence in the field. As a consequence they never had to be involved in large-scale development projects, before oil was discovered.

Moreover, this "divide and rule" policy sought to carve up the region in order to allow survival of small political entities without direct interaction between each other. On the basis of these sheikhdoms whose raison d'être was the ruling dynasty, the British compartmentalised social and political activity into small local arenas, under the supervision of a ruler whose visibility was institutionalised. The signing of multiple bilateral agreements between London and the various emirates reinforced the fragmentation of sovereignties and the sometimes "artificial" peculiarities of one compared to the other. Indeed, the establishment of separate relationships between London and each of them increased each state's self-perception of a genuine identity, all the more so as London encouraged them to create their own symbols of sovereignty, such as passports, national anthems or merchant marine flags. This trend was to be strengthened when oil companies burst into the region; as they negotiated with each ruler the clauses of the contracts as well as the concession areas, they favoured the strict delimitation of territories of sovereignty. Yet, because the disparities in oil and material resources disrupted the regional balance, tensions exacerbated, and so did the perception of belonging to distinct political entities.

In Oman, London's action reinforced the hierarchisation of society with, at the top, the ruler, who was granted protection and immunity when facing political demands from other members of the royal family. In exchange, the latter were themselves distinguished from the rest of the people, thanks to the establishment of a "civil list" for their personal expenditure, taking up one-third of the Sultanate's total budget in the 1930s.[43]

As long as the established rulers respected the treaties and their duties, they enjoyed full British support—political, sometimes military, but above all financial—in internal affairs. On their side, however, the British were not too reluctant to drop rulers who had rebellious attitudes to the game imposed on them; in 1871 they backed without reservation the overthrow of Imam 'Azzan, who had succeeded in doing without them to expel the Wahhabis from the Buraimi oasis. The interference was more subtle in 1895, when the tribes, mostly Hinawi, identifying with the Imam conquered Muscat and Sultan Faisal had to take refuge under the protection of the British political agent. Sultan Faisal was allocated a huge sum of money by the British and the Indian merchants of Muscat, so as to buy the support of some Ghafiri tribes and convince the Hinawi tribes to withdraw; the ruler was then able to return to his palace. This funding only strengthened the dependence of Muscat on the British India government, which was illustrated by the Zanzibar subsidy and the 1891 treaty, under which the ruler committed himself never to cede a part of his territory without British agreement.

Unfortunately for the British, the result was not as they had hoped. The beginning of the twentieth century was marked by complete dereliction of their official duties by Sultan Faisal and his son Taimur (1913–32). Rulers in name only, without enough field knowledge and means of action, they showed no desire to get involved in public affairs at all. Their feeling of powerlessness regarding Omani political issues they did not control in fact soon changed into lack of interest. Faisal, who spoke Gujarati and Swahili, had very bad command of Arabic, which cut him off from the people he was supposed to rule. The gulf of separation from the British India government reached its climax with Taimur, who soon became aware of the trap the dignity of Sultan of Muscat represented: "Both were determined that the other party should govern".[44] The conditions were all the more difficult for Taimur because, a few months before his accession to the throne, the Imamate renaissance had been proclaimed in Nizwa.

The Seeb agreement (1920). In May 1913, at Sheikh 'Abd Allah al-Salimi's call, an assembly of tribal notables, mostly Ghafiri, gathered in Tanuf, the fiefdom of the noble branch (al-Nabhani) of Bani Riyam tribe, and elected Sheikh Salim al-Kharusi as Imam. The new Imam did not belong to a major tribe but was Sheikh 'Abd Allah al-Salimi's son-in-law and enjoyed good relations with the Bani Riyam.[45] *Jihad* was immediately proclaimed against the Sultan and his British allies.

While the Ghafiri tribes had usually been closer to the Sultan throughout the nineteenth century, this confederation was paradoxically at the origin of the most important uprising in Inner Oman since 1868. The explanation of this U-turn has to be found in the lucidity of a handful of *sheikh*s about the disintegration of Muscat authority. Until then, polarisation had been established around two clans of the al-Busa'idi tribe, the Turki bin Sa'id and Qais bin 'Azzan branches. These lineages had been instrumentalised by both Ghafiri and Hinawi factions in their struggle for the political control of the territory. In the twentieth century's first decade, the economic difficulties in Inner Oman, linked in people's minds to the British tutelage over Muscat authority, and accompanied by a halt to the financial aid allocated by the Sultan to the most powerful *sheikh*s, led the latter to reject the status quo.

One month later, Nizwa, Manah and Izki towns fell into the hands of the Imam's allies. Soon Sheikh 'Isa bin Salih al-Harthi, the Hinawi leader, joined the insurgents so as not to be marginalised. From then on a pact, which would last for more than forty years through their descendants, bound together two men whose personal ambitions, until then contradictory, concurred for the purpose of taking control of Oman: Himyar bin Nasir al-Nabhani, *sheikh tamima* of the Bani Riyam tribe and the Ghafiri confederation's leader, and 'Isa bin Salih al-Harthi, *sheikh tamima* of the Hirth tribe and head of the Hinawi. Even though their mutual mistrust prevented both of them from gaining the position of Imam, they soon understood that sharing power at the top of the Imamate, as the Imam's *éminences grises*, was the cost of safeguarding the Inner Oman tribes' interests.

In the autumn of 1913 Sultan Faisal asked for Indian contingents to be deployed to defend the town of Muscat, a decision which did nothing but arouse the tribes to reject a ruler who depended, according to them, on British goodwill. Faisal's death in October and the accession of his son Taimur, who was better considered by the Omanis, together with Taimur's attempts to divide the other side, slowed down the Imam forces' progress. In January 1915, when attacking Muscat, they suffered a big defeat by British India regiments, composed of Baluchi mercenaries. For a while, both sides put up with a *de facto* partition of the territory, but several factors quickened diplomatic contacts in early 1920.

Among the Imam's supporters, Himyar bin Nasir died in May; his 14-year-old son Sulaiman succeeded him as *tamima*, but the Ghafiri confederation's political power declined. Two months later, the death of Sheikh Salim al-Kharusi allowed 'Isa bin Salih to have Muhammad al-Khalili, his own father-in-law, elected as Imam. Viewed as a moderate, Imam al-Khalili was straightaway in favour of negotiations with the Sultan. On the British side, the Government of India was not satisfied with a precarious stability which placed an unpopular Sultan at the mercy of a new attack by the Imam's side, and thus forced it to provide constant military and financial support to Taimur. The British therefore thought it necessary to secure official mutual recognition by a treaty binding both sides.

This happened on 25 September 1920, with the signature of the Seeb agreement (*sulh*).[46] It takes the form of two identical letters in Arabic, the first signed on behalf of the Sultan by his representative and minister, Sayyid Muhammad bin Ahmad al-Busa'idi, the other one by eighteen tribal *sheikh*s, including the Imam. The introduction stipulates that there is a reconciliation agreement "between the government of Sultan Taimur bin Faisal and the Omani [...] by the mediation of Mr. Wingate, political agent and consul of Great Britain in Muscat, who is conferred by his government the authority [...] to act as intermediate between them".[47] The preamble implies that the Sultan would settle an agreement with his own people ("the Omani"), who were officially represented during the negotiation by 'Isa bin Salih. This odd wording came from the British refusal to accept that peace could be signed directly between the Sultan and the "Imam of the Muslims", because it would have meant the "open recognition by [Britain] of another ruler"[48] in the territory, and so challenged all the efforts accomplished since the mid-nineteenth century.

More generally, the negotiations were conducted personally between the political agent and 'Isa bin Salih. The diplomatic notes confirm that the Sultan had no knowledge of what he would have to undertake to respect. Ronald Wingate does not mince his words regarding his ultimate purpose: "Our interest has been entirely self-interested, has paid no regard to the peculiar political and social conditions of the country and its rulers; and by bribing Sultans to enforce unpalatable measures which benefited none but ourselves and permitting them to misrule without protest has done more to alienate the interior and to prevent the Sultans from re-establishing their authority than all the rest put together."[49]

While this agreement did not establish an independent government in Inner Oman under the Imam's authority, the interpretation made by some observers—that the signature of 'Isa bin Salih attests "an explicit acknowledgment of [the Sultan's] government, and by extension, of its legitimacy"[50]—is unfounded.

The text is organised in a double list of four pragmatic conditions to be respected by the Sultan, on the one hand, and the "Omani", on the other. Four paragraphs (three requested by the Omanis, one by the Sultan) concern the security of goods and people and freedom of movement between the coast and the interior. Two other articles, in favour of the Sultan, deal with non-interference by Inner Oman's political forces in coastal affairs, and with the protection of Muscat traders, whose complaints to the Imam must be taken into account. This agreement marked a shared desire for peaceful coexistence to allow the revival of trade between the coastal towns, for which trade was a raison d'être, and Inner Oman, autonomous politically. Significantly, it contained no map which would have delimited the territories under the respective authorities of the Sultan and the Imam: this is understandable in view of the British side's categorical refusal to recognise any sovereignty of the Imamate in the interior.

By this agreement, the British achieved a *de facto* division of Omani territory. The decisive impact their actions had on the fragmentation of the Omani political authority, both globally (between Imam and Sultan) and locally, with the exacerbation of the tribal variable, resembled the imperial strategy they pursued in Africa at the same time, which is described by Bruce Berman: "The strategic logics of political control in the colonial state rested on [...] a practice of fragmenting and isolating African political activity within the confines of local administrative sub-divisions [...] Each administrative unit ideally contained a single culturally and linguistically homogeneous 'tribe' in which people continued to live within the indigenous institutions and were subject to 'tribal discipline' through local structures of authority."[51]

Besides, the Seeb agreement ratified a sharing of roles between three actors that John Wilkinson calls the Omani "old guard".[52] The interior tribes, who enjoyed effective control over the greater part of the territory, had the feeling of having gained their independence; Sultan Taimur could consider that he had saved face in preserving a territory, even if it was restricted to the Batina, Muscat and Salalah, over which he enjoyed full sovereignty, while retaining formal the authority over the whole territory. Lastly, the British kept the upper hand over a divided and weakened Oman, whose future depended directly on their goodwill. The agreement established the foundations of a political situation that Frederick Bailey called "encapsulation"[53] of two structures. The leaders of the encapsulating structure, here embodied by the British, in fact allowed those of the encapsulated entities to keep control at a local level, as long as the prevailing political order fitted the needs defined by the larger structure. This "subcontracting" of social control, in which each of the three actors would have an interest in maintaining the existing conditions, was a very effective instrument for preserving the political order. In 1920, in fact, a status quo of more than thirty years started; it would be challenged only by the intrusion into the game of new players, attracted by the smell of oil.

2

TWO LEGITIMACIES AND NO STATE

Those three decades after 1920 are characterised by a notable socio-political stability, which however coincided with harsh economic conditions. There was a cartelisation of the game by the three actors, who agreed on sharing the scarce dividends of the economic control defined by the 1920 agreement. But this conjunction of interests did not lead to open collaboration to develop the territory.

The break with the principle of the Sultan as primus inter pares

At the end of 1920 Taimur once again asked the British if he could abdicate; his more and more frequent journeys to India illustrated the awkwardness of his position. Two successive compromises were reached with the British. The first, in 1920, established a council of ministers, chaired by the Sultan's elder brother, Nadir, and composed of four members, among whom Zubair bin 'Ali, of Baluchi origin, was responsible for justice issues. In addition, Taimur was required to spend at least three months per year in Muscat, after being granted a financial allowance. Nobody had illusions about the viability of these institutional expedients, as the 1923 report of the British political agent shows: "[The council] functions with delatoriness and, during the absence of His Highness to Dhofar, found a new excuse for procrastination [...] *Sayyid* Nadir the president, when remonstrated with averred that it was impossible for the council to arrive at a unanimous decision, as [...] the Member of Finance

33

invariably opposed any suggestion he made and [...] the minister of Justice not being an Arab is treated by the other three as a nonentity, but has to be tolerated by them as he is the only one who can read or write."[1]

From the beginning of 1920, a British adviser was appointed to establish the beginnings of an administration and to control the finances according to the Government of India's interests. From 1925 to 1931 a British financial adviser, Bertram Thomas, had a full-time seat on the council, where he acquired more and more influence. British control over Oman's affairs had never been so direct, as shown in the 1923 treaty, which laid down that no oil concession could be granted on the territory before the Government of India had given its approval, and in the direct British military interventions to crush local rebellions, as in Khasab and Sur in 1930.

The supremacy of the Sultan over the al-Busa'idi tribe. Taimur had five sons and one daughter, but only Sa'id's mother, Fatima bint 'Ali, granddaughter of Sultan Salim (1866–68), belonged to the royal family. The British placed great hopes in him. Educated at Mayo College in India, he felt at ease in Arabic as well as Hindi, and was described as "a young Sultan who, if tactfully handled, should turn out a good ruler [...] while we should try at the same time to build up a façade of independence in the eyes of the world".[2] In 1929, when Nadir decided to retire, Sa'id, who was just 18, assumed the functions of chairman of the council. Two years later, Taimur announced to the British his abdication in favour of his son, who acceded to the throne officially on 10 February 1932. London made Sa'id sign a similar letter to the one they had asked his father to sign, in which he had to recognise that he owed his position to them and would fulfil all obligations towards them. From that date, Taimur did not interfere any more in Omani politics, especially as Sa'id did not allow him to come back before his death in Karachi in 1965.

As early as 1929 and his accession to the position of "regent", Sa'id demonstrated his strength of character. He was resolved to establish his supremacy over the al-Busa'idi tribe and then over the territory dependent on Muscat's authority. He was successful in a tussle with his uncle Hamad bin Faisal, who had taken advantage of the lack of leadership in Muscat to establish an almost independent authority in Sohar, and forced him to proclaim his allegiance.

Like his father and his grandfather, Sa'id did not have at his disposal any kind of political legitimacy, as his authority relied first and foremost on the British support. But he stood out from his predecessors by his determination, and soon succeeded in imposing himself as the actual political leader of the family. This was shown by a fall in the share of the budget devoted to the royal family, from 30% in the 1930s to less than 2.5% in 1968.[3] His most noteworthy success was to drive the other al-Busa'idi members to make in a short time an unequivocal choice: either accept his authority and become assistants of his power, or renounce for good any political role in Oman and, at worst, go into exile. Sa'id wished to end the quarrels over legitimacy which had troubled the tribe since the eighteenth century, and the ways in which the tribe had been used by the other socio-political forces.

Among his half-brothers, Majid, Tariq and Fahr were limited to *wali* positions, at the best. Tariq, who would play a major role in putting down the revolt in the Jabal Akhdar (see chapter 3) and be appointed to head the Muscat municipal authority in 1957, was slowly sidelined by the Sultan, who perceived him as a potential competitor. In 1958, he was to be appointed *wali* of Inner Oman, after this sensitive region was officially regained by the Sultan's troops; he chose to leave the country out of spite in 1962, followed shortly afterwards by Fahr.

Logically, Sa'id chose to rely on his uncles without any suspicion. The most loyal was Shihab bin Faisal; Sa'id entrusted him with foreign relations in 1939, then appointed him his representative (*wakil*) in Muscat when he decided to settle in Salalah, in 1958. In internal affairs, Sa'id relied mainly on Ahmad bin Ibrahim, Imam 'Azzan bin Qais's nephew. Ahmad, who was recognised for his knowledge of the country and his relations with the tribes, seems to have always enjoyed the Sultan's consideration, as he was kept in charge of internal affairs from 1938 to 1970. In duet with Shihab, he ruled Muscat on behalf of the Sultan and ensured for the latter a necessary connection with the tribes, while serving as a filter for their claims. As far as internal affairs were concerned, Sa'id soon demonstrated his determination to arrange peaceful coexistence with the Imamate, in order to preserve his power from any hostile initiative.

Cordial relations between Sultan and Imam. One of the first steps taken by Sa'id was to dissolve the Cabinet and replace it with three departments that he would supervise: finance, internal affairs and justice (under Zubair bin 'Ali). In June 1933, when R.G. Alban, a Briton in charge of finance, finished his mission, Sa'id succeeded in preventing the appointment of a replacement; this allowed him to personally take care of financial affairs, which he would do until his deposition in 1970. A *wali*, usually born into the royal family, represented the Sultan in every town, and was assisted by a *qadi* responsible for resolution of conflicts. This pair of officials constituted in most cases the entire local state apparatus. One of the rules, which would live on under Qaboos, was to appoint a *wali* in a town far from his native region, so that he could be assumed to be impartial towards the local tribes.

In order to strengthen the basis of his power and guard against tribal rebellions, Sa'id sought to link his legitimacy, which was precarious, with those of the traditionally influential families. So he soon had good relations with the Imamate authorities. For instance, he encouraged scholars from Inner Oman to serve in his administration. Not only were personalities allowed to move between the services of both Sultan and Imam, provided that they did not threaten authority; in addition, the Sultan's payments were much more attractive than the Imam's. Among these personalities were the Imam's adviser, Sheikh Ibrahim al-'Abri, who carried out the function of *qadi* for the Sultan from 1939[4] and would become later the first Mufti of Oman under Qaboos (1971–75), and the Imam's own brother, 'Ali al-Khalili, *wali* of Bawshar until his death in 1949.[5]

Another standard practice, described by John Townsend as an "old-age Omani method of overcoming enemies",[6] was the regular payment of allowances to the most powerful *sheikh*s, in order to buy peace in the interior of the country. On various pretexts (political recriminations or injustice they considered they had suffered), Inner Oman notables came to visit the Sultan in Muscat, spent several days with him and went back with gifts. Particular favours were reserved for the leaders of both the confederations, Sulaiman al-Nabhani (Ghafiri) and Salih al-Harthi (Hinawi). For these personalities, the double recognition by the Imam and the Sultan, but also the opportunity to make use one against the other, were the best guarantees of their political pre-eminence in Inner Oman.

Co-operation even developed between the Imam and the Sultan on the basis of the Seeb agreement, especially in the judicial field. Besides, the Sultan was never opposed to the Imam inviting the Muttrah medical mission's doctor, given that the Imamate had no medical structure at all. As Major Chauncy, consul general in Muscat, noticed in 1951, "Both they seem to apply the 1920 Seeb agreement, maybe even more in the spirit than in the letter, and the tribes themselves enjoyed since that date a period of peace without comparison in the history".[7] For instance, both leaders agreed in 1946 to work for restoration of order in Sharqiyya province, when troubles involved the Bani Bu 'Ali tribe.

Even the personal relations between the Sultan and the Imam seem to have been respectful. While Sa'id made the point, in his letters, of addressing the

Imam by the title of *'alim*, on account of the political significance the word "Imam" held, the latter used the word "Sultan" and "recognized that the Sultan sought the well-being of the people of Inner Oman".[8] This cordiality can certainly be explained by the favourable image the Sultan enjoyed over the whole territory, given his rather independent attitude to the British until the early 1950s. But it was also a consequence of the ruler's skills, as he sought to benefit from proximity to influential people of the Imamate to take back control of Inner Oman at the Imam's death.

Standing up to traditional political pressures? One of the main aims of Sa'id's policy was to reduce the Sultanate's huge debt to the British and to the Muscat traders; Sa'id was aware that as long as his government remained insolvent he would be strangled by the British tutelage. On the assumption that he could only spend what he had, all the expenditure he considered useless was cancelled, like infrastructure projects, or drastically reduced, like the allowances to the members of the royal family. His limited income, mainly consisting of British subsidies and customs duties, never allowed him to start development projects outside Muscat. This austerity was to be intensified in the 1960s after his departure to Salalah. His dependence was particularly important in the military sector. In fact, following the Seeb agreement and given the vulnerability shown by Taimur in the face of tribal attacks, the British decided in 1921 to create an embryo army, the Muscat Levy Corps. Mainly composed of Baluchis, this 300-strong corps had the advantage of allowing a British officer to be based continuously near the Sultan and occupy the unofficial position of Minister of Defence.

However, the Second World War represented a turning point in the administrative organisation of the Sultanate. The growing pressure of American oil companies and their Wahhabi allies, eyeing Omani territory, but also Sa'id's increasing mistrust of some of his family members, accounted for his decision to rely on foreign mercenaries as being less dangerous and more docile, or on individuals who owed everything to him and would remained loyal. Sa'id divided responsibilities in the administrative sectors so as to avoid any individual developing power that would weaken his own authority.

Sa'id was assisted successively by various Indian experts, among them Maqbul Husain, the former accountant of the British agent in Muscat, who remained in charge of finance from 1941 to 1966. In foreign affairs, the ruler could not resist pressure from the British, who thought his diplomacy aimed at too much independence for their liking. From 1948 to 1958 a British person dealt with these issues, before the office in charge of foreign affairs was simply cancelled, as London did not consider it necessary any more. In the Muscat municipal authority, Sa'id made a point of balancing the responsibilities of Ahmad bin Ibrahim with a Palestinian expert, Isma'il al-Rasasi, who was to occupy several positions (*wali* of Muttrah, chairman of the municipal council, and even Oman's first ambassador to Iran), and a loyal-to-the-Sultan Pakistani officer, who also stayed until 1970.[9]

This desire to rely on partners outside the Omani social forces (the royal family and the Inner Oman tribes), partners who owed their social rise to their proximity and their loyalty to the Sultan only, was especially striking in Muscat. Sa'id gave a few families the possibility to build and consolidate their political and economic positions, in exchange for their support for him. Their independence from the traditional factional alliances gave these families the freedom to spread their networks without any other consideration than their rational interest, which depended directly on Sa'id's political survival.

A new economic order

Despite the dichotomic perception conveyed by contemporary historiography, post-1970 Oman has been built on the social and political foundations inherited from the first half of the last century. Although the socio-economic structure of the Sultanate has changed dramatically within thirty years in a way no other region on earth has experienced, it is necessary to emphasise that many current fortunes are derived from the skilful reconversion of prominent positions built during the twentieth century. To use Jill Crystal's phrase about Kuwait, "in a few generations, families had made a transition from wealthy traders and pearl merchants to extremely wealthy modern contractors".[10]

This process finds its roots especially in the alliance developed between Sultan Sa'id and the merchants who were active in sectors in which they held monopoly positions. Politically harmless, these merchants' families were able to take advantage not only of their personal proximity, but particularly of the protection this brought them in consolidating their economic interests, usually thanks to direct intervention in the decision-making process. In return the merchants, who were active in the export and import trade in Muttrah and Muscat, showed skill in proving indispensable to the ruler's political survival; not only were they the only ones able to provide the Sultan's growing need for liquid assets, but the Sultan deducted from their resources huge taxes, which represented one of the major sources of the Sultanate's revenue. These mutual advantages lay at the heart of this enduring alliance from 1930 to 1970.

The Indian merchants of Muscat. The Indian traders had played, since the eighteenth century at least, a major economic role in the prosperity of the Omani empire. As early as the end of the nineteenth century the Hindus, as well as the Lawatiyya, who were settled in the Omani ports benefited from the extra-territorial protection of the British India authorities. In practice, these families stood above the laws of the Sultan and they could ask for British help in case of damage or loss suffered, especially during Inner Oman tribes' attacks. Calvin Allen developed the argument that the economic recession Muscat suffered after Sultan Saʻid bin Sultan's reign (1804–56) was actually a transfer of resources from the ruling dynasty to the town's Indian traders: "The trade of the port did not dry up, it simply changed hands".[11]

From the beginning of the twentieth century, and in a decisive way under Saʻid bin Taimur, these families consolidated their position in the Omani economy, since they had a monopoly of imports, only shared with Saʻid himself. Many Omani tribes were forced to mortgage their lands every year to the Indian merchants of Muscat as security for advances on basic goods which were not produced in Oman and only available through imports, like rice and sugar.[12] This huge economic dependency, combined with the traders' proximity of interests with the British, explains that, when attacking Muscat, the interior Omanis usually raided Banyan and Lawatiyya goods. The British understood this situation, as the political agent explained to his superiors in 1902: "The British Indian (Hindu Banya) traders [...] who are mostly usurers, have become a necessity to the Arabs, but at the same time occupy in their eyes much the same position as the Jew usurer does in Europe."[13]

Ratansi Purshottam is one of the most striking examples of one of this wealth built up more than one century ago. He went to Oman to work for his uncle when he was 14, but he established his own business in 1870 in Muscat. He specialised in rice and dates import and export, and became at the end of the nineteenth century, thanks to his family networks in Bombay and Karachi, one of the most powerful arms traders in the Gulf.[14] While he held at the same time the post of customs director of the port, this Banyan trader was the main creditor of Sultan Faisal, who was usually forced to borrow from one of the traders to refund another one. Nowadays, Ratansi's descendants only own a small shop on the Muttrah Corniche. But other families, for which the determining factor in success was the economic-political alliance with Saʻid bin Taimur, took over.

One of these families is another Banyan one, known today as Khimji, whose ancestor came to Oman around 1870 from Gujarat. The family business grew during the Second World War, when it became the Sultan's most important contractor: the Khimji group was the exclusive supplier of the royal palace, and was granted the monopoly of distribution of food products in Dhofar region. Several contracts were signed with the American and British armies, dealing with the building of military bases in Salalah and Masirah and supplies to those bases.[15] In the 1960s the Khimji were able to settle in Dubai also, before they benefited from the economic boom following Qaboos' accession to the throne.

One of the oldest Omani merchant dynasties is the al-Sultan family. In 1866 a US citizen, W.J. Towell, founded a shipping transport company in Muscat. In 1906 Muhammad Fadl, a Lawati born in Bombay who had been a clerk and then a partner in the company, became its full owner. The company, which kept the name of WJ Towell, was the representative in Oman of the British India shipping line and of the Standard Oil Company.[16] Muhammad Fadl's grandson, 'Abd al-Rida, decided in the 1930s to set up a branch in Kuwait, which three of his brothers would manage. Quickly, the choice proved profitable, as the family prospered thanks to the import of sugar and the acquisition of the monopoly on basmati rice from Pakistan in the 1960s. In Muscat *hajj* 'Ali, 'Abd al-Rida's younger brother, became the agent of international brands like Mazda, Buick, GMC and Unilever and changed WJ Towell into the most powerful economic group in the Sultanate on the eve of the Qaboos coup.

Business on the fringe of society. Most of the Omani trading dynasties were not from the Ibadi tribes of the interior. Their longstanding involvement in trading activities can undoutedly be explained by the concentration in Muscat of "peripheral" social groups, as a consequence of the previous centuries' processes of immigration. Belonging to a small minority group, independent of Omani political affiliations, contributed to directing these people towards the only economic activity which did not require any particular integrative process: trade.

Thus the Lawatiyya's predisposition for maritime trade, given both their isolation in a closed area of Muttrah trading port and their connections with the Indian subcontinent, can be observed as early as the end of the nineteenth century. Many families benefited from the conjunction of interests with Sultan Sa'id and from the extremely close-knit nature of the community, marginalised within Omani society as a whole. Even if they are an ultra-minority (less than 5% of the total population in 2017), Lawatiyya business families currently hold a very important position in the country's economy, while their ancestors usually started a century ago with a small shop in Muttrah.

Similarly, the Zawawi family soon used relations with Muscat rulers to build an economic empire which is still among the most powerful in Oman today. Their ancestor, Yusef bin Ahmad al-Zawawi, was a native of Hijaz and came to Muscat at the end of the nineteenth century to establish a trading company. He became one of the unofficial advisers to Sultan Faisal.[17] His son, 'Abd al-Mun'im, acted later as commercial agent of Sultan Sa'id in Karachi.[18] Both 'Abd al-Mun'im's sons, 'Umar and Qais, were to be very close to Qaboos when he took power. The case of the Darwish family is also enlightening. The Darwish brothers, of Bahrani origin, came to Oman at the beginning of the twentieth century and founded a trading company in 1921. During the 1950s and 60s one of the sons, Muhsin Haidar, was awarded several contracts with major foreign companies, like British Leyland, with Sultan Sa'id's blessing.

If Muscat has been a place of intermingling where Sa'id found his best allies, Dhofar also played a major role in the establishment of personal relations between the Sultan and some of the most influential families today; not only did Sa'id spend most of his time after 1958 there, but so did Qaboos in his youth. The royal palace of Salalah was the place where the Sultan's close relations and courtiers mingled. Within this context two Dhofari families, who are originally from sections of the Bait Kathir tribal confederation, were especially close to Sa'id and have kept their prominent positions until now: Shanfari and Rawas. The Shanfari family ran Sultan Sa'id's personal economic interests in Dhofar.[19] This family is said to have been the first to call on the Sultans of Muscat, at the end of the nineteenth century, to assert political control of the province.

The al-Zubair family also owes a part of its later economic success to its old connections with the Sultans of Muscat. 'Ali al-Hutti, from Baluchistan, who ran a shop in Muttrah *suq* at the end of the nineteenth century, held unofficial ministerial positions under Sultans Turki and Faisal. His son Zubair was appointed to be responsible for justice issues in the council of ministers established after the Seeb agreement in 1920. In 1936 he was appointed governor of Dhofar and Sa'id entrusted him with running his real-estate projects. In Dhofar, Zubair married a girl from the Shanfari tribe and had two sons, Muhammad and Ahmad. This proximity led Muhammad al-Zubair to be one of the main supporters of Qaboos during the war effort in Dhofar.

The Imamate: the myth of 'traditional democracy'

The Imam, a temporal ruler with limited powers. The Seeb agreement did not plan geographical borderlines between Imamate and Sultanate. Nevertheless, a tacit consensus established that Imam Muhammad al-Khalili's power covered the territory inhabited by tribes which recognised his authority. Concretely, this represented all the southern fringe of the Hajar range (from 'Ibri to North Sharqiyya governorate), but also the whole of the Jabar Akhdar, including towns like Rustaq, Nakhl or Sama'il. In the twentieth century the Imam's residence was the Nizwa fort. The Imam, who was a spiritual head, was a political chief above all. He took the decisions which involved the whole Imamate after consulting his advisers, who were the *sheikh*s of the most important tribes as well as the *'ulama'*. He appointed *wali*s, usually natives of the most influential tribes, who were assisted by small numbers of troops. A *qadi* administered justice on account of the Imam.

Yet the Imamate's financial resources (*bayt al-mal*) were weak, which explains why its administrative apparatus remained undeveloped. The revenue was composed of taxes under the headings of *zakat* (alms) and exploitation of *waqf* (religious endowments). The Imam had no army. But he had the possibility to levy a military force against any group which did not comply with the decisions taken by the Imamate, and even to pronounce an anathema on any individual considered as an "enemy of Islam". At the international level, Imam Muhammad was never interested in establishing foreign relations. Implicitly, he left this responsibility to Sultan Sa'id, as if there was a division of labour: the management of Oman internal affairs under the Imam, that of foreign affairs by the Sultan. Passports for the few Imamate personalities who went abroad were, until the early 1950s, issued by the Sultan's administration and signed by Sa'id.

Yet in practice, the Imam's freedom of action was not as large as one could have imagined from his prerogatives. First, it is necessary to mention the principle of "consultation" (*shura*), which was at the centre of the process of contemporary political legitimacy in Oman; it echoed the double Ibadi tradition of the choice of the Imam and the collegiality of decision-making under his direction. Concretely, the *shura* principle was displayed every day in the *sabla*, a meeting during which the tribal *sheikh*, assisted by the *'ulama'* and the other notables, received the group's members who wanted to tell him any problems. In the same way, the Imam listened to supplicants every morning, while he remained inaccessible to foreigners.

The sheikhs' influence in the Nizwa Imamate. A recurrent analysis of Omani political history, which is based on historical "cycles", establishes a direct link between the powers of the Imam and the tribes. Among the works which developed this approach, the most elaborate one is to be found in John Wilkinson;[20] inspired by the Khaldunian theory of life and death of Muslim empires, the author explains how the Ibadi Imamate changed inevitably into a dynastic authority when the return of unity and peace allowed the rulers to build a prosperous empire, relying on overseas trade. Then the role played by religious doctrine and ethics slowly moved aside. This led to economic weakening and polarisation of interests through emergence of tribal confederations, whose purpose was to lay hands on diminishing resources. A civil war became unavoidable, so that foreign forces were led to interfere in the political game, either as arbiters or as direct actors called upon by one of the Omani factions. This moment was chosen by marginalised tribes to use the Ibadi legitimacy as a symbol of national pride, and proclaim the Imamate's renaissance, a rallying flag to reunify the territory under a single religious authority. The cycle of expansion and decline of Ibadism could then start again.

This theorisation is all the more attractive in that it provides an exhaustive interpretation of Omani history, and hence includes all the explanatory political factors of the local political game in an iterative scheme. Nevertheless, for the modern and contemporary eras, this cycle presents two difficulties. First, the foreign influences are widely underestimated; they were not only peripheral forces whose irruption can be seen as the consequence of an already marked internal weakening, they had an impact by themselves on major political developments in Oman. Moreover, it does not seem as clear as John Wilkinson's model suggests that the symbolic flag of the Imamate can definitely be seen as the origin of political upheavals in Oman. If such a historical reading appears valid for the 1913 Renaissance, it does not apply to the first years of the al-Busa'idi dynasty, nor to the Imamate's temporary resurgence in 1868. That affirmation of Imamate legitimacy was nothing but a way to confirm an already established temporal authority; this contradicts John Wilkinson's cycle theory, according to which the religious legitimacy (Imamate) precedes in time the temporal legitimacy (Sultanate, dynasty, etc.). Moreover, it does not help understand political events like the attempt to overthrow the Sultan in 1895 or the noteworthy peaceful coexistence of two legitimacies during the first half of the twentieth century.

This theoretical approach contributes, unintentionally of course, to the political myth of the *nahda*. This reference, which is constantly used in Oman nowadays, was brought back to light and popularised in Ibadi intellectual circles by Muhammad al-Salimi's book,[21] and then taken up by Sultan Qaboos' regime after the mid-1970s. In fact, the cycle theory relies on the idea of a virtuous Imamate which comes back at regular intervals, usually after the reign of a monarch considered as responsible for political and economic chaos, to allow Oman to recover peace, unity, independence and moral values. At a larger level, this picture finds its place, together with the principle of *shura*, within another national myth: "traditional Islamic democracy". Oman, it is suggested, possesses an atavistic democratic culture inherited from Ibadism, which explains the intrinsic ability of its people to get rid of authoritarian rulers. John Wilkinson seems to identify with this self-perception which, above all, pertains to a process of rewriting history.

Moreover, this cycle is based on a perception of Omani history as unchanging and timeless. The author describes Inner Oman as a "sociological *cul de sac*", in which "change from the outside world is absorbed by 'Muscat' [...] The Imamate takes on an unchanging form, the minimal state apparatus that a tribal order is able to develop to maintain some form of regional cohesiveness and [...] subsistence".[22] Even though the political isolation of Oman in the twentieth century is not deniable, the extremely troubled history of the Imamate, whose peoples were constantly in contact with the outside world, does not support the hypothesis of a banal repetition of events. The fact that the actors themselves invoke an immutable, fundamental past does not mean that they should be taken at their word.

Lastly, this theory leads to focus on the balance of power between Imam and tribes. An opposition between Imam and tribe usually exists in the work of observers: the existence of a strong Imamate would necessarily mean weak tribes, and conversely. In this connection, it is fundamental to recall that the dignity of Imam is then the indirect work of tribal *sheikh*s, and by consequence of the tribes themselves, as the *sheikh*s did not stop remodelling the legitimacy of the Imamate throughout history, by altering this symbolic reference to suit their own interests. The office of Imam cannot be seen as autonomous from the social forces supporting it. It is illusory to set the question in terms of separate entities whose respective influences are inversely proportional. On the contrary, the authority of the Imam certainly depended on negotiated relations with the tribal *sheikh*s coming under it, so that an Imamate could be powerful with an Imam who had no freedom of action, through tribal chiefs who would use its political legitimacy to assert their own interests. This happened in 1868, but the most striking example is given by the period starting in 1920. Two major individuals played a leading role under the rule of Imam Muhammad and were masters of the Imamate's policy's orientation.

'Isa bin Salih and Sulaiman bin Himyar were respectively *sheikhs tamima* of the Hirth and Bani Riyam tribes. 'Isa bin Salih became in 1896 the head of the Hinawi confederation; he was opposed to the conservative line of Imam Salim, who was supported by the Ghafiris. 'Isa naturally imposed himself as the Seeb agreement's negotiator on behalf of Imam Muhammad whose election he had just secured. He remained the strong man of the Imamate until his death in 1946 and enjoyed wide prestige even among his enemies. While he did not hesitate to resist the Imam, especially over the positions to assume towards the Sultan, 'Isa bin Salih, who always enjoyed regular relations with Sa'id, liked to use the title of *amir al-sharqiyya* ("Prince of Sharqiyya").

Sulaiman bin Himyar, who styled himself "Prince of Jabal Akhdar", succeeded in the 1920s, following his father's tradition, in establishing his ascendancy over the tribes who were allied to him. He stood out from the other personalities of the Imamate by his pragmatism, as it seems that he planned, in the 1950, to pay for a road between the coast and Inner Oman, in order to open that region to the outside world. Wilfred Thesiger said of him that "he was not a tribal sheikh ruling by consent, but an autocrat accustomed to obedience." His personal ambition led him to try, in 1949, to secure recognition from the British government as head of a semi-independent Jabal Akhdar, extended to the west, with the same status as the Trucial Coast sheikhdoms.[23] In addition, he worked secretly to negotiate directly with the oil companies on exploration rights in Inner Oman.[24] When 'Isa bin Salih died, Sulaiman became the brains of the interior forces, especially when the balance established since the Seeb agreement was suddenly upset.

Oil and the breakdown of the political balance. The Buraimi oasis, shared nowadays between the Emirate of Abu Dhabi and the Sultanate of Oman, has been a strategic stake since the eighteenth century. In 1869 Imam Azzan's troops succeeded in taking control of the oasis from the Saudis.[25] In 1925 the D'Arcy oil company signed an agreement with Sultan Taimur concerning the very first exploration rights in the Buraimi and 'Ibri areas. The political difficulties in this region, which was claimed by the Saudis and several Trucial Coast emirates, made the exploration fruitless; in 1937 the same happened with the exploration by an Iraq Petroleum Company (IPC) subsidiary, Petroleum Development (Oman and Dhofar),[26] after the signature of a 75-year concession agreement with Sultan Sa'id for the whole of Omani territory. The

Second World War put an end to these hopes. Prospecting started again in 1948, but IPC representatives soon realised that the Sultan did not have any control over the territories which today constitute the Dhahira governorate, despite his generosity to the tribes. This feeling was confirmed by declarations of Imam Muhammad, who refused to allow the IPC to prospect on his territory. In 1949, Ibn Sa'ud awarded a concession to the Arabian American Oil Company (Aramco) in the western part of Abu Dhabi Emirate; quickly, the company started exploration south of Buraimi. But the British, aware that their area of influence was threatened by this oil alliance between United States and Saudi Arabia, created a military force in Abu Dhabi, the Trucial Oman Levies.[27] They organised at the same time two joint commissions with the Saudis, in order to establish the borders once for all. Nothing came of these negotiations; then the Saudis decided to send troops to occupy Buraimi in August 1952, and to appoint a governor in charge of the area.

They tried also to get the support of the Oman Imamate, which had to solve a dilemma: should it support the Sultan and continue the trial of strength with the Saudis, in the name of Omani unity? Or should it take advantage of the situation to adopt an independent position and start direct discussions with Riyadh, as Sulaiman bin Himyar as well as Ghalib and Talib al-Hina'i, respectively *qadi* and *wali* of the Imam in Rustaq, favoured? Finally, the Imam rejected the Saudi deal and agreed with the Sultan of Muscat to join forces to expel the Saudis from Buraimi, catching the oasis in a pincer movement. In October Major Chauncy, British consul general in Muscat, forced the Sultan to abandon this plan, probably at the request of the American government. A temporary agreement was signed between the Saudis and the British on 26 October 1952, to start discussions about the Buraimi issue and appeal to outside arbitration.

If the underlying cause of the Sultan's change of mind was Britain's will to prevent a political rapprochement between the Imam and the Sultan, which could free them from British tutelage, the consequences were crucial. This was the last time the British used the divide-and-rule principle in Oman. For Sa'id, this forced turnaround only confirmed his lack of political freedom and increased the contempt he aroused among the most determined actors of the Imamate. Even more important, the interference of the Saudis and the irruption of the oil issue into the Omani political game had the tacit assent both of London and of the Imamate's *éminences grises*. In fact, they could do nothing else but agree to the end of the tripartite political order derived from the Seeb agreement and of the peaceful coexistence which had been introduced, particularly since the arrival of Sa'id bin Taimur. In order to avoid a direct trial of strength with the United States, whose purpose was the control of eastern Arabia's oil areas, London set in motion a process it did not bring under control. For Oman a new era was starting, an era to be marked by two conflicts which would prove decisive in the formation of contemporary national identity.

3

THE FOUNDING CONFLICTS
OF THE MODERN NATIONAL IDENTITY

The end of the Imamate (1955–59)

In May 1954, Imam Muhammad al-Khalili died. The Imamate's future strategic line was at the heart of the confrontation between two political sides. When continuation of the conservative order proved unworkable, a small group led by 'Abd Allah bin Zahir al-Hina'i, the Bani Hina *sheikh*, and Ahmad bin Muhammad al-Harthi, Salih bin 'Isa's nephew, called for fusion with the Sultanate, which meant refusal to elect a new Imam. Sulaiman bin Himyar and the brothers Ghalib and Talib al-Hina'i supported an independent line; they stood their ground and were in favour of a rapprochement with the Saudis. Finally, this latter political option won and Ghalib bin 'Ali, who was 35, rose to the dignity of Imam.[1] Nothing seemed to stand any more in the way of a direct confrontation.

Sa'id's first successful offensive. The Sultan's political priority was established in the spring of 1954: to take control of the territories which were supposed to hold oil reserves. In February an oil prospecting mission had already entered Duqm, north of Salalah, with the aim of reaching as soon as possible the northern borders of the Rub' al-Khali, near Fahud, where the chances of discovering oil were the best. The mission was funded by PDO, which set up a 500-man military escort, the Muscat and Oman Field Force (MOFF), composed of Baluchi and Batina tribesmen, under the official supervision of Sultan Sa'id. Things moved quickly in the summer of 1954, when Talib and

49

Sulaiman bin Himyar, opposed to this intrusion into the Imamate's territory, decided to recapture 'Ibri. This town took on a strategic importance because it commanded the Fahud area but also the road to Buraimi, which was still occupied by the Saudis. Yet the British took the initiative, more than ever convinced that there was no alternative to reunifying Oman. In the face of the Saudi-American threat, determination to preserve their influence area took precedence over the fragmentation principle extolled in the past. The Sultan convinced the Duru' Bedouin tribe, in the majority in the Fahud area, to assist oil production in return for his guarantee to protect them. With the agreement of this group, the MOFF reached Fahud, which allowed PDO to start exploration, and took 'Ibri in October without opposition.

At the same time, in Geneva, the official Saudi-British negotiations on Buraimi dragged on, as Riyadh openly supported the Imam, supplying his side with food, weapons and ammunition. In October 1955 the British stopped the discussions unilaterally; the Trucial Oman Scouts, based in Abu Dhabi, recaptured the Buraimi oasis at the end of the month. Saudi Arabia was to wait until 1974 to recognise the shared sovereignty of Abu Dhabi and Oman over this area.

Nothing now prevented the British from launching a head-on attack on the Imamate. On 15 December 1955 the MOFF captured the Imam's fortress in Nizwa without resistance, while in Rustaq, Talib surrendered on the 17th to the Sultan's Batina Force. Imam Ghalib withdrew to his Jabal Akhdar fiefdom, Bilad Sait; his brother found shelter in Saudi Arabia, and later in Cairo. Sulaiman bin Himyar chose to come back to Tanuf, while Salih bin 'Isa, seeing it was impossible to plead his cause before the Sultan, embarked for Zanzibar, before joining Talib in Egypt.

Sa'id bin Taimur made a several weeks' motorised tour of the interior.[2] He was the first Muscat ruler to come to the area since his great-grandfather Turki in 1886.[3] He visited the Fahud oil complex under construction, and then received the allegiance of many tribal leaders, like Sulaiman bin Himyar, who had asked his tribesmen not to fight when the MOFF troops entered Nizwa. In this town, the Sultan proclaimed that he granted amnesty to all those who would help him. This formal submission bore an unprecedented symbolic value, before all Inner Oman people's eyes, as they did not know another political authority than that of their *sheikh*s.

Strangely, Sa'id was not to change his authoritarian and distant way of governing. While many Omanis who had emigrated to neighbouring countries to find work pinned hopes on Sa'id for getting the interior of the country out of destitution, the ruler merely relied on the *sheikh*s: he imagined he controlled them by encapsulating them into a rudimentary bureaucratic structure and buying their peace, through continuation of a policy based on allowances and regular gifts. No deliberate strategy of development was started, except the building of a road to the interior—to provide access to the Fahud oil wells. Entrenched in his Salalah palace, Sa'id proved reluctant to meet the tribal chiefs. He entrusted his *wazir* Ahmad bin Ibrahim with the task of running Muscat, and appointed as *wali* of Nizwa *sheikh* Ahmad bin Muhammad al-Harthi, who was *tamima* of one of the tribes involved in the recent events, but was himself in favour of the Sultan.

The short-lived rebirth of the Ghalib Imamate. At the same time, Talib bin 'Ali established in Dammam, in Saudi Arabia, an Oman Liberation Army (OLA) of 300 soldiers, and then opened in Cairo, with Salih bin 'Isa, an office devoted to promotion of the Imamate ideas. Moreover, the Arab nationalist radio Sawt al-'Arab (the Voice of the Arabs) broadcast a weekly programme dedicated to the Imamate's struggle. In May 1957, in Sharqiyya province, Ibrahim bin 'Isa, who was the *wali* of Nizwa's uncle and Salih's brother, rose against the Sultan. When invited to Muscat to negotiate, Ibrahim was immediately sent to jail by Sa'id. But this first skirmish proved to be a diversion to facilitate Talib's return to Oman by the Batina coast. Both the Sultan and his British advisers had been warned about such steady infiltration of weapons and fighters into Oman more than a month beforehand by tribal chiefs loyal to them as well as by Tariq bin Taimur; but this information was not taken seriously.[4] Talib joined his brother in the Jabal Akhdar, so that in mid-June Ghalib proclaimed the rebirth of the Imamate. The Oman Regiment,[5] outnumbered by its adversaries, was routed near Bilad Sait and had to retreat to Fahud.[6] Within a month the most important interior fiefdoms, like Nizwa, Bahla and Izki, and also the Sama'il gap on the route to Muscat, flew the Imamate's white flag once again. On 16 July the Sultan was forced to ask officially for British help, as Muscat was threatened, given the weakness of the troops which defended it.

It seems that the Imam's supporters counted on British non-intervention. Behind this confrontation there emerges between the lines a new British-American (IPC versus Aramco) tussle over oil-bearing areas in the east of the peninsula. Britain's historic supremacy in the region was directly called into question by the Saudi authorities, who were backed secretly by an American company that some British protagonists described as "more Saudi than the Saudis".[7] As for the Americans, the consequences of a possible deterioration of the situation were feared, as the uprising in Oman could result in modifying King Sa'ud's policy towards the West.[8] Stormy debates in the House of Commons displayed the fear of a "second Suez";[9] but the London Cabinet reconciled itself to a military intervention which would involve as few of its troops as possible in the field. It allowed the British authorities in the Gulf to decide the necessary steps, without excluding air action against the Imamate fiefdoms. Around 25 July, preliminary bombing by the Royal Air Force (RAF), based in Sharjah, destroyed the Izki and Bilad Sait forts and reduced Barkat-al-Mawz to ashes. In August the Trucial Oman Scouts (TOS) and the Sultan's regiments seized control of Nizwa, Bahla, Izki and Tanuf (Sulaiman bin Himyar's fiefdom, which was blown up at the Sultan's orders) without meeting resistance. The Imam's supporters found shelter in the Jabal Akhdar. At the end of the month, the situation was considered stable enough to allow the British troops to leave the country, in order not to give the international community an opening to talk of military occupation of Oman. At the beginning of 1958 the Sultan's Armed Forces (SAF), funded by the British government as well as the sale of the Gwadar enclave to Pakistan, were established to prevent another uprising.

But this tactical withdrawal could not hide the inadequacy of the Sultan's authority, which was completely kept away from both political and military decisions. In fact, nothing was settled. The Sultan's already weak credibility was sapped by the explosion of mines, laid by Imamate supporters who were entrenched in the Jabal Akhdar, when the SAF patrols and PDO teams passed, or bombs aimed at the oil and military installations near Muscat. The various steps the SAF took, like the imposition of a blockade around the Jabal Akhdar, but also summary arrests and torture[10] and destruction of hamlets and agricultural infrastructure around which a mine had exploded,[11] proved to be ineffective, given the sympathy for the Imamate cause among Inner Oman's population. The SAF chief, David Smiley, decided in October to call in British elite troops of the Special Air Services (SAS), to launch a large-scale operation in the Jabal Akhdar. Despite the easy capture of the adversary's positions with the help of intensive air bombing, this action, which was carried out between November 1958 and January 1959, was only a mixed success because most of the fighters could return to their villages and the three Imamate leaders, Ghalib, Talib and Sulaiman bin Himyar, reached Saudi Arabia. Harsh reprisals were taken against the Jabal Akhdar; houses, *aflaj* and village palm groves belonging to the families most involved in the conflict were destroyed, the inhabitants were ostracised in order to cut them off the neighbouring towns and prevent them from going abroad to look for work.[12]

Yet the prospect of a new rebellion would not last long. The exiled Imamate's struggle turned into intimidation actions (explosions of mines or bombs, sabotage, etc.). In Inner Oman, the situation was so difficult to manage for Muscat's ruler that the Nizwa-Muscat road was to stay closed for five years.[13] An SAF British officer gave an account: "We had, with extreme difficulty, climbed victoriously out of a conventional war with a shooting enemy and a recognizable front line, only to find ourselves up to the chin of a guerilla war with an invisible enemy, and a front line which was assuming two dimensions instead of only one: it was us against the whole country, not just the *Jebel*."[14] Until 1964 there would be explosions and other incidents over the whole territory, which maintained a strained climate, extending to the capital. But Imam supporters would now concentrate on political action, with the internationalisation of the conflict.

The 'Oman question' in the international arena. Paradoxically, the legitimisation process on which the Imamate supporters focused from the late 1950s took place within the framework of the nation-state register of references. In 1955, when the Imamate office in Cairo was established, its members were already getting closer to the Arab League to defend their positions. An application for membership was even made, supported by Egypt, Syria and Saudi Arabia, but unsuccessfully.[15] While Saudi support had weakened, because of the desire to settle the Buraimi issue, the Imamate spokesperson in Cairo called on the United States and China for help, and representation offices were opened in Damascus, Dammam and Beirut. The Oman question was regularly discussed in UN commissions from 1958 on, with debates concerning the respective political legitimacies of the Imam and the Sultan, and the interpretation of the Seeb agreement. In 1961, informal discussions started in Beirut between the services of the British political resident in the Gulf, who negotiated on account of the Sultan, and Talib bin 'Ali and Muhammad al-Salimi, for the Imam.[16] Nothing came of them. These would be the last direct contacts between the two sides until Sa'id's overthrow in the summer of 1970.

The argument invoked by the British and the Sultan in refusing to recognise the UN's right to interfere was that the Omani question was a strictly internal affair. In the early 1960s the British finally accepted a UN information mission. In the spring of 1963, an envoy of the UN Secretary General completed a visit to Oman, and then went to Dammam and Beirut to meet Imamate supporters in exile. The envoy's report, which was favourable to the British point of view, established that there was no more military opposition in Oman, but was not able to take a position on the respective political legitimacies. In December 1963 the UN created an *ad hoc* committee on Oman. The Sultan did not agree to let the committee members enter the territory; the conclusions presented stressed the international nature of the Omani question, as a result of "imperialistic policies and foreign interventions in Muscat and Oman".[17] At the end of 1965, a resolution of the UN General Assembly recognised the right of Inner Oman to political self-determination and called for British withdrawal from the country. This resolution, which had no concrete effect, was renewed in December 1970; it preceded another unfruitful meeting between the Imamate authorities in exile and Sultan Qaboos' representatives, in August 1971.[18]

Imam Ghalib's supporters did not succeed in solving the contradictions inherent in the internationalisation of a movement which quickly went beyond their control. Whereas their legitimacy relied on perpetuation of a religious legacy peculiar to Omani history, in which one of the main motivations was the fight against the "infidel" British occupying force, the struggle's political language gradually switched from a religiously-inspired discourse to one of an anti-imperialist struggle for national emancipation. The Saudis, initially international godfathers of the movement, were slowly replaced in that role in the early 1960s by Nasser's Egypt, and then by General Qassim's Iraq. While senior figures of the Imamate resistance took the name of the Revolutionary Council of Oman, the importance of the offices in Cairo and Baghdad increased as the Imamate's official bulletins, *Nizwa* and *Free Oman*, were issued from there. These accounts, while they spoke in the name of a "State of Oman Imamate" (*dawla imama 'uman*), used pan-Arab themes, echoing the other struggles in the region. For instance, more and more references were explicitly made to "the Arab revolution (*thawra*) in Oman", a "fair struggle in which is engaged the Arab people (*sha'ab*) of Oman".[19] Moreover, as the replacement of supporters and activists, trained in Iraq and Dammam, became more and more difficult, appeal was made to the Omanis who had emigrated to Gulf countries for economic reasons. Their progressive political ideas had tremendous influence on the goals the movement pursued: the central aim became less the restoration of the Imamate as a political authority than economic modernisation, improvement of living standards, and the simple removal of an authoritarian Sultan, seen as responsible for the country's backwardness.

This doctrinal shift added to the difficulties the resistance faced after 1962. The slogans of the Imamate authorities in exile were not able to hide their remoteness from the Omani reality, so that they were slowly condemned to marginalisation. In a desperate attempt, in the summer of 1962 Talib bin 'Ali made contact with Dhofari personalities, to support an uprising in this region.[20] Two of the future Dhofari movement's leaders, Musallam bin Nufl and 'Abd Allah al-Ghazali, went in the spring of 1963 to Dammam and Damascus to meet Talib. This strategy relied on shared resentment against the Sultan, who lived permanently in Salalah. While he administered this region as his personal domain, no development policy had been launched. Progressively, Dhofar became the epicentre of a struggle against Sa'id bin Taimur's power.

The Dhofar War (1965–75)

Dhofar is the most southerly province of the country. Usually compared to an island, because of its isolation from the rest of the country, it is inhabited by 386,000 people, of whom 51% are Omani.[21] It has three geographical parts: the coastal plain of Salalah (*al-madina*); three mountain ranges (*al-jabal*) which overlook the plain; and lastly, the desert hinterland (*al-sahara*). The second town of Oman, Salalah, where 80% of Dhofar's inhabitants live, is the meeting point of these various regions. The whole Omani population of Dhofar is Sunni. The area was roughly independent until the end of the nineteenth century but came under the rule of the Sultans of Muscat in 1879, when Turki appointed a governor there. This political subjection increased with the special relationship that Sa'id established with the province after 1958. In practical terms, however, until the 1970s Muscat's political control was limited to the coast.

All Dhofari populations are affiliated to a tribe (*'ashira*), even though Arabic is far from being the only spoken language. Several "south-Arabic Semitic" dialects, which are related to the Ethiopian languages but not mutually understandable with them, are spoken nowadays in Dhofar, like Mahri, Jabbali and Shahri. Four main tribal confederations inhabit Dhofar: the Bait Kathir, Mahri, Qarawi and Shahri confederations. The confederations usually spread over the plain, the mountains and the desert plateau. For instance, the Bait Kathir include not only sedentary groups inhabiting the mountains, but also urban tribes (Shanfari, Rawas, etc.) and a large proportion of the nomadic pastoralists living in the desert. Two smaller groups add to the picture: the Sada, who are descended from Prophet Muhammad and constitute the religious aristocracy of the region, and the Mashayikh. Similarly to northern Oman, some groups who are descendants of clients or slaves from East Africa have a lower social status.

From rebellion against Sa'id to a revolutionary political front. In the early 1960s, many people from Dhofar emigrated to the Gulf countries to escape a deprived existence at home. Clerks, oil workers, soldiers, these migrants came into contact with the intellectual and political turmoil in the region at that time, as well as the connections between some of the Dhofari elite and the exiled Imam. At the same time, in 1964 more exactly, oil exploitation in northern Dhofar began, though Sa'id wished to exert close control over the oil rent in order to maintain the status quo.

British officials were far from imagining what was to come: "There is no serious threat against the Sultan's authority here. The Sultan likes to keep this province as separate as possible from the remainder of the country."[22] But the strained climate favoured the emergence of several underground organisations, such as the Benevolence Society of Dhofar (*al-jama'iyya al-khayriyya dhufar*), a charity association whose slogan was "Dhofar for the Dhofaris", and even the local branch of the Arab Nationalist Movement, which took more violent action. These operations multiplied around Salalah as early as 1963; there were several explosions in the new oil installations, while sabotage targeted SAF convoys. Under the impulse of the revolution in the neighbouring Yemen, these various circles progressively merged into the Dhofar Liberation Front (DLF, *jabha tahrir dhufar*). The first DLF congress took place in June 1965.[23] Among the members of the executive committee were Yusef bin 'Alawi, the DLF representative in Cairo and leader of its Nasserist tendency, and Muhammad al-Ghassani, a supporter of Arab nationalism. On this occasion, 9 June 1965 was proclaimed officially as the "beginning of the revolution".

In April 1966 Sa'id escaped miraculously unharmed from an assassination attempt at the Salalah air base by some Dhofari DLF-supporting soldiers of his own guard. The core of the movement was mainly tribal and popular, and won the inhabitants' sympathy more easily because the restriction measures Sa'id imposed after the attempt kept on increasing. Fawwaz Trabulsi explains that DLF ideology "was neither a call for the right to self-determination of an oppressed group, nor a rallying cry against the autocracy of the al-Busa'idi dynasty and its British overlords [...] but something on the borderline between the two."[24]

The second DLF congress, in September 1968, represented a major turning point in the movement's history: it took the name of the Popular Front for the Liberation of the Occupied Arabian Gulf (PFLOAG). The rebels adhered to the "scientific socialism" doctrine, declaring themselves "Marxist-Leninist".[25] While a socialist regime was established in South Yemen in

1967, the Dhofar insurgents had to face Saʿid's radicalisation of the war. The ruler decided to implement a blockade of the mountain area and to prevent its contacts with Salalah. Furthermore, greater freedom of action was given to the army, as a British officer explains: "[We blew] the wells, [...] burnt the rebel villages and shot their goats and cows... Any enemy corpses we recovered were propped up in a corner of the Salalah market as a salutary lesson to any would-be freedom fighters."[26]

The action had until then been limited to Dhofar, but now the movement set as its objective the extension of the struggle to the whole of Oman and the Trucial Emirates. The idea of social revolution went with the armed struggle: education for all (linked to the spread of Mao, Lenin and Che Guevara texts), abolition of slavery, women's emancipation (abolition of polygamy and dowry), and the struggle against tribalism were proclaimed. However, the PFLOAG central committee had to face the departure of several founding members, like Yusef bin ʿAlawi and Musallam bin Nufl, who were to head a new DLF for some time, before going over to Sultan Qaboos in 1970. At the international level the Egyptians, suffering from the 1967 war, had to reduce their help, and Saudi Arabia did the same as the Front's discourse became more and more radical; Riyadh finally made up with the Sultan's and British side in Oman when South Yemen proclaimed its independence. The PFLOAG progressively established closer links with China, Iraq and Palestinian movements such as Nayef Hawatmeh's Popular Democratic Front for the Liberation of Palestine.[27] This new support allowed the Front to take the whole Western Dhofar in the summer of 1969. South Yemen acted as an intermediary with the Socialist bloc but also as a sanctuary and rear base for the rebels all through the war; it also provided equipment and personnel on an extensive scale, especially at the end. By early 1970, when Jabal Samhan had also fallen into the rebels' hands, the Sultan's forces only controlled the Salalah plain and a few fortified positions on the Muscat-Salalah road. Their remaining means of action consisted of air raids by the RAF on the positions and ruined villages controlled by the PFLOAG.

The victory of the new central government. The rebellion spread to northern Oman in June 1970. The newly-established National Democratic Front for the Liberation of Oman and the Arabian Gulf (NDFLOAG) claimed three failed attacks against the Izki, Nizwa and Saiq bases. The British had no other solution to counter this situation but a psychological blow, with Sultan Saʿid's forced abdication in favour of his son Qaboos. This coup, announced in advance,[28] enjoyed the support of the other Gulf emirs as well as the Shah, all worried by potential revolutionary contagion.

The Sultanate authorities had a radical change of heart, as they decided to use the oil rent in wide-scale development programmes (education, health, agriculture), but also in establishing tribal units (*firqa*) under the *sheikhs'* authority, in order to involve their credibility directly in the results of the operations. Defence expenditure increased in 1971 to 50% of the State budget.[29] Thousands of tracts announced that a general amnesty, combined with financial help, would be granted to rebels who surrendered. These measures would prove effective only in the long term: in May 1971, the Muscat road passed under the PFLOAG's control.

In October the SAF, supported by the SAS which had arrived in August 1970, launched a large-scale land and air operation in eastern Dhofar. The results remained below expectations. Jet fuel was still being massively dumped from aircraft at the beginning of 1972 in order to burn vegetation and fields around the rebellious villages.[30] In May 1972, a new attack focused on the western part of the province (operation Simba) was repelled by the PFLOAG.[31]

The summer of 1972 represented the turning point of the conflict. While the rebels succeeded in coming through the two hardest attacks of the war, marked by massive attacks by the RAF and the Sultan of Oman's Armed Forces (SOAF) on mountain villages, they were heavily defeated when they tried to take the coastal towns of Taqa and Mirbat in July. The PFLOAG then sought to increase the range of opponents of the British by opening a new front in northern Oman while establishing connections with northern underground groups, like the Arab Workers' Party of Oman,[32] and others from other Gulf countries. 1972 also witnessed the arrival of the first Iranian experts on the side of Sultan Qaboos;[33] this support showed its efficacy when a victorious offensive was launched in December 1973 to take back the Muscat-Salalah road. At the same time, a containment strategy conceived by the British as early as 1971 was implemented. The goal was to divide Dhofar into three hermetical segments, perpendicular to the coast, in order to isolate the rebel forces in the "cleaned" zones. The rebels still controlled the western part as well as the major part of the eastern *jabal*, but had to act in an autonomous way because of the positions held by the Sultan in the centre of Dhofar. The Arab League tried to act as go-between in March 1974, but it failed, while dissensions began to appear within the rebellion movement. A new change of name was adopted: the PFLOAG became the Popular Front for the Liberation of Oman (PFLO). It illustrated the will of the Gulf-native members to turn to a more political struggle, which the Dhofaris, for whom the armed fight remained primordial, were reluctant to do. The PFLO decided on a decentralisation of decisions, to give every local fighting unit the possibility of responding to particular requirements.

In November 1974, a PFLO cell was dismantled by the Sultan's forces in Rustaq, and then a weapons cache in Muttrah in December; these events highlighted the activity of underground movements in northern Oman, and their infiltration into the government apparatus. The year 1975 saw the offensives led by the SAF and the Iranian forces intensified on an unprecedented scale; they progressively overcame the most solid PFLO positions, at a very heavy human and material cost. The rebels, who were decimated by defections but supported by South Yemeni soldiers, were forced to transfer their infrastructure to the other side of the border. The PFLO stronghold of Sharshati, on the Yemeni border, fell just before the town of Dalkut on 1 December. Most of the rebels reached South Yemen, and on 11 December 1975 Sultan Qaboos proclaimed the official end of the war. However, small well-equipped rebel groups kept on fighting fiercely for three years.[34] In 1982 the arrest near Muscat of rebels who were carrying weapons to Dhofar confirmed the opinion of a SOAF officer who took part in these late operations: "The situation for the British around 1980 was comparable to Afghanistan for the Americans in 2003".[35] The fighting would actually cease between 1983 and 1985.

Foreign help proved decisive in reversing a situation which was extremely difficult for the Muscat ruler in the early 1970s. Among these external forces, the British played a deciding role. Besides their support in equipment, their forces numbered between 1,000 and 1,500 in Dhofar in December 1975;[36] they represented the overwhelming majority of military, medical, technical and even intelligence officers on the field and were divided into three categories: SAS members, officially there to train the Omani forces; individual "contract officers", usually former RAF members; and staff "seconded" from the British Ministry of Defence to the Sultan of Oman.

In the Arab world, only Jordan backed Qaboos' regime without reserve. King Husain went personally twice to Dhofar, but also allocated large-scale equipment supplies and made intelligence staff available to the Sultan. On a much lesser scale, Saudi Arabia's support, through financial and material help since 1972, indirectly convinced South Yemen to moderate its involvement in the conflict. Lastly, Egyptian military advisers helped the Sultan's army in the mid-1970s.

Iran actively involved itself in the conflict after 1972; 5,000 Iranian personnel were in Dhofar in 1975.[37] The Dhofar war was used by the Shah as a training ground for his youngest troops, which explains both the frequent turnover and the heavy losses Iran suffered. Pakistan and Sri Lanka, by their considerable help, and India, which put military instructors at Oman's disposal, also participated in the war effort.

In a sociological perspective, the tribal variable never constituted a decisive factor to explain the polarisations observed during the war. Some tribes which are only present in Salalah, like the Shanfari, the Rawas and even the Marhun, soon positioned themselves on the Sultan's side because of the economic interests they shared with the central government long before the conflict. Some isolated personalities, like the Bait Ma'ashani *sheikhs*, followed the same path. As for the others, all Dhofaris, either from the mountain region or from the town, felt sympathy for the revolt and participated more or less actively in it—a fact confirmed by a British officer in 1970: "The Qara tribesmen and most of the coastal Arabs were sympathetic to, if not actually engaged in, the struggle against the Sultan."[38]

The situation began to change only after the coup. The promises Qaboos made to ensure people's security and impunity, but above all to help these families to rebuild their livestock herds decimated by the war or build houses, had a determining effect on their surrender. It was not uncommon to see families torn between a member in Salalah who had given allegiance to Qaboos and another still fighting on the rebels' side. In a period when the outcome was still uncertain (1970–74), this behaviour made it possible to position a pawn on each political side so as to reclaim collective virginity for the group, at the watershed of a conflict.

The 1960s: the decade of remoteness

In 1958 Sa'id bin Taimur decided to retire to his palace in Salalah; he was not to go to Inner Oman any more, or even to Muscat. The daily running of the capital was entrusted to Ahmad bin Ibrahim and Shihab bin Faisal, but also to the foreign experts. From then on, features of Sa'id's mode of government which emerged in the 1930s and 40s—deep suspicion towards the Omanis and corresponding increased presence of the British in the corridors of power—were to be exacerbated.

British tutelage in political affairs. The pre-eminence of mercenaries, mostly British, within the Omani circles of power in the 1960s clearly illustrates both the Foreign Office's will to keep its grip over a regime it sought to maintain and Sa'id's generalised distrust of all who surrounded him. Except for Ahmad bin Ibrahim, all the Sultan's advisers were British. They had usually served in other Middle East regions under British rule (Jordan, Egypt, Sudan, etc.). Among the most important, it is necessary to note Sa'id's personal adviser from 1958 to 1970, Major Chauncy, a former consul in Muscat from 1949 to 1958, and Hugh Boustead (1959–63) and D.N. Ogram (1963–68), who headed the Development Department successively from its creation. This presence was particularly strong in the military and security fields, which consumed seven-eighths of the British government's annual payments to the Sultan. The unification of various former military formations into an army, the Sultan's Armed Forces or SAF, in 1958 hardly masked the tutelage to which the Sultan was tied. Thus, after the appointment of a new SAF chief, who was a seconded officer, the British political resident in Bahrain explained his function to him like this: "Your master is the Sultan. But if he should give you any order you consider contrary to British interests, you have the right to appeal to me, and through me to the Foreign Office."[39] Colonel Waterfield, a former British India officer, became Secretary of Defence and remained until his leave in January 1970 the individual closest to Sultan Sa'id; he controlled internal intelligence with Major Dennison. As for the Masirah and Salalah bases, they were at Britain's disposal from 1936.

Moreover, a large number of expatriates, recruited by private contract to fill executive and technical positions, came to Oman. They were usually retired members of the military and civilian administrations of British India. Some of them had already served officially in Muscat. For instance, C.J. Pelly, who was appointed as director of Plan and Development in 1968, and L.B. Hirst, Secretary for Oil Affairs from 1965, had respectively been Political Agent in Muscat and military adviser in the 1940s. Even such a specialised position as Secretary for Internal Affairs was occupied by a US citizen, John Shebbeard, in 1968.[40]

The telegrams sent by London revealed nevertheless the obstacles these individuals faced in transmitting their plans to the Sultan. The simplest way was usually the best one: "If the Sultan had been equally passive in all respects, matters might have been easier; but his attitude was on many occasions simply obstructive [...] To be effective, decisions would have to be taken unilaterally. When we thought that measures were necessary, we took them and told the Sultan afterwards."[41]

Sa'id's decision to stay in the Salalah palace was taken above all to escape the direct financial requests of northern Oman peoples who would have come to give their allegiance; the latter were then forced to use Ahmad bin Ibrahim as an intermediary in order to submit a request to the Sultan. Nevertheless things changed after 1967, as oil production had begun in Fahud and the Sultanate's revenues increased dramatically. After a speech in January 1968 by the Sultan, several large-scale urban projects—which would only come to fruition under Qaboos—were launched, such as the building of Muttrah port, three hospitals, two power plants (Ruwi, Salalah), the Sohar road and a girls' school in Muscat.[42]

But the extreme precautions with which Sa'id implemented these projects show that his aversion to any excessive expenditure cannot be explained by financial necessities only, particularly as Sa'id's personal wealth was considerable, thanks especially to his speculative operations in Africa started as early as the 1930s.[43] Despite Sa'id's dependence on the British regarding his own political survival, the unconditional protection they provided contributed to social and political immobility, as it exonerated him from any need to adapt or reform. The British were highly aware of this paradox: "[The Sultan] is probably fundamentally loyal to the British connexion as his family have been for 150 years [...] In negotiations, however, he does not hesitate to exploit what he assumes to be the fundamental weakness of our position, namely that we depend totally on him to secure an interest vital to our own position in the Gulf, that is control of the interior of Oman. Our whole line of conduct towards him since the outbreak of 1957 rebellion has led him to conclude that we will rescue him from any trouble at any cost to ourselves, and it is almost certainly this assumption which has made him so resistant to proposals for internal reform."[44]

Social and political stagnation in the 1960s. Besides this castrating tutelage, the Sultan and the British shared the idea that out of control social and economic development would inevitably lead to the emergence of political opposition. The second half of Sa'id's rule was marked by the constant fear of having to face such problems. At that time a wide range of restrictions, directed at the Omanis while British or PDO employees were exempted, were in force. Anything that could favour, even indirectly, the exchange or spread of "foreign" or "modern" ideas had to be opposed. Owning a car or projecting a film, importing newspapers, books or even medicine, all this has to be submitted strictly to the Sultan's agreement. Drinking alcohol, smoking in public, opening restaurants, riding bicycles, playing football or music, and wearing glasses, closed shoes, trousers or any "foreign dress"[45] were prohibited.

Similarly, all entry permits for the country, even for journalists or diplomatic missions, were stopped after 1965, when an unfavourable report by the

UN ad hoc committee was published. The Sultan maintained no diplomatic relations, as his only official foreign representation was a British honorary consul in London who also administered his financial interests. Any Omani who wanted to travel within the country or abroad had to ask for special permission from the Sultan. Three hours after twilight, the doors of Muscat and Muttrah were shut down until the morning and nobody was allowed to go in and out without the permission of Ahmad bin Ibrahim. Anybody who moved within those towns after sunset had to carry a lantern at eye level to be recognised by the police. Moreover, the authorities proved reluctant to make the territory benefit from development, even a minimal one. Running water and electricity, provided by electricity generating systems, were reserved to the Sultan's residences and those of his *protégés* in Muscat and Salalah, and the PDO compound near the capital, which was equipped with air-conditioning from generators, a running water system, a small hospital and a school.

These dreadful conditions had consequences at the social level; until 1970, the Sultan proved hostile to the development of education and health services in his country. He considered for instance that the education system established by the British in India was the basic cause of the unrest which led to independence in 1947: "The teachers would come from Cairo and spread Nasser's seditious ideas among their pupils. And what is there here for a young man with education? He would go to the university in Cairo or to [...] London, finish in Moscow and come back here to foment trouble."[46] In 1970, the whole territory had only three "Western" elementary schools—in Muscat, Muttrah and Salalah—with 1,200 pupils, but also almost fifty Koranic schools which welcomed 4,800 children.[47] In a very cynical way the Sultan justified his rejection of health planning: "We do not need hospitals here. Oman is a very poor country which can only support a small population. At present many children die in infancy and so the population does not increase. If we build clinics many more will survive. But for what? To starve?"[48]

In 1970, there were forty rudimentary health centres in Oman—most of them established under Hugh Boustead's administration in the 1960s—including five hospitals.[49] The poverty of the health service structures explained the appalling health conditions in the country. Malaria, trachoma, leprosy were common diseases, as well as malnutrition and anaemia due to meat deficiency. Pneumonia proved usually fatal for Inner Oman inhabitants, because the journey to Muttrah by donkey took so long.[50] This disastrous economic and social situation was the main reason for the increase of Omanis' expatriation. At the end of the 1960s, more than 50,000 Omanis lived in the other Gulf emirates, including 11,000 in Bahrain (28% of the foreigners in Bahrain in 1971) and 14,000 in Kuwait.[51] They occupied usually subordinate positions, in particular the ones neglected by the nationals: crew on the pearl boats in Bahrain, unskilled workers in agriculture and in the oil sectors in Kuwait and Bahrain. The Dhofaris clustered in Saudi Arabia, Kuwait and Qatar in the armed forces, police and in the building sector.

As Robert Landen observed in 1967,[52] none of the most influential Omani political forces throughout the twentieth century took care to promote any sort of economic development or modernisation. Both the Sultan and the British had nothing to get out of it, as the lack of change made it possible to keep the territory safe from the upheavals the Middle East endured at the same time. This attitude was shared by the Ibadi religious authorities for a long time. Similarly, the Indian traders could not take the risk of putting commercial pre-eminence in doubt for uncertain gain. As for the foreign powers, nothing attracted them into this isolated land, a land also locked up by the British—until oil dramatically changed the existing order.

Qaboos' coup. Qaboos bin Sa'id was born in 1940 in Salalah; he is the son of a Bait Ma'ashani *sheikh*'s daughter from the Dhofari Qara tribe. When he was 16, his father sent him to Sandhurst for military studies; he completed his training with the British Army of the Rhine, before serving a one-year training period with Bedfordshire County Council, so as to study local government. When Qaboos came back to Salalah in 1964 after a world tour, Sa'id put him under house arrest. Qaboos, who was instructed only to concentrate on Islamic studies, tried to convince his rare visitors, mostly British, to talk to his father in order to entrust him with responsibilities. Qaboos' situation in Salalah thus recalled that of the potential successors of Ottoman sultans in the seventeenth century, who were kept in confinement to prevent them from fomenting a coup.[53]

The British authorities' role in the coup was fundamental. Officers who served the Sultan—like the Secretary of Defence, Hugh Oldman, and the intelligence chief—and the official representatives of London in the Gulf, like the British Consul in Muscat and the Political Resident in the Gulf, were all involved.[54] None of the Al Sa'id family members participated directly, as most of them were in exile in the Gulf.

In the evening of 23 July 1970, Sheikh Buraik al-Ghafiri, son of the Dhofar province *wali*, broke into the palace with Omani soldiers; in the gunfight started by Sa'id's slaves, the Sultan was injured, and soon he was forced to sign his abdication in favour of his son. He was evacuated to Bahrain by plane on the following day, and then to England. He would spend the end of his life in London, where he died on 19 October 1972.[55] When Qaboos entered Muscat for the first time of his life on 30 July, he was warmly applauded by a dense and colourful crowd, whose immense hopes gave him a foretaste of the task which awaited him.

4

LEGITIMISATION BY THE WELFARE STATE

Brought to power with the benevolence of a foreign power, Sultan Qaboos inherited a territory without a state, about which he knew almost nothing. His room for manoeuvre with regard to the British was reduced to a minimum, and so was his legitimacy vis-à-vis the Omani population. The Dhofar military campaign, in which he was personally involved, gave him only a short time to dedicate to the country's development during the first years of his rule. And assertions about the Sultanate of Oman as a true unitary state throughout the twentieth century were not based on a genuine feeling of a nation bound together around its sovereign. Paradoxically, Sultan Sa'id's active opponents who took refuge abroad, united by common rejection of the system, were certainly the only ones to display a feeling of belonging to an Omani community.

Nevertheless, no political system can show such durability and stability as Sultan Qaboos' regime has shown if it does not enjoy the trust or the support of a part of the population it leads. Soon Sultan Qaboos had to enlarge the traditional basis of power (composed of the allies of the Sultan) by weaving personal ties with the population, so as not to be dependent on a single social force. To do this, Sultan Qaboos has used the "homogenisation power" of the central state. Exploitation of the new oil rent, growing in an exponential way, has made possible economic and social development unknown before, in which the state, in all-out expansion over the territory, has played a pivotal role. In short, the Sultan's idea has been to make Omanis individually rely no longer on the 'asabiyyat, but on the state for day-to-day life. This is the conclusion Joel Migdal reaches when he states that "state leaders and their agencies have sought ways to change those they rule from disconnected subjects of state rule to some other status that would connect their personal identities to the continued existence and vitality of the state. And state rulers have sought to establish this connection while [...] remaining the ultimate authority and arbiter, standing in a continuing object-subject relationship with them."[1]

In the Omani case, it was necessary for Qaboos to de-legitimise, to discredit the other *'asabiyyat* by raising himself to be the only authority able to conduct the oil rent redistribution. The primary goal was to replace the *'asabiyyat*, traditional sources of legitimacy that were dwarfed by the new state's economic and social achievements so that they could no longer provide what was their raison d'être, the protection and socio-economic well-being of their tribesmen. This trend has gone with a symbolic process of national unification, through the reinvention of the frames of identity references around the person of the Sultan, assimilated in new historiography to the state and subsequently to modern Oman as a whole. To sum up, Sultan Qaboos has been able to set up the legitimacy of his authority by building both an Omani state and an Omani nation.

The key to the Sultanate's stability since 1970 lies in the incorporation of so-called "traditional" values into the state apparatus. The central authorities have sought to de-autonomise the traditional solidarity groups, rendering them fully dependent on a political game that the regime controls and whose rules the regime establishes. In parallel, the *'asabiyyat* have also attempted to reappropriate the state in their own interests, seeking power positions that can ensure their members' survival. As both the author and the object of redistribution, the state is thus the framework that is reshaping and reinventing the *'asabiyyat* while simultaneously being reshaped by them.

Oil as fuel of the 'development war'

Oil in commercial quantity was discovered between 1962 and 1964 in the Fahud, Natih and Jibal Petrol Development Oman (PDO) fields. Soon it was decided to build a pipeline to convey the oil to the Mina al-Fahal terminal, near Muttrah. In July 1967 oilfields exploitation by PDO, which was held 85% by Shell, 10% by the Compagnie Française des Pétroles and 5% by the Gulbenkian Foundation, started. In 1969, production stabilised at 327,000 barrels per day. That year this godsend represented forty times the total annual revenue of the Sultanate in the early 1960s! On 1 January 1974 the Omani state took a 25% stake in PDO's capital; this was raised six months later to

60%. Like the other countries of the area, Oman took advantage of the oil crises of the 1970s and multiplied its revenues by 15 in ten years. The late 1970s saw a fall in production, which was counterbalanced by the discovery of huge oilfields in Dhofar, like Marmul.

The all-time peak of the country's production came in August 2000, with 1,010,000 barrels per day. Nevertheless, Oman's oil production costs are still high by comparison with the other Gulf producers, especially because of the extreme dispersal of resources over many small fields. In 2001 Oman produced 47.4 million tons of oil, compared with 423 million in Saudi Arabia, 113 million in the UAE and 104 million in Kuwait. Despite Oman's relatively small oil production, this rent allowed economic take-off and financed the Omani state-building process for the last thirty years. Over this period, oil revenue has never represented less than 70% of total state resources (except in 1998, 1999, 2006, 2007, 2008 and 2009); since 2010, the rate has stabilised around 70–72%.[2]

The state monopoly of oil rent management, which has been considered for two decades by the Omanis as an inexhaustible source of revenue, has been at the heart of the control policy the ruler has implemented. In fact this rent has made it possible not only to set up the state as the symbolic framework of reference for all, but also to build it up as the crux of development, by the redistribution system the state organised for all social and ethnic groups. This process has helped to reduce the audience of competitive legitimacies—such as tribes, ethnic groups and regional factions—which were forced to adapt to new rules of the game, rules whose definition they were not consulted on. Hence it has been possible for Qaboos to build a nation on these new state foundations.

Building a new framework of collective references

International law defines a modern state[3] as a territorial unit (a "material" element), containing a stable population (a "personal" element), under the authority of its own government (a "formal" authority), and recognised as being able to enter relations with other states. In his quest for political legitimacy, Qaboos' priority was to establish, for the first time in Oman's history, a state which could be both a political control apparatus at the central authority's disposal and a geographical and symbolic territory defined by physical boundaries. It was for Sultan Qaboos to determine what Oman was, that is, to establish what was "inside" and what was "outside" the new national community; concretely, he had to settle the issues of Omani nationality (the people) and the Omani state's boundaries (the territory). Once this frame was defined, Sultan Qaboos had to reassert his sovereignty by being recognised at the international level, but also by spreading common rules and references all over the territory, which was symbolically and materially invaded by the state and its values.

Demographic and geographical boundaries. Omani independence has never been officially proclaimed by Qaboos, as the British considered for long that the Sultanate was a sovereign country "in special treaty relations" with London. Oman was admitted to the Arab League on 29 September 1971, to the UN on the following 7 October, and then to the International Monetary Fund, the World Health Organization, etc.

The "Arab" and "Muslim" character of the country was emphasised by Qaboos without any explicit reference to Ibadism. This last issue was crucial as it made it possible to avoid establishing any difference of status among the Arab-Muslim populations settled on the territory—the sedentary or nomadic tribes from the north and centre of Oman, whether Ibadi or Sunni; but on the other hand it raised questions about several "peripheral" groups, like the Dhofari peoples, the Baluchis, the Lawatiyya and the Banyans, as well as all the Omanis who had emigrated to Africa and the Gulf.

The uncertain military situation in Dhofar, combined with a series of unfruitful oil explorations, led some British officers to think of unilateral withdraw from this province, but the Sultan clarified the situation in 1971: "Dhofar is an integral part of the Sultanate of Oman, to precisely the same extent that Muscat is [...] We will sacrifice lives in order to [...] provide our people there with the same decent life enjoyed by all Omanis throughout the Sultanate."[4] The "Omanity" of Dhofar and Dhofaris would not be the subject of any compromise.

As for the emigrants, who were mostly from tribes of Inner Oman, and the Baluchis who were living in Oman, Qaboos' political calculation was the same: despite the linguistic handicap of both groups, who usually did not speak Arabic fluently, there was no choice but to grant them citizenship, given their strategic significance for him. The Baluchis were invaluable allies of the Sultan. This group constituted the framework of his army but no threat in terms of political demands. Similarly, the "back-from-Africa" Omanis, since they had not been involved in internal political and tribal matters in Oman, could be an asset for Qaboos, and they soon made contact with the new power in quest of political allies. Besides, they were relatively more educated than those at home. Many of them had been trained in technical fields in Europe, East Africa or other Gulf countries, so they could make a significant workforce for the ruler's planned modernisation. Qaboos had then no option but to grant them Omani citizenship, as soon as they returned, without any consideration of the time their families had spent abroad.

Unlike the Lawatiyya who had wished to remain British subjects after Pakistan's independence in 1947, the Banyans had rather taken Indian nationality, as before 1960 only a minority among the Banyans was born in Oman. Women, with few exceptions, did not join their husbands in Oman, as the latter went back to India for summer holidays.[5] Moreover, this community was involved in family networks spreading all around the Indian Ocean rim, whose connections were in Muttrah as well as in Zanzibar or Bombay. Given this historical legacy, Sultan Qaboos granted Omani nationality only to a minority of Banyans but to the whole Lawatiyya community, on whom he knew he was highly dependent from an economic point of view.

More generally, decree no. 1/72 of 1972, which prohibited dual nationality, established that a child whose father was Omani would automatically get Omani nationality, and so would a child whose mother was Omani while the father was unknown, and the descendent of an Omani who had never had another nationality. The latter case applied directly to the Omanis who had emigrated before 1970. Similarly, tough preconditions were instituted for obtaining Omani citizenship or for marrying a non-Gulf Cooperation Council (GCC) foreigner. According to the royal decree no. 5/86 and a 1993 ministerial decision (*qarar wizari* no. 92/93), any national who is not disabled, who is under 60 years of age, and who marries a non-GCC foreigner risks losing Omani citizenship. The only alternative is to file a detailed request to the Ministry of the Interior. Since April 2005, Omanis can marry GCC citizens without preliminary agreement from the authorities.[6] According to decree no. 3/83 (article 13), any person acting against the national interest (*al-maslaha al-watani*) can be deprived of his Omani citizenship by the Sultan.

Similar emergency action was required in the early 1970s to determine Oman's geographical boundaries. While the time was not right for such a project in the south, the situation was favourable regarding relations with the United Arab Emirates, after their independence in 1971. From the early 1950s, with increasing Saudi pressure in the Trucial States region, and exacerbation of tension over oil concessions, several groups settled in the border zone made use of the Abu Dhabi-Muscat rivalry to hold on to their autonomy; this happened with the Bani Qitab, Bani 'Ali and Al Bu Shams tribes. At the end of the 1960s, the oil rent allowed Sheikh Zayed Al Nahyan to exert a growing influence on the western territories of the Sultanate.[7] Despite the financial help the latter provided to Qaboos during the Dhofar war and the employment of many Omanis in the new Emirates' armed forces, relations between Zayed and Qaboos remained tense: while Muscat recognised the new state, it refused to appoint an ambassador in Abu Dhabi. Mutual relations even deteriorated after the 1974 agreement between the UAE and Saudi Arabia over Buraimi, as Oman considered that other parties had reached agreement over a part of Omani territory. Tension reached its height at the end of 1977 between Oman and Ra's al-Khayma about sovereignty over a 10-kilometre coastal strip. After more than a one year of negotiation conducted by Sheikh Zayed, an agreement was signed in April 1979 to fix the border. But it concerned less than 10% of the total length of the Oman-UAE border! The Sultan then became aware that too much inflexibility would have made economic and social cooperation with the UAE, which was vital for Oman, more difficult.

The rulers came closer personally during the 1980s; this led to enhanced economic relations and to the first exchange of ambassadors in 1991.[8] In April 1992 Oman and UAE citizens were granted permission to move freely across the border. A joint commission was then entrusted with examining the border issue. In 1993 an official from the Omani Ministry of Foreign Affairs declared that "Oman and the Emirates were twin palm-trees on the same land",[9] while the Dubai daily *al-Khaleej*, at the beginning of the negotiations, had the headline: "One nation, two states".[10] In May 1999 a treaty on the southern part of the border was signed in Muscat by Sheikh Zayed and Sultan Qaboos, and an agreement on total final delimitation was ratified by the rulers in Abu Dhabi on 22 June 2002.[11]

Oman's original diplomacy in the Arab world. Many studies have been devoted to Oman's foreign policy.[12] The purpose here is to tackle it from the angle of the regime's stability pursued by Sultan Qaboos. Omani diplomacy since 1970 has directly depended on the ruler and his policy orientations. To quote Calvin Allen and W. Lynn Rigsbee, "Oman's foreign policy is that of Sultan Qaboos and his interpretation of the State's national interest."[13] As early as January 1972, when the first government was constituted, the ruler kept the position of Minister of Foreign Affairs, while an assistant, Fahd bin Mahmud, had the official but misleading title of "Minister of State for Foreign Affairs". The latter was replaced in May 1973 by Qais al-Zawawi, and in 1982 by Yusef bin 'Alawi, until then undersecretary in the same ministry. In 2017 Yusef bin 'Alawi still held the position of "Minister responsible for Foreign Affairs".

Traditionally on the fringe of the Arab world, Oman has displayed under Qaboos a two-sided aim: to find its place in that region, while underlining its originality. Franck Mermier has perfectly summed it up: "Differentiate to affirm the peculiarity of a national territory and its historical destiny, include in order to bring out its belonging to the Islamic and Arab communities."[14] Particularly significant from that point of view has been the relationship between Oman and its Gulf neighbours. The initiatives taken in international crises in order to open negotiations and maintain stability in the region—especially during Qatar-Bahrain crisis in 1986 and the Yemen war in 1994[15]—and the ambition to make GCC something more than a ratification instrument for Saudi policy showed evidence of that approach. Thus at the end of 1976 Sultan Qaboos decided to invite the Gulf countries' ministers of Foreign Affairs (future GCC states, Iraq and Iran) to discuss a regional joint security policy.[16]

In 1981, at the Abu Dhabi summit which established the GCC, Oman reiterated its proposal for close collaboration between the six countries in security and defence domains, which would be based on a special partnership with the United States, but said it was hostile to any transformation of the organisation into an anti-Iran coalition.[17] Qaboos was less inclined than his GCC counterparts to see in his domestic Shi'i minority an Iranian Trojan Horse; he was convinced that Oman's internal stability would fit well with a consensus-oriented, pragmatic foreign policy. Sultan Qaboos did not break diplomatic relations with Teheran in the Iraq-Iran war; he considered that he had no interest in presenting Iran as the sole source of regional tensions, as such an attitude could not lead to any opportunity of cooperation in the long term. In the summer of 1987 the Sultan's special representative acted to smooth the way for diplomatic contacts between Iran and Iraq, and later Oman tried to convince Teheran to approve the UN resolution putting an end to the war.[18] When Iraq invaded Kuwait in 1990, Oman disapproved of this as a violation of international law. But it proved unwilling to agree to a military solution and did not break its relations with Baghdad. The Sultanate constantly called for lifting of the sanctions imposed on Iraq.

This pragmatism was also present throughout Oman's relations with its Yemeni neighbours. In 1982, talks were started in Kuwait with South Yemen; this led to diplomatic and economic exchanges from the late 1980s. As soon as such a lull happened in the relations with Aden, the first informal contacts took place with the USSR. Not only did the Sultan consider Moscow as an instigator of détente in South Yemen, this was also an occasion for him to strengthen stability in Dhofar and to demonstrate the independence of his diplomacy vis-à-vis the GCC.[19] In 1994, when the civil war broke out in Yemen, the Sultan initiated talks between the two sides in Salalah; then, despite his own convictions, he agreed to host several Southern leaders in exile. For ten years now, Oman has considered that the proper course for the GCC is to extend not only to Yemen but also to Iran and Iraq.[20]

Within the GCC framework at present, Muscat held that the Iraq-Kuwait crisis should be a lesson for the rulers to prevent the emergence of future conflicts by strengthening multilateral links. Moreover, Oman has usually shown freedom of action vis-à-vis the Saudi kingdom. History had left in Omani minds a perception of Saudi Arabia as an imperialist neighbour, and hence there is still a suspicious attitude to Riyadh. More broadly, the Omanis have had ambiguous relations with their Arabian Peninsula neighbours, derived from a double complex of inferiority and superiority. In interviews Omani pride in a rich history, which was marked by international influence long before the oil rent, is heard intermingled with bitterness at having to admit the development gap with the UAE, Qatar and Kuwait, and the heartache at having to endure the arrogance of regional neighbours who consider the Omanis as "peasants"—according to the stereotype inherited from the 1950s, when they were employed in subaltern functions in Bahrain and Kuwait—and "sorcerers". This commonly shared feeling, even among the elites, finds expression in the public arena. In the religious field, the Sultanate usually starts the month of Ramadan one day later than Riyadh. The *fatwa*s fixing the date, which are proclaimed by the highest religious authorities of the Sultanate, are officially justified by longitude and have a clear political meaning. Similarly, the Sultanate has never joined OPEC, out of a desire to keep its—more symbolic than real—independence in working out its energy and budget needs.

Relations with Riyadh became strained during the Yemeni civil war, when Saudi Arabia and Kuwait supported the Southern leaders against the Sanaa government, which had sided with Iraq on the occasion of the Kuwait invasion. But the fluctuating climate since 1970 never led to major disagreements between Muscat and Riyadh, as the latter has granted substantial financial help to the Sultanate for a long time. An agreement on delimitation of the common border was signed only in 1995.

Outside the Persian Gulf area, Qaboos' international policy orientations can be understood better through his double hatred, which he inherited from his father, for both socialist or progressive movements and Islamist ones. The inescapable corollary of this desire to perpetuate an independent policy among the Arab world has been that "Britain's oldest friend on Arabian Peninsula"[21] has never been able—and has certainly not wanted—to question the strategic and economic British influence in its territory. As we will see below, this foreign grip was responsible for Tariq bin Taimur's decision to resign from his position of Prime Minister in December 1971. Although British forces officially left Masirah and Salalah bases in 1977, at the end of the Dhofar war, these positions were used in 2003 as operations bases by the British-American coalition during the Iraq air offensive, as had happened in 1991. Moreover, the renewal of the military cooperation agreements with both Britain and the USA in 1985 and 1995,[22] but also joint exercises—as in 2001 in the Omani desert, on the occasion of the biggest deployment of British troops abroad since the 1980s—only confirmed this Omani strategic dependence. Even if the special relationship with Britain grants the ruler very wide freedom of action against recalcitrant social forces at home, it causes recurrent criticism from the Sultan's GCC counterparts.

Sultan Qaboos has maintained an equally long-lasting relationship with two pro-Western Arab countries: Hosni Mubarak's Egypt and Jordan. The similar political obstacles King Husain and Sultan Qaboos have had to face certainly brought them close to each other. This personal proximity has been unfailing since Husain's support during the Dhofar war, one illustration being their shared vision of the Israel-Palestine conflict. In the 1990s the Sultanate, which only recognised the existence of a Palestinian leadership in 1988, financially aided the Palestinian Authority, but established relations with Israel in 1993; Prime Minister Yitzhak Rabin was a guest in Muscat in December 1994.

Just as Oman supported the Israel-Jordan peace treaty, it displayed solidarity with Egypt on the occasion of the 1978 Camp David agreement and refused to participate in the March 1979 Arab League summit that expelled Egypt.[23] Under Hosni Mubarak's rule, the close relations between the two countries never faltered, as was shown by Sultan Qaboos' frequent visits to Egypt in a private or official capacity and the constant help from the Egyptian intelligence services in dismantling underground Islamists cells in Oman after 1994.

Within the framework of this foreign policy which claims to be independent from neighbouring states' pressure, it is possible to detect some wrong notes, especially regarding Africa. Economic interest took precedence in the 1980s, when the Sultanate bought weapons from South Africa despite the embargo.[24] Moreover, Muscat waited until 2005 to establish official diplomatic relations with Tanzania, out of dislike for the latter's "African socialism" ideology. Similarly, Oman has been reluctant to grant work permits to Nepalese, Palestinians, Syrians or Yemenis because of the obsession with a danger of Oman being infected by socialist ideas. This explains that workers from other Arab countries represent only a small minority of all foreign employees, half of them being Egyptians.[25]

Planning as a means to spread the influence of the state. A necessary condition for recognition of the Sultan's power by the other social and political actors has been access for all Omanis to the same state-provided facilities. As early as the 1970s, the government emphasised national planning, through the first urban development plan for the Muscat area and a policy of long-term projects in transport and communications in the rest of the country. The whole capital had fewer than 20,000 inhabitants, but the drift from the land, coupled with the arrival of expatriates, made direct measures necessary in the housing field to extend the capital to the west, into desert areas.[26] Thus the Ruwi business centre was born, but also the Madina Qaboos quarter—modern villas set aside first for well-off expatriates—and al-Khuwair north, allocated to ministries and embassies. In 1972, a royal decree guaranteed the right to each Omani to own four plots of land: for housing, agriculture, business and industry.[27]

A Ministry of Land Affairs was established in January 1972 to plan the registration of title deeds—a tribal *sheikhs*' privilege until then. But given the extent of housing needs, following the general spread of nuclear families and the return of emigrants to Oman, this institutional supervision could not stop the Muscat conurbation expanding out of control; between 1975 and 1980 80% of the public investment was devoted to the capital, which housed only 10% of the total population.[28] In 1984, a new Ministry of Housing was organised in decentralised branches; its policy aimed at curbing the exodus to Muscat and favouring settlement of people in their native regions with financial assistance. In 2007, 96% of Omani families were connected to electricity and/or gas, and almost 95% of the population was supplied, by piping or tanks, with drinkable water.

The new regime also had to face the various regions' isolation from each other, due to the paucity of the means of communication outside the capital. Because of this situation no regular contacts, and hence no means to become aware of belonging to a national community, were possible. The government endeavour focused first on the most "profitable" sectors, in term of political visibility and penetration of territory and mentalities: roads and television.

The first asphalted road connected Muscat with Sohar in 1973, and was extended to the UAE border the following year.[29] Nizwa, Sur, Rustaq and Buraimi were linked by road to Muscat before the end of the 1970s. In 1975 Sultan Qaboos decreed that every Omani inhabitant must be reachable by a road suitable for motor vehicles, which meant that many tracks had to be enlarged, or the most isolated populations transferred to live near to improved roads.[30] The same year, Salalah was connected by asphalted roads to Thumrait in the north, Taqa in the east and Raysut in the west. In 1985 the road link from Muscat to Salalah was completed, after building of the monumental Nizwa-Thumrait section going across the country from north to south. In the 1980s and 90s, a special effort was devoted to improving access to the most remote regions, like Musandam, the Jabal Akhdar and western Dhofar. In 2013, the asphalted road network covered more than 32,600 kilometres.[31]

Development was also extremely fast in civil aviation. Before 1972, the few planes coming to Oman landed at Bait al-Falaj, a military airfield established where the Ruwi business centre is located today. At the end of that year the new Seeb international airport opened, thirty kilometres west of Muscat. The Sultanate soon acquired 25% of Gulf Air, which started a Muscat-Salalah flight in 1976. In 1993 Oman, arguing that its nationals would suffer discrimination within that company, created a national airline, Oman Air, which took over Muscat-Salalah route, opened a new one between Muscat and Musandam's main town Khasab, and slowly widened its connections to Gulf countries, the Middle East, the Indian subcontinent and East Africa. In 2013, Seeb airport hosted more than 200 daily flights, carrying 8 million passengers.[32]

Except for Sultan Sa'id's relatives and PDO employees, who had their own radio-phone network, there was no telephone network in Oman in 1970. The national company Omantel was created in 1974, and a network was extended to the whole territory during the 1980s and 1990s; digitalisation came in 1998. In 2013, 351,000 fixed lines, half of them in Muscat, were working. GSM ones increased sevenfold between 2004 and 2013 and are now sixteen times the number of the fixed lines—more than 1.5 GSM line per inhabitant.[33]

Another basic step in the encapsulation of the territory and its inhabitants into state-building has been the administrative redivision of the country, in the early 1990s. Five new regions (*mintaqa*) were created—Batina, Sharqiyya, Dakhliyya, Dhahira and al-Wusta—and three governorates (*muhafadha*): Dhofar, Muscat and Musandam.[34] Each region has been organised around a central urban pole, intended to reduce the overload on the Muscat urban area and to impose itself as a driving force for local economic and social development, and micro-poles, centres of the 59 new *wilayas*.[35] Through the devolution structures that were created, the old solidarities have had to reconsider their strategy, by coming closer to the regional centre, as the latter has appeared as the new local redistribution pole for the oil era: the state has thus made itself indispensable as a mediator between periphery and periphery, that is between the various local solidarity networks.

Thus, by its sudden and practical breaking into Omanis' daily life, by building asphalted roads, creating borders and delivering required building permits, the state has succeeded in undermining over time the Omanis' traditional definitions of inside/outside and, with them, the definition of authority. The multiple aspects by which the state has become concrete in the eyes of everybody have had a central role in legitimisation of the Sultan's authority; this process has been all the more convincing because the state has brought services unknown before and has thus given proof of its efficacy.

The state as a driving force in economic development

The education infrastructure, "too large and costly for any organization other than the biggest one of all, the State"[36] to take it in charge, and the health infrastructure and the social programmes started, have brought huge prestige to the ruler. But above all, the state's role as "universal employer" has put the final touch to his symbolic grip on Omanis' daily life.

Between 1980 and 2000, state expenditure amounted to 40–45% of GDP. Thanks to this huge state public investment, the Sultan's authority has achieved a concrete dimension to the detriment of old structures of solidarity that were unable to compete in the very area of their traditional legitimacy: the socio-economic protection of the group. The Sultan's allies have slowly come to include many individuals whose fate is connected to the state and and its ruler.

The state's social and educational role. When Qaboos came to power an ambitious programme of primary education was launched by the new Ministry of Education. It focused on a massive school building programme and an adult literacy campaign. The official figures mention 200 new built schools between 1970 and 1976, among which were 23 preparatory secondary schools, educating 65,000 pupils, a quarter of whom were girls. Nevertheless the authorities had immediately to cope with a complete lack of skilled teaching staff; besides the Omani hired staff, among whom 25% did not even have a primary level of education,[37] expatriates from countries Qaboos was in good relationship with were called in, like Jordanians, Egyptians and Sudanese, and later Tunisians and Algerians. The quality of education suffered from the lack of any planning for teaching methods and contents until the late 1970s; in 1977, the International Bank for Reconstruction and Development (IBRD) estimated that 60% of children did not go to school.[38] Some years later, Sultan Qaboos admitted, "We have made mistakes. In the first five years we did everything in such a rush. We had to. But there was waste here and there and things of dubious quality. Some schools were thrown up too quickly so we had to build them again."[39] At the moment, primary schooling lasts six years and ends with examinations in Arabic language, religion, English, sciences, mathematics and social sciences; pupils passing these tests qualify for entry to the three-year preparatory level. Girls are also taught domestic science, including cooking or embroidery courses. The three years of secondary school, divided into arts and sciences sections, lead to a certificate which, until the mid-1980s, allowed 2,500 young Omanis to carry on higher studies abroad.

Places at government schools as well as the university are reserved to Omani children.[40] Among the teachers in the public sector, the Omani rate has never stopped increasing; from 10% in mid-1980s, it rose to 46% in 1994 and 86% in 2012.[41] Over the 1993–2003 period women's illiteracy went down from 54.1% to 24%, and men's from 29% to 11.8%. Overall, people who can neither read nor write numbered only 14% in 2010, while the rate was 21.9% in 2003 and 41.2% in 1993.[42] Females constitute 60% of the illiterate, of whom 88% are over forty.

In 1986, Sultan Qaboos University opened near Muscat with five faculties (education and Islamic sciences, engineering, science, agriculture and medicine), to which a department of arts was later added in 1987 and a department of commerce in 1993. Students who obtain 90% or more in their secondary school certificate are admitted. A Ministry of Higher Education was established in 1994 to cope with the huge need in training and technical education. In 2011–2, 15,345 students, half of them female, were registered at Sultan Qaboos University. There are no fees to pay and all female students can enjoy free housing on the campus. A monthly allowance is available for male students coming from areas beyond 100 km from the campus.[43] Moreover, Oman has several private universities—two in Muscat, one in Sur, Salalah, Nizwa, Sohar and Buraimi—and around twenty private technical institutes. More than 18,100 Omanis (55% female) were studying abroad in 2011, 46% of them being registered in the UAE.

In the health sector, the impulse for an ambitious programme of building local health centres was given by a small team managed by Dr 'Asim al-Jamali, who was appointed Minister of Health in August 1970. Less than five years later, twelve hospitals and thirty-two clinics were already working. Nevertheless, in 1978, a United Nations study established that 67% of children still suffered from anaemia.[44] Today the Ministry of Health runs sixty-six hospitals and 195 health centres spread all over the territory, plus twelve hospitals and 1,026 clinics dependent on the private sector.[45] Until 1996, services and medicines were completely free for the nationals; since then, a family card has to be bought for one rial every year and consultation costs 200 baisas. Medicines are not automatically provided any more and have to be picked up at pharmacies on prescription only, without refunding.

The overall consequences of this fast development in public health were not slow in coming; average life expectancy at birth went up from forty in the 1960s to sixty-six in 1990 and seventy-six in 2013. The infant mortality rate has fallen greatly to reach ten per thousand today.[46] It is not all a bed of roses, as a former senior international organisation official who served in Muscat has testified: "There is a huge gap between Muscat and Inner Oman, where a series of problems still persist: malnutrition of many babies; increase of AIDS, which can be explained by many Omanis travelling to Dubai and Bangkok or by demographic exchanges with East Africa; female excision, still overspread, in particular in Dhofar, where the hospitals' authorities connive at it."[47]

Social assistance programmes were set up by a Sultan's decree in 1984 (no. 87/84) to help needy sections of the population, in particular orphans, disabled, widows and divorced or abandoned women. In 2013, 86,200 people benefited from such state financial protection.[48] Similarly, the implementation of a minimum wage for Omanis (see chapter 7) and Sultan Qaboos' acts of benevolence on great occasions reinforce the role of the welfare state in people's life, but also their belonging to the new national community. On the other hand almost nothing material is required from the citizen, who until recently was not subjected to any taxation.

Since 1976, Sultan Qaboos has established five-year plans officially intended to set out the state's priorities; in fact, they have been a means to channel the new state's inclination to devote money to politically "effective" policies. The Ninth Five-Year Plan (2016–2020) was announced in January 2016.

Bureaucratisation as a means to spread the influence of the state. The inexhaustible pool of jobs offered by the public sector, following the explosion of oil revenue, represents an even more decisive step in confirming the new Sultan's political legitimacy and hence his social grip. In 1971, while expatriates working in Oman numbered 7,000 and Omanis employed abroad 15,000, the number of active Omanis in the Sultanate was estimated at 100,000. Of these 78,000 worked in agriculture and fisheries, compared with 5,500 in the state apparatus.[49] The share of civil service jobs within total employment of Omanis was to keep on growing until the late 1990s, while in the private sector there was a heavy expatriate presence (90%) until 1998. The number of Omani civil servants went up from 25,000 in 1980 (compared with 15,000 expatriates) to 75,000 in 1995 (compared with 27,000 expatriates).[50] In 1992, 76,000 Omanis (and 455,000 expatriates) were registered as in employment, 84% of them working in the civil service sector. The latter proportion then declined, after the various programmes aimed at favouring both the recruitment of young Omanis in the private sector and the early retirement of government employees who wished to create private businesses. In December 2012, 50.8% of all active Omanis—that is, 172,066 people out of 339,000 working nationals—were registered in the private sector.[51] As for the security forces (army, police, intelligence), which consume 35% of the state expenditure,[52] even if no official figure is available, their strength is estimated in 2014 at over 150,000, both nationals and expatriates.

The main public sector employers are the Ministries of Education (69,300 Omanis in 2012), Health (22,500) and Regional Municipalities, Environment and Water Resources (7,050), as well as the *Diwan* and the Royal Court (22,600 together). These sectors have developed not only in the capital but over the whole territory. They have not only participated in physically and symbolically anchoring the state in the daily proximity of every Omani—thanks to the presence of a school, a health centre or a cooperative belonging to the Public Authority for Commercialisation of Land Products—but have more broadly contributed to giving the citizen autonomy from the *'asabiyya*, thanks to state jobs and social services that he depends on more and more tightly.

The bureaucratisation of society illustrates the political and social control the ruler has implemented over the territory. As Nazih Ayubi has explained, "through the creation, expansion and maintenance of a bureaucracy, the rulers of the oil-state are paying the citizen [...] Instead of the usual situation of the state taxing the citizen (in return for offering him services), here the citizen is taxing the state—by acquiring a government payment—in return for staying quiet, for not invoking tribal rivalries, and for not challenging the ruling family's position."[53]

Nevertheless it is the state—and through it the one who controls it, the ruler—that commands the game, as no other actor is able to provide individuals with such benefits. A bureaucratic position of power, at any hierarchical level, grants first a regular and quite high salary, and consequently an important addition to social prestige; it provides, above all, opportunities for creating personal networks but also for enrichment in the private sector, to such a point that fraudulent misuse of public goods and clientelism are implicitly tolerated by the authorities. Personal proximity and the ability to serve one's own and one's relatives' interests have become values of social promotion. The state apparatus has been the shortest and the most effective way to access wealth; the opportunities are all the greater when one's position is high in the hierarchy and interpersonal knowledge within the elites is extended—thanks to the sparse population. The state apparatus then holds a pre-eminent role in the actors' strategies, as everything is provided by it: it grants legitimate dividends (salaries, social allowances), but it is also seen as a more unofficial democratic mechanism of redistribution. Thus these thousands of state employees, who have benefited from the new opportunities for personal enrichment that the oil godsend has offered, have shown themselves for two decades to be the most reliable and pragmatic allies of the ruler.

A state budget dependent on one main source of revenue, an active population mainly employed by the state, no direct taxation—these elements, among others, seem to make Oman a rentier state.

The rentier state. Introduced in 1970,[54] the "rentier state" notion was conceptualised in the 1980s to explain the socio-economic structure of Arabian countries of the Gulf after the oil booms. Michel Chatelus highlighted the similarities of these economies, following the sudden arrival of a tremendous godsend which it was impossible to spend in a rational way. These countries' rulers, facing similar temptations[55] to buy the nationals' welfare through a generous redistribution of the rent, under the pretext of ensuring socio-political stability, succumb to the urge to build "prestige infrastructure" (ports, airports, highways, etc.) and an over-extended security system. While Chatelus acknowledged that there are huge opportunities, especially for improvement of living standards and economic development, he cautioned at an early stage against the basic contradictions of such an economy, which bears the risk of upsetting ways of life and leading to non-reversible disruption, while perpetuating a double dependence: of individuals on the tutelary authority's generosity, and of political leaders on a foreign workforce and on oil itself, as a pretext to avoid starting industrial diversification.

According to Hazem Beblawi, a "rentier"[56] economy relies first on substantial external rent: more than the "production" itself, it is the "allocation" by the state of revenue drawn from the sale of this raw material abroad that plays a prominent role.[57] In such an economy, the state is the main beneficiary of the rent and only a few nationals are engaged in its extraction or production. Most people are involved in spending of this wealth, which produces the advent of a "rentier mentality": "For a rentier, reward becomes a windfall gain, an isolated fact [...] accidental as against the conventional outlook where reward [...] results of a long, systematic and organized production circuit".[58]

In the early 1990s this theory was used to explain the political stability of authoritarian Arab regimes, especially in Libya[59] and the Persian Gulf;[60] a state which profits from a large external rent, and which is thus able to grant its citizens goods and services viewed by the latter as unlimited, without requiring anything in exchange, is in a position to create a consensus that exonerates it from any need of democratic legitimisation.[61] Indeed, the state's financial sufficiency allows it to avoid resorting to taxation of citizens. This hypothesis of a correlation between financial crises of the state and democratisation echoes the principle "no taxation without representation", raised during the United States' War of Independence by supporters of political liberalisation.

Before oil, a tacit arrangement linked Qatari and Kuwaiti rulers to the local traditional merchant families; in exchange for their financial support, the former granted the latter wide influence in political decision making, so that they could preserve their interests. The merchants provided the rulers' financial needs while in return their interests were protected. This historical alliance was disrupted by the unexpected material sufficiency of the rulers, after oil was discovered. The rulers were thus freed from their economic dependence on the merchants, and hence from the need to involve them in the political process. The economic elites were bought off by the state, as the ruler reserved them a substantial part of oil rent, against their agreement to renounce their claims to a political role.

Nevertheless this compromise allowed them to strengthen their economic pre-eminence: "Where merchants wanted to invest—trade, construction, services—the state stayed out, or offered encouragement."[62] These favours took various forms, particularly very tough laws governing foreign investors' rights, to protect the well-established local merchant dynasties. The most important difference between Qatar and Kuwait lies in the comparative influence of these dynasties; while in Kuwait the ruler was forced to promise to keep royal family members out of business, in Qatar, because the merchant community was weaker and smaller, the ruler allowed his relatives into the merchants' economic territory.[63] If eventual confusion of political and economic actors can be seen in Qatar, it can be explained first by the ruler's relatives' intrusion into the economy, but also by the economic actors' exclusion from the decision-making sphere. Thus, in the Gulf, the terms of the famous formula have been reversed to become: "no representation without taxation".

Two incompatible conceptions of Oman's future. Given Qaboos' youth and lack of experience, but also his full-time involvement in the Dhofar war, the first months of his rule allowed two groups with influence to appear in Muscat. An "Interim Advisory Council", which proved to be "advisory" in name only, was established, chaired by the Defence Secretary, Hugh Oldman. It was mostly composed of British expatriates who were in charge of routine matters of government and took decisions in the Sultan's name.[64] John Graham, the Sultan's forces commander, who was to be replaced in the autumn of 1972 by Tim Creasey, David Ogram, the Director of Development department, and Robin Young and William Heber-Percy, in charge of the Planning and Development Board, were members of the Council; the only Omani member was Thuwaini bin Shihab, Sa'id bin Taimur's cousin. Influential figures in the former regime, like Ahmad bin Ibrahim and Shihab bin Faisal, were placed under house arrest.[65]

Qaboos' uncle, Tariq bin Taimur, had been in exile in Germany and Lebanon since the late 1950s; he had been considered by the Council as the main threat to the regime's stability, as he was popular among the Omanis abroad, but in August 1970 it was proposed that he should return to Oman to occupy the post of Prime Minister, even though his functions had not been determined. Most of the new state's future top officials (Fahd bin Mahmud, Faisal bin 'Ali, 'Asim al-Jamali, etc.) also returned from abroad, where they had spent most of their lives.

On 8 August 1970 Tariq announced a four-member cabinet, with Sa'ud al-Khalili (in charge of Education), 'Asim al-Jamali (Health), Badr bin Sa'ud al-Busa'idi (Interior) and Muhammad bin Ahmad al-Busa'idi (Justice). These last two portfolios could not be given to an Inner Oman main tribal *sheikh*— given the political sensitivity of these issues—or to a member of a "peripheral" community (Baluchi or Shi'i) which had historically been less involved in political and tribal affairs. This cabinet was steadily completed by addition of departments for Foreign Affairs—a position occupied by Fahd bin Mahmud from November 1971—and Social Affairs, Information, etc.[66] Tariq spent most of his time abroad, dealing with the new Sultanate's diplomacy; this left the Interim Council a clear field to run internal affairs, while the Sultan himself was involved in the Dhofar war.

At the same time, two deep-seated trends were already evident in the new regime's organisation: first, Qaboos' inclination to personal power, even though Tariq opposed this, working towards a constitutional monarchy; secondly, a clear propensity to appeal to British experts, who reported directly to the ruler, short-circuiting the Omanis. Thus from the viewpoint of concepts of authority, continuity between before and after 1970 was palpable. The most striking example was in financial issues, as the oil revenue, which amounted in 1971 to almost the entire state resources, was directly transferred to the Sultan's bank account, the oil concessions being registered in his name. The ruler refused to establish a state budget, as he explained in an interview: "Why should I do it? It is only a technical issue about which almost all our subjects know nothing. We take decisions in the country's interest, and it is better if they are not questioned by ignorant people."[67] No Omani but he, not even Tariq bin Taimur, was then supposed to know what was in the agreements with PDO or the British; in the latter case, the ruler declared: "I will not publish it or transmit it to my cabinet and my Prime Minister [...] Such an issue comes within the Sultan's competence alone".[68]

Until 1975 a British expert, who was answerable to Qaboos only, occupied the position of Secretary for Finance; a Central Bank was set up only in 1974. In the military field, the only people involved with the Sultan in the decision-making process were the Secretary of Defence and the SAF Commander, both British citizens. Thus, in three primary fields like oil, defence and finance, everything was in Qaboos' and his foreign advisers' hands.[69] Tariq declared in May 1971: "Nothing good will be accomplished in this country without a Constitution and a Parliament [...] Unfortunately the Sultan does not want to hear about such an evolution before three or five years; he has arrogated himself competences which go beyond those a constitutional monarch has usually at his disposal [...] [But] he will finally understand his mistakes and will know how to correct them."[70]

In December, on the occasion of a visit to Germany, Tariq resigned. His departure allowed the ruler to redefine responsibilities. On 2 January 1972 he announced a more elaborate Cabinet, in which he himself assumed the functions of Head of State, Prime Minister, Minister of Foreign Affairs (assisted by Fahd bin Mahmud, who was officially Minister of State for Foreign Affairs), Minister of Defence (assisted by Hugh Oldman, Secretary of Defence) and Minister of Finance.

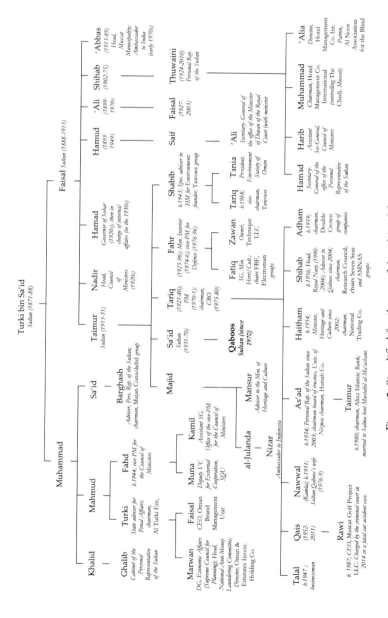

Figure 2: Simplified family tree of the Al Saʿid family

An Interim Planning Council was set up in March 1972 to be responsible for the country's general development issues;[71] its composition highlights the new state's extreme dependency on the Omani emigrants whom Sultan Qaboos called upon in 1970 to join forces to develop the country. The Omanis abroad were relatively more educated than those at home and had not been involved in the internal political and tribal issues in Oman during the last decades: in Qaboos' eyes, they could be an asset to him as his natural allies. Of the ten Council members, except its chairman Thuwaini bin Shihab, six had been educated in Eastern Europe, while two were born in Zanzibar and had never been in Oman before 1970.[72] As it had no precise attributions, the Interim Planning Council was undermined by rivalries with the other ministries and was soon dissolved. But its members were moved into new decision-taking positions.

In November 1974, after the next cabinet reshuffle, the ruler seemed to have reached a sort of balance of power, which would be confirmed by the new cabinet in 1979. There was no state matter the Sultan was not in touch with. The increasing improvement in the Dhofar situation allowed him to take up the leadership of government, to chair the Council of Ministers and to pass his own decisions.

In security and defence matters a National Defence Council, to advise and assist the ruler, was formed in June 1973, when Hugh Oldman retired. In 1975, this Council consisted of three Omanis—the new Minister of State for Foreign Affairs, Qais al-Zawawi, the Deputy Defence Minister, Fahr, and the new Dhofar governor, Buraik al-Ghafiri—as well as the SAF Commander, the Director of Intelligence, the Advisers for Security Affairs and for the Economy, the Chief of Police and the Chief of Defence Department: all British.[73] One of closest advisers to the Sultan at that time has said: "[The Sultan] would have fought tooth and nail to avoid the establishment of any popularly elected constituent assembly. He always liked to believe that he was the only decision-maker in Oman. Any other organisation with power would constitute a threat to his personal security [...] Other rulers in the area are not so free to disregard the views of their subjects as is the Sultan. There is no effective means of questioning national decisions and policies, no means of putting forward alternative policies for national debate, no vehicle for debating the national budget."[74]

From the mid-1970s, Sultan Qaboos would draw from three main "banks of personalities" to fill cabinet positions. First and foremost, there have been members of his family who came back from exile in 1970 and could be said to know nothing about Oman. But Oman cannot be compared with the other Gulf monarchies, where the sovereignty ministries (*wizarat al-siyada*)—of the Interior, Foreign Affairs and Defence, and the Prime Minister's office—have been monopolised by the ruler's relatives; as Michael Herb says, "while the Al Sa'ud rule Saudi Arabia and the Al Sabah Kuwait, Qaboos rules Oman".[75]

Secondly, there have been members of collateral branches of Qaboos' tribe, usually belonging to the families John Peterson defined as "the traditional al-Busa'idi civil servants";[76] they have served on a large scale under the twentieth-century sultans, especially as governors. Last but not least, 1974 marked the entry into the new top administrative positions of personalities descended from families who were Sultan Sa'id's closest allies; they either belonged to Muscat merchant elites or were political allies of the former ruler, from Salalah or from Inner Oman, and they knew perfectly how to make themselves essential to the new ruler in his endeavour to political and economic legitimacy.

In contrast, tribal personalities were conspicuous by their absence, at least at the beginning; their political role suffered greatly from their involvement in the 1950s events, but also from their lack of technical and intellectual skills.

The royal family. Since 1970, a clear distinction is established between the royal family—which is composed of Sultan Sa'id bin Sultan's (1804–56) descendants, bearing the name "Al Sa'id"—and all the other branches of the al-Busa'idi tribe, who kept the surname "al-Busa'idi". Qaboos belongs to both the Al Sa'id family and the al-Busa'idi tribe.

Let us focus first on the royal family members who have been in decision-making positions (see figure 2 above). One of Sa'id's brothers, Sayyid Fahr, held until his death in 1997 the position of Deputy Prime Minister for Defence and Security, while Sayyid Tariq, who returned to Oman in 1974, was given the honorific position of Personal Adviser to the Sultan. Public reconciliation between both men was sealed by Qaboos' marriage in March 1976 to Tariq's daughter Nawwal. Tariq died in 1980 while holding the office of governor of the Central Bank.[77]

The youngest brother, Sayyid Shabib, who was born in 1943, held the Environment portfolio (1984–91), before he became Special Adviser to the Sultan for Environmental Affairs, a position he still holds. In 1982 he created Tawoos group; currently chaired by his half-brother Samir J. Fancy, Tawoos has become one of the leading Omani business groups, involved in various sectors from agriculture, telephone and services (through its main division, Renaissance Services) to leisure and oil, and concluding contracts with PDO,

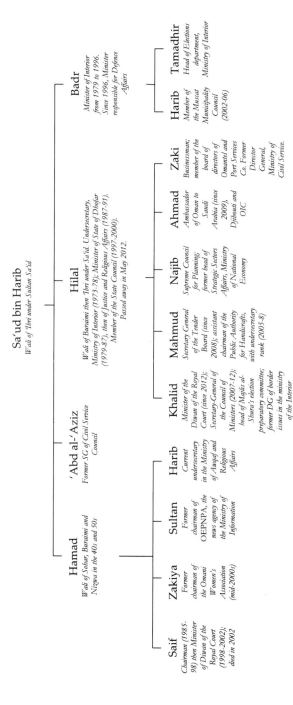

Figure 3: Simplified family tree of the Al Harib branch of the al-Busa'idi tribe

the Diwan of the Royal Court and the Ministries of Defence and Oil. If Shabib and his son Tariq, Tawoos' vice-chairman, were among the first Al Sa'id members being directly active in the economic sector, the involvement in business of royal family members, including the sons of Tariq bin Taimur, has become much more visible in the 2000s.[78]

Several more distant uncles have played leading roles during the last thirty years. As Personal Adviser to the Sultan, Sayyid Thuwaini bin Shihab represented the Sultan when he was absent; he held in parallel a position his own father had held, that of governor of Muscat. He died in 2010 while holding the position of Personal Representative to the Sultan. Thuwaini's cousin, Sayyid Faisal bin 'Ali, who came back from exile in 1970, after a short stay in the post of Minister of the Economy between March and July 1971 became Minister of Education in 1973, then Ambassador to the US; he was afterwards appointed Minister of National Heritage, then of National Heritage and Culture until he resigned in March 2002. He died in January 2003, while holding the post of Special Adviser to the Sultan for Heritage Affairs.

Another senior office holder who is personally close to the Sultan, Fahd bin Mahmud, held the Ministry of Foreign Affairs for a short time before he was appointed in 1973 as Minister of Information and Tourism. He left this position to become Deputy Prime Minister for Legal Affairs. In 1994 he was appointed to his current position, Deputy Prime Minister for the Council of Ministers' Affairs. His brother Turki, who is State adviser for Penal Affairs, is also the president-founder of Al Turki Enterprises, one of the leading Omani companies in the construction sector. It has been a contractor for the building of several ministries, Sultan Qaboos University and the Great Mosque in Bawshar.

A new generation has slowly come to prominence for ten years now: the generation of Tariq bin Taimur's sons. Born in 1954, Sayyid Haitham was appointed in 1996 as Undersecretary in the Ministry of Foreign Affairs and became in March 2002 Minister of National Heritage and Culture. His brother Brigadier-General As'ad briefly held command of the Sultan's Armoured Corps. In March 2002 he was promoted to be Representative of the Sultan, presumably in anticipation of Thuwaini's succession, and in March 2017 he was appointed as Deputy Prime Minister for International Cooperation. Sayyid Shihab, who has had military training, was appointed in 1990 as Commander of the Sultan of Oman's Navy; since February 2004 he has served as Adviser to the Sultan.

Other cousins of Qaboos currently hold less pre-eminent positions, like Fatiq bin Fahr, who is Secretary-General of the Ministry of Heritage and Culture and a businessman, through the FBF group, and 'Ali bin Saif, who is Secretary-General of the Minister of the Diwan of the Royal Court's Office.

The al-Busa'idi tribe. We shall now examine the role of the collateral branches of the al-Busa'idi tribe. As the state apparatus has expanded tremendously since 1970, more and more senior public positions have become available. Jill Crystal explained about Kuwait that "the successive rulers strengthened family networks to provide more reliable elite recruitment pools for the increasingly large and bureaucratic governments catalyzed by oil".[79] Sultan Qaboos, who could not rely on an extensive family, has heavily resorted to al-Busa'idi tribesmen, who have been seen as neutral in internal affairs. This has led to perpetuation of the bureaucratic role played by some lineages that have been working for the sultans for a long time.

Among these families, the one of Sayyid Hamud bin Hamad, who was *wali* of Sur under Sa'id bin Taimur, is particularly interesting. Hamud's son, Sayyid Hamad, was Sultan Sa'id's secretary. In 1970, Hamad supported the coup and became Qaboos' personal aid. He was Minister in charge of the Diwan from 1974 to 1986; at that time, Hamad held the role of a *chef de cabinet*, as he prepared meetings of the Council of Ministers and occupied the ruler's seat in his absence. From 1986, when he was appointed as Personal Adviser of the Sultan, until his death in 2002 Sayyid Hamad concentrated on his own activities as businessman. He used his position to become the Omani partner of many foreign companies, including Shapoorji, an Indian group, which was awarded contracts for the building of the Sultan's palace in Muscat and the Diwan. His own assets are split among many companies, like Omasco, in partnership with Al Futtaim group (Dubai). His sons Sami (who died in the 1980s), Khalid, Badr and Aiman have taken over the Sabco group, which was founded in 1983 by their father. Sayyid Badr bin Hamad is also Secretary-General of the Foreign Ministry with ministerial rank. Sayyid Hamad's daughter Wafa' is married to Qaboos' mother's brother Mustahil al-Ma'ashani. Wafa' and Mustahil's daughters Salma and Basma are married to Sayyid Taimur bin As'ad and to Badr bin Hamad's son Nasr. Hamad's great-nephew, al-Mu'tasim bin Hamud, who had successively been Minister of Regions and Municipality Affairs, of State for Defence Affairs and then of Labour in the 1980s, was governor of Muscat, with minister of state rank, from 1991 to 2011. Al-Mu'tasim's father's sister, Shawana, is the mother of Sayyid As'ad bin Tariq.

Another al-Busa'idi branch is the Al Sammar branch, which produced *wali*s for generations through the twentieth century.[80] Hilal bin Hamad, a former minister of Interior and Justice in the 1970s and 80s, became state counsellor for Judicial Affairs. He chaired the State Security Court which in 1994 and 2005 tried people accused of attempting to overthrow the regime (see chapter

7). His son Sa'ud, previously governor of Musandam, has been governor of Muscat since 2011, while Hilal's brother, Sultan bin Hamad, was governor of Muscat between 1983 and 1991, before becoming the first Ambassador of Oman to the United Arab Emirates.[81]

Similarly, the Harib family of the al-Busa'idi tribe has been close to Muscat authorities for a long time (see figure 3). Under Sa'id, Sayyid Hamad bin Sa'ud was *wali* of Sohar, of Buraimi and then of Nizwa, a town from which he was driven by the Imamate supporters in 1957.[82] His brother Hilal succeeded Buraik al-Ghafiri as Minister of State for Dhofar from 1979 to 1987. For three years he was Minister of Justice and Religious Affairs. Hilal's son, Sayyid Khalid, has been Minister of the Diwan of the Royal Court since 2012 while his brother Mahmud is secretary-general of the national Tender Board and his other brother Ahmad is the current ambassador to Saudi Arabia. Sa'ud bin Harib's youngest son, Sayyid Badr, was appointed Minister of the Interior in August 1970 for a short period, and returned to that position in May 1979, then holding it until November 1996. Since then, he has been Minister in charge of Defence Affairs.

Sayyid Saif bin Hamad was appointed in December 1985 as chairman of the Diwan of the Royal Court and was given the title of "Minister of the Diwan of the Royal Court" in 1998, while holding also the chair of the Higher Education Council. He died in October 2002. Among his brothers, Sayyid Harib is currently undersecretary at the Ministry of Justice and Religious Affairs, while Sultan is the former chairman of the Oman Establishment for Press, News, Publication and Advertising (OEPNPA), the official news agency of the Ministry of Information. Sayyid Saif's successor as Minister of the Diwan was Sayyid 'Ali bin Hamud, who had held the charge of Minister of the Interior from November 1996 and had been replaced by Sayyid Saif's uncle.

Other al-Busa'idis occupy leading positions, like Sayyid Hamud bin Faisal, a former Secretary-General of the Council of Ministers, and Minister of Interior since March 2011; also Sayyid Musallam bin 'Ali, Minister of State, governor of Dhofar from 1987 to May 2001. Finally, today's Minister of Higher Education, Sayyida Rawiya bint Sa'ud, who was appointed in March 2004, has been the second Omani woman to reach this rank but the first to be granted a full portfolio.

Despite the direct involvement of several families from the al-Busa'idi tribe in the decision-making process for thirty years, in Oman there has been no massive entry into strategic positions by royal family members. The capacity for influence or political nuisance of Qaboos' close relatives is much more limited than in the neighbouring monarchies. In contrast, while the "sovereignty ministries" have never been the al-Busaʿidis' private ground—or, *a fortiori*, the Al Saʿid's—Sultan Qaboos has always taken care to surround himself with members of his tribe, especially from those al-Busaʿidi lineages who have served the rulers for generations, for internal affairs positions like the Ministries of the Interior, Justice and the Diwan of the Royal Court. The al-Busaʿidi tribe has strengthened the impression it gives of a-political office holders without any territory and allegiance connections, only working for the central government. The decision to grant al-Busaʿidis positions linked to internal issues, given their politically sensitive feature in post-1970 Oman, has not been surprising.

Thus it is not possible to talk about an "Omani ruling family" as such, but instead of a sole ruler whose mode of government has been very much in keeping with his father's. He has used the al-Busaʿidis as a bank of loyal office holders, who have been all the more useful for him in that they had no legitimacy to aspire to the throne. The Sultanate of Oman is not under the rule of a tribe constituted in a ruling *ʿasabiyya*, but under that of a monarch with his own legitimacy, who has relied on various allies, taking care to balance influence to perpetuate the regime's stability.

Consolidation of business positions inherited from the twentieth century

With the new political order in 1970 came consolidation of the positions the already prominent actors occupied. As Hazem Beblawi has pointed out, in a rentier state "citizenship is not only an affective relation between the individual and its nationhood; it is also, and above all, a pecuniary relation."[83] This is especially true when the individual is in an economic position of strength vis-à-vis the state.

If the state has been the Omani economic development's major actor for thirty years, it is not only through the mechanisms of "direct" and un-individualised redistribution we studied above (bureaucratisation of employment, no taxation, health and education for all, etc.) but also through individualised favours, which benefit only some citizens to whom the regime considers itself particularly indebted. Whereas in the other Gulf monarchies wealth distributed to the citizens by the state as salaries, social allowances or price subsidies is regained by the ruling elite (mostly the royal family) through the ownership of companies winning public contracts,[84] in Oman the old allies of the Sultans

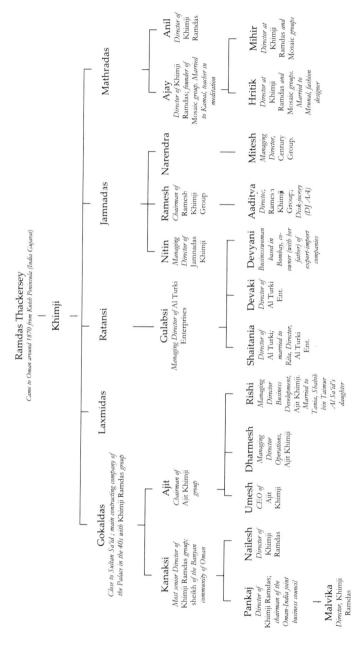

Figure 4: Simplified family tree of Khimji Ramdas descencants

have played this role and have received the greater part of the rentier state's subsidies, so as to become rentiers *de facto*.

First, one sort of subsidy has consisted of the fabulous public contracts in all sectors dealing with infrastructure and urban planning (roads, public buildings, etc.), as Oman started from zero in 1970. The "public works" branch has played a decisive role in the building of the leading Omani economic groups' wealth. The government granted another favour to the local private sector by protecting the national market, through the *kafil* (sponsor) system which obliges any foreign individual or company wishing to work in Oman to be associated with a local partner who receives regular payment; the Omani's name must be used for the foreigner to be allowed to work in Omani territory. For business purposes this favours the already well-established national companies, which enjoy political contacts in top political circles, as these leading business groups' connections are sought by foreign investors willing to take only minimum risks. This process has become even more important with the rise in living standards; as a result there has been growing demand for consumer goods produced abroad, which has made local intermediaries necessary for entry into the market. Finally, some top Omani civil servants even believe that a few businessmen were awarded fixed percentages of oil revenue in 1970 in order to give them a direct stake in the new regime's stability.[85]

The Muscat merchant elites. The Khimji Ramdas group is currently the main Omani wholesaler[86] and covers many other sectors, like building, computers, leisure, etc. It is the exclusive agent in Oman for Rolex, Motorola, General Electric, Fujitsu, Procter and Gamble, Philip Morris, Marlboro and Pizza Hut. Khimji Ramdas has been involved in the military sector since Sa'id's time. In 2000, the third generation (see figure 4) split the family group into four holdings: Khimji Ramdas, Ramesh Khimji, Jamnadas Khimji (JK) and Ajit Khimji. The latter is involved into hypermarkets, banking, advertising and public works. Finally, Gulabsi and his children are in partnership with Turki bin Mahmud Al Sa'id in the Al Turki group of companies.

Other families of Banyan origin have benefited from the oil rent, like the Naranjee Hirjee family—owner of the eponymous group—and Karsandas Hamlai's descendants. He founded in 1947 the Al Bahja company, which is currently active in various sectors like leisure, distribution, metallurgy and pharmacy. Finally, it is worthwhile to mention the Dharamsey Nensey family, who belong to the closest circle around Qaboos and are entrusted with management of the Sultan's personal assets.[87] Bipin and his son Shikhar sit on boards of a number of financial and banking groups.

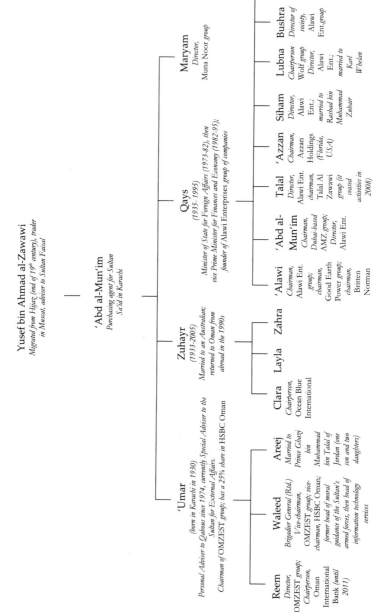

Figure 5: Simplified family tree of al-Zawawi family

Similarly, post-1970 Omani development benefited the Lawatiyya, who have been able to use their contacts in the whole Gulf region to enhance their economic positions. 'Ali Salman's sons raised the Al Hassan family company to the leading position in Oman in electricity and electrical supplies distribution. Khadija bint Hasan bin 'Ali has been the first Omani woman ambassador. She was appointed to the Netherlands in 1999 and until 2009 held at the same time the post of non-resident Ambassador Plenipotentiary to the European Union.

Other leading companies are owned by Lawatiyya; there is OHI, chaired by Maqbul al-Salih and representative in Oman of Alcatel or UPS; Ali Redha Trading is ruled by the businessman of that name, who had almost a monopoly of sugar refining and distribution in Oman when he ran into big financial problems in 2001.[88] Another Lawatiyya merchant family is that of Sulaiman Ja'afar's descendants, prominent among them Muhammad 'Abd al-Husain Baqr, who served as member of the Muscat Municipal Council from 2006 to 2010. The family occupies a leading position in the import and distribution of rice, sugar and tea, through its Muttrah-based company Bhacker Suleman Jaffer Co.

Finally, the descendants of 'Abd al-Latif bin Fadl, who was already active in Muttrah at the end of the nineteenth century in trade to India and Europe (arms, pearls, fish, etc.) and was close to Sultans Taimur and Sa'id, retain wide influence nowadays. The family group, Bhacker Haji Abdullatif Fazul, is chaired by Sa'id bin Ahmad bin 'Ali and is in a quasi-monopolistic position in Muttrah industrial port in the maritime freight sector. Husain bin 'Ali, who who was the ambassador of Oman to the United Kingdom until 2009, is currently Adviser at the Diwan of the Royal Court.

The 1970s were good for the Mohsen Haider Darwish company's development. The group is run by Muhsin Haidar himself, who represented Muscat in the Consultative Council between 1991 and 1994, and his daughters Lujaina and Areej. Lujaina was Muscat representative on this Council between 2000 and 2007, and a member of the Oman Chamber of Commerce and Industry (OCCI) board of directors from 2003 to 2007. In January 2005 Muhsin's brother, 'Adnan bin Haidar, became Director General of the Oman Housing Bank.

Descendants of several leading Baluchi traders who have settled in Muttrah have benefited from trade positions they inherited from their ancestors. We can mention Musa bin Abd al-Rahman al-Ra'isi's grandsons. Husain bin 'Ali and 'Abd al-Rahman bin 'Ali run the Mussa Abdulrahman Hassan group,

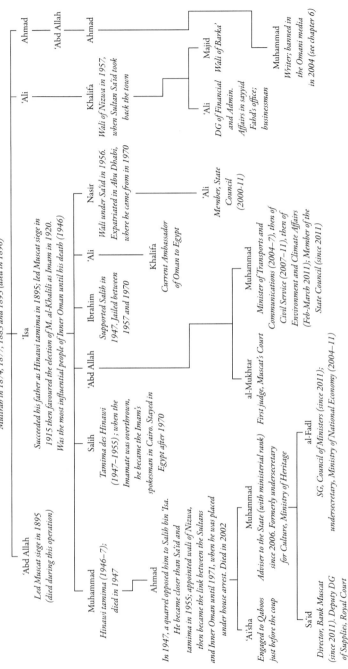

Figure 6: Family tree of Salih bin 'Ali al-Harthi descendants

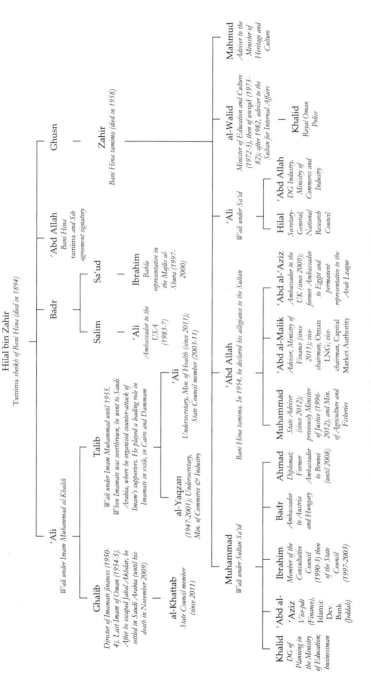

Figure 7: Simplified family tree of Bani Hina noble branch

Omani agents for GMC, Opel and Suzuki, while their father 'Ali bin Musa al-Ra'isi had a seat on the State Council between 1997 and 2003. Muhammad bin 'Awad bin 'Abd al-Rahman has been the Omani Ambassador to Russia since 2009.

Another example is the Al Nasib family. Since the 1980s, Yahia Muhammad Nasib has built up one of Muscat's leading business groups, through the Yahya Group holding. His brother Habib chaired the most important Omani government newspaper, *'Uman*. Yahia's son Nasib is the holding's managing director and Natasha bint Yahia, the former head of the OCCI businesswomen forum (2007–2011), is the group's CEO. Also director of the group, their younger sister Nashia is head of the HIV section at the Ministry of Health.

Finally, one must mention the powerful Bahwan trading family from the al-Mukhaini tribe. The brothers Suhail and Sa'ud, from Sur, have been close to Sultan Qaboos since the beginning and built up the SSB holding group. They became Omani exclusive agents for Toyota, Ford, Continental, Kia, Hertz, Sony Ericsson and Seiko. In 2002 they split the group into two entities bearing their names, Suhail Bahwan and Saud Bahwan. Their activities range from public works to agriculture, motors, chemicals, the travel trade, etc. Suhail's son Sa'ad, the chairman of OTE group of companies (representing LG, Hyundai, Bosch in Oman) was elected to the Consultative Council in 2011.

However, oil not only strengthened inherited economic and social positions, through the conversion of trade dynasties to rent wealth; it led to a profound disruption of the boundary between politics and economy.

Two-way economic-political interference after 1970. Sultan Qaboos has had no objection, in term of conflict of interests, to cabinet members and senior office holders developing, personally or through their relatives, their own businesses through which they can benefit from public contracts and enrich themselves; it seems that he has considered it an effective means to make sure that they are loyal, as his ministers and advisers' personal wealth would depend directly on the regime's survival.[89] The Sultan issued a law in December 1974 forbidding any member of the government to hold a stake in a private business involved in contracts with the government, with no retroactive effect. In 1982 this ban was extended to relatives, but with the same exemption.[90] These opportunities given by the ruler allowed decision-makers to build and consolidate powerful economic groups.

The obvious examples are found among Sultan Qaboos' kin, including his mother's brother Sheikh Mustahil al-Ma'ashani, a former Minister of Labour and Social Affairs in the late 1980s. He has chaired since 1974 the Muscat Overseas business group, which is very active in the agriculture, banking and real estate sectors. His son Salim, vice-chairman of the group, is an adviser to the Diwan of the Royal Court, with ministerial rank, while another of his sons, Khalid, is chairman of the most important Omani banking group, Bank Muscat. Another of the families closest to Sultan Qaboos is that of Sheikh Hamud al-Ghafiri, who was governor of Dhofar under Sa'id bin Taimur. While Buraik bin Hamud succeeded his father from 1970 to his death in 1979, Hamad bin Hamud has built up the leading Dhofar business group, Hamdan Trading.

Their old loyalty to Muscat's authority has allowed the Salalah-based al-Rawas branch of the Bait Kathir tribe to benefit from the rewards of the new state. Sheikh 'Abd al-'Aziz, who was a member of the DLF in the 1960s, held the position of Minister of Information and Youth (then only Information) between 1979 and 2001, and then was appointed Adviser to the Sultan for Cultural Affairs, a post he still holds. Since 1970 Sheikh 'Abd Allah bin Sa'id's family has established the Al Rawas holding, which is active in various sectors and has been taken in charge by the founder's sons. Salim bin 'Abd Allah, a former Majlis al-Shura member, was an OCCI board member between 2011 and 2014. His brother Muhammad was treasurer of the OCCI (2003–7). Their cousin Sheikh 'Abd Allah bin Salim was chairman of the OCCI until May 2004, then Minister of Regional Municipalities, Environment and Water Resources (2004–07) and of Municipalities and Water Resources (2007–11).

Among the Sultan's historical allies, who after 1970 were given cabinet positions because of their support during the previous decades' wars, members of the Hirth tribe's noble lineage are a rather special case (see figure 6). The family was torn apart from the 1940s by a quarrel over the post of *tamima*, and divided between supporters of Sultan Sa'id and the Imam. Only the descendants of people who declared support for Sa'id straightaway or remained out of the conflict retain political influence nowadays. Thus, Sheikh Muhammad bin 'Abd Allah, a State Council member since 2011, held various Cabinet positions in the 2000s while Sheikh al-Fadl has been Secretary General of the Council of Ministers since 2011.

The same is true of the Bani Hina tribe's noble lineage, which split into two factions after 1954 (see figure 7). While Ghalib and Talib were pre-eminent supporters of the Imamate, Zahir bin Ghusn's sons, and especially 'Abd Allah, who was *sheikh tamima* of the tribe, gave allegiance to Sultan Sa'id. This stance earned them top administrative positions after the coup, as al-Walid entered

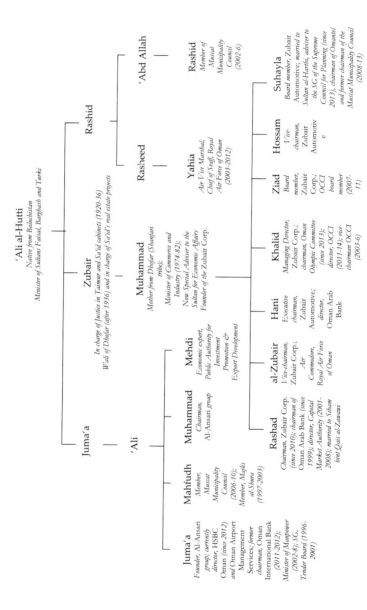

Figure 8: Simplified family tree of 'Ali al-Hutti's descendants

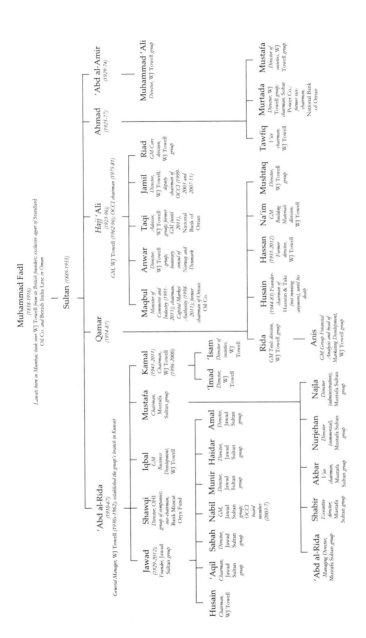

Figure 9: Simplified family tree of al-Sultan family

the government in 1972. Afterwards, several of his nephews took advantage of the opportunities the new regime offered: Sheikh Muhammad bin 'Abd Allah was Minister of Justice until 2012, his brother 'Abd al-'Aziz is Ambassador to the UK. Their cousin 'Abd al-'Aziz bin Muhammad is vice-president of the Islamic Development Bank while Badr is Ambassador to Austria and 'Abd Allah bin 'Ali is Director General of Industry at the Ministry of Commerce and Industry.

Other members of Sultan Qaboos' Cabinet personally took advantage of these opportunities. One was Lieutenant Colonel Sa'id al-Wahaibi, head of the Diwan of the Royal Court from 1970 to 1985. This position has given him the opportunity to build up since 1976 one of the leading Omani business groups, the Assarain group. His son Khalid currently heads the group. Since September 2004 Sa'id's brother Ahmad has been executive manager of the state corporation Oman Oil, which bought up all BP Oman filling stations in the same year and has become the long arm of the state in several industrial megaprojects, in Sohar port for example.

Similar is the case of Sheikh 'Amr bin Shuwain al-Husni, whose tribe was in the 1960s and the 70s one of the main recruiting areas for the Sultan's armed forces based in Dhofar. Sheikh 'Amr was Minister of the Environment (1991–96), then of Labour and Social Affairs (1996–2001) and then of Social Development between November 2001 and October 2004. His brother 'Abd Allah served as undersecretary at the Ministry of Information until 2011. Since 1975 the two brothers have built up, concurrently with their official positions, a major business group, Al Hosni.

Ahmad bin 'Abd al-Nabi Makki illustrates a similar advance by decision-making actors into the economic sector. After serving as the first Omani Ambassador to the UN in the 1970s, then as Ambassador to the United States (1975–78), he was appointed Minister of the Civil Service (1991–95). From 1995 to 2011, he served as Minister of the National Economy. His brothers Habib, Munir and Mahmud sit on many boards of directors of companies listed on the Muscat Stock Exchange. Moreover, Habib was director of urban planning in the early 1970s.[91] Also a former ambassador, Munir founded Oman's first financial company, Fincorp, while Ahmad Makki's son Sami, a former director of Bank Sohar, is Managing Director of Al Mashriq group. Finally, Salim bin Hasan Makki, who was in charge of oil affairs in the Interim Planning Council in the early 1970s, and then an ambassador in the 1990s, chairs the OOSC group which specialises in oil industry supplies. His sister Zamzam sat on the Muscat Municipal Council between 2002 and 2006.

Finally, it is necessary to mention Muhammad bin Musa al-Yusef, who was successively undersecretary for Financial Affairs (1981–89) and Minister of State for Development (1994–97); he also chairs the Al Yousef group of companies. In May 2001 this Lawati businessman was sentenced to six years' imprisonment for embezzlement and fraud on the Muscat Stock Exchange, but pardoned by the Sultan;[92] his sons Qais and Faisal have taken over his economic functions.

Thus, direct interference by decision-making people in the economic and financial sectors is undeniable. But there is an exception to this political-economic mixing: noble clans from Saham of the al-Maʿamari tribe did not conquer economic positions as powerful as the ones described above. Their influence in the decision-making process has nevertheless not faded; thus General ʿAli bin Majid held between 1989 and 2011 the posts of Minister of the Royal Office and head of the office of the Sultan's Armed Forces Chief of Staff (see chapter 6), while his brother Sheikh Fahd was vice-chairman of the Majlis al-Shura between 2000 and 2007. Moreover, ʿAli bin Majid's brother-in-law, Sheikh Muhammad bin Marhun, was Ambassador to the UAE until 2007, then Minister of State and governor of Dhofar from 2007 to 2012. The noble branch of the al-Maʿamari tribe has also been a reservoir for recruitment of civil servants under Qaboos. Sheikh Yahia bin Hamud has been *wali* of Nizwa, then governor of Buraimi (2006–11) and of North Sharqiyya (since 2011), ʿAbd Allah, was a State Council member from 2007 to 2011, and another brother, Hilal, a former Assistant Head of Liaison at the Royal Office and chairman of Sohar Bank, was transferred to the Foreign Ministry in 2012 and granted a minister's rank. Finally, Sheikh Hamad bin Hilal, who was Ambassador to Jordan, has held since 2005 the post of undersecretary for Cultural Affairs in the Ministry of Heritage and Culture. As for Lieutenant General Malik bin Sulaiman, whose father was one of the closest advisers to Saʿid bin Taimur in the 1960s, he was Inspector-General of Police and Customs until 2011.

But the most interesting process has been a reverse movement: the takeover of decision-making positions by members of the traditional economic elite. An example was Qais al-Zawawi, who was appointed in December 1973 as Minister of State for Foreign Affairs, a position he held until 1982 (see figure 5). At the same time he assisted the Sultan in running the Finance[93] and Development Councils. In 1982 Qais al-Zawawi became Deputy Prime Minister for Finance and the Economy; he died in unexplained circumstances in 1995. His brother ʿUmar, who was appointed in 1974 as Personal Adviser to Qaboos, currently holds the post of Special Adviser to the Sultan for External Affairs. Economically speaking, Omar Zawawi Establishment (OMZEST), which represents many foreign brands (BAE, Daimler, Microsoft, Nokia, Oracle, Siemens, etc.), has become one of the leading Omani holding companies. While the founder's children, Waleed and Reem, are taking over the OMZEST management, the Zawawi economic empire is composed of several other holdings, including Alawi Ent. owned by Qais's children. Brigadier (Rtd.) Waleed bin 'Umar, a former head of information technology services of the Sultan's forces, is vice-chairman of HSBC Oman.

Another businessman who was involved in the decision-making process early on is Muhammad Zubair, who was appointed in November 1974 to the post of Minister of Commerce and Industry; he left it in 1982 to become Personal Adviser to the Sultan for Economic Affairs, his current position (see figure 8). The Zubair Corp. group has become one of the most influential in the Sultanate. Muhammad Zubair's son, Khalid, was OCCI deputy chairman between 2003 and 2006, and board member from 2011 to 2014, while his brother Ziad was a board member from 2007 to 2011. Moreover, the former Minister of Manpower, Juma'a bin 'Ali Al Juma'a, is related to the Zubair family, as his father is Muhammad Zubair's first cousin. Juma'a bin 'Ali is the founder of the Al Ansari group, which is active in construction and information technology. Finally Air Vice-Marshal Yahia bin Rasheed, the chief of staff of the Royal Air Force from 2003 to 2012, is Muhammad Zubair's first cousin's son.

Sheikh Sa'id bin Ahmad al-Shanfari is another businessman to occupy a cabinet position, responsible for Agriculture, Fisheries, Oil and Minerals since November 1974. He became Minister of Oil and Minerals in a 1979 reshuffle, a position he held until 1996. The powerful Shanfari business group, managed by Sheikh Sa'id, his son 'Adil and his cousin 'Abd al-'Aziz bin 'Ali, was originally centred on motors but diversified into several sectors, like tourism, construction, the electrical appliance industry and oil services. Sa'id bin Ahmad also chaired the Dhofar International Development and Investment Co., set up to promote local investments. Two other sons of Sheikh Sa'id, Nizar and Thamer, are pre-eminent businessmen: Thamer was chairman of the Oryx group, created in 1990, which was mentioned in 2002 in UN reports on the illegal exploitation of natural resources in DR Congo. As for Sheikh 'Abd al-'Aziz, he chaired Salalah Port Services, a mixed public-private company in charge of promotion and development of the port Free Zone.

Another merchant dynasty which has taken positions in the decision-making sector is the al-Sultan family (see figure 9). In the 1970s *hajj* 'Ali bin

Sultan was already chairman of the first Omani consultative institution, the Agriculture, Fisheries and Industry Council. Afterwards he was appointed vice-chairman of the State Consultative Council between 1981 and 1983. In addition, he was chairman of the Chamber of Commerce and Industry from 1975 to 1981. His son Maqbul, who chaired the Chamber of Commerce from 1987 to 1991, held the post of Minister of Commerce and Industry from 1991 to 2011. He was simultaneously chairman of the Capital Market Authority from its creation in 1998 to 2011. Several holding companies are wholly owned by more than 35 cousins descended from Sultan bin Muhammad Fadl; the leading company is WJ Towell, which is involved in more than forty sectors (motors, telecommunications, construction, computer engineering, insurance, etc.) and represents in Oman brands like Mars, Unilever, Nestlé, Mazda and Bridgestone. Two other holding groups (Mustafa Sultan and Jawad Sultan) show al-Sultan's economic dynamism.

The involvement in the decision-making process by historically pre-eminent actors in the Omani economy has spread over more than twenty years. It illustrates the Omani merchant elites' flair in converting their traditional activities to the new economic order, responding also to opportunities the Sultan has given them. Qaboos has thus aligned himself with the traditional political and merchant elites, giving strategic positions to secure public contracts and control over the distribution of the oil wealth to the merchants. This strategy has increased both the elites' dependence on the state and the stability of Sultan Qaboos' rule, because the economic survival of the trading families has become indissolubly linked with his political fate as a ruler. These allies have certainly had no alternative to supporting him. The symbolic debt imposed on the merchant elites by Qaboos at the beginning of his rule (when he relied on their funds to consolidate his authority) has thus gradually turned into a weapon in his hands, forestalling any challenges to his reign by turning the most powerful societal forces into unfailing allies.

Never, until the late 1990s, were the Omani merchants "forced to choose money over formal political influence".[94] This can be explained by Qaboos' extreme vulnerability in 1970; unknown among his subjects, abandoned by his father's family, denounced by opponents as the last card played by the British who were about to leave the game, Sultan Qaboos had no other choice than giving guarantees to merchants' networks.

But thanks to the oil rent, Sultan Qaboos has endeavoured to undermine the other political actors' legitimacy and to impose his as the arbiter; through various strategies, but with the same arm at his disposal—the state apparatus—the new ruler tried to win over both the whole population (by universal redistribution) and the politically most threatening social categories (by individualised redistribution).

Giacomo Luciani considers that, with such a machine overpowering opposition, an "allocation State does not need to refer to a national myth and, as a matter of fact, will usually avoid doing so".[95] Nevertheless, the Omani ruler could not allow himself to rely only on the destruction of the former political order, the one combining the Imamate, tribes and merchant towns. It was crucial for Qaboos to build his own legitimacy at the same time, to overcome the alternative political and social allegiances offered to his subjects. To do that, he has endeavoured to promote an original Omani national identity for which his own person has constituted the keystone. Thus, he has followed kings Hasan II of Morocco and Husain of Jordan, examples Lisa Anderson quotes when she explains that in the Middle East "the monarchs who have been able to sustain and build their own power are [...] adept at the politics of state formation" and nation-identity building.[96]

5

NATIONAL IDENTITY BUILDING

Since its origin, in the middle of the eighteenth century, the al-Busa'idi dynasty's legitimacy has had nothing to do with any nation-building; the Omani sea empire owed more to successful trading than to political conquest, and the sultans themselves, who spoke Gujarati more than Arabic and spent most of their time in Zanzibar or Bombay, ruled over regions inhabited by Arabs, Indians, Baluchis, Africans and others. In parallel to the process detailed in the previous chapter, which aimed at linking contemporary Oman inextricably to the modern idea of the state, Sultan Qaboos has had to create among the inhabitants of this territory a feeling of belonging to a common "imagined community"[1] while at the same time raising this feeling, as fast as possible, above the other allegiances people were used to referring to, such as tribes and local communities. The national ideology the Sultan has developed comes within this perspective: it has aimed at promoting a timeless Omani national identity, which has relied on standardised collective references and helped his authority's legitimisation.

In this chapter, we will follow Eric Hobsbawm's view that "nations are more often the consequence of setting up a State more than they are its foundation".[2] We will work to display the voluntaristic political strategies that the central state has pursued in order to root an Omani national identity which, even if "made up", could become obvious in everybody's eyes and could strengthen the Sultan's image as the nation's natural representative. Promotion of the Omani nation has been the occasion to develop what we call identity engineering, in which history, heritage (*turath*) and symbolic references have helped to anchor the awareness of a new political community and to serve the central authority's legitimisation.

The standardisation of cultural references

A parallel with nineteenth-century European national identity building helps to illustrate the path the Sultanate has followed since 1970. Words used by Alain Dieckhoff to describe the role of public education in national identity building in France at that time echo post-1970 Oman:

> The nation as a collection of individuals remained an abstraction, a meaningless slogan [...]. It was absolutely necessary to make it an experienced reality [...], an all-the-time experience [...]. This nationalisation of minds could proceed only from a formidable process of inculcation, which had to be led, through its school network, by the state, zealous propagator of "refined culture."[3]

The state school network: melting-pot for identities. Within three decades, the Sultanate of Oman experienced a tremendous increase in the number of schools; in 2013 there were 1,043 schools, half of them mixed, with around 503,000 pupils until the end of secondary school, while 71,500 were registered in 444 private or community schools.[4] Girls represent 49.1% of all pupils registered until secondary school certificate.

This process of introducing universal standardised teaching was part of the efforts driven by the authorities to spread Omani national ideology. This is confirmed by the language policy: if all Omanis were able to speak Arabic, they were more likely to be reached by the regime's ideology. In Inner Oman especially, local dialects which have been officially presented as archaic and viewed with condescension by younger generations are slowly disappearing in favour of standard Omani Arabic which is spoken all over the territory, for which Muscat set the tone. The areas where Arabic is least spoken, even at school, are those where the state, and hence national feeling, have faced the greatest obstacles in getting established. In the Jabru and Wadi 'Aday quarters, in Western Muttrah, children were still in 2004 using the Baluchi and Swahili languages as vernaculars, to the great displeasure of schoolteachers from Inner Oman.[5]

In Oman, a very large proportion of people speak two or three languages fluently, the use of a particular language depending on the person one is talking with and the social situation. But in Oman's nation-building process, language has never held the central position that it had in comparable processes in nineteenth-century Europe. This can be explained by the fact that

Sultan Qaboos' main political allies in the 1970s—Baluchi soldiers, Omanis returning from overseas, and Muscat merchants—did not have Arabic as their mother tongue, and never played the role of a scholarly elite at the origin of a separate national culture; these groups on the fringe of Oman's historical heart could not lead the nation-building process.

At school, "not only nation's language, history and geography are taught, but also how to be and how to think as a national".[6] Without mentioning teaching contents, the perception conveyed of the national school system has been of an effort to inculcate individual feeling of belonging to the nation, wrapping it with outwards signs of sovereignty, like raising the national flag and singing of the national anthem before entering school. The school-promoted symbolic repertoire was spread uniformly across the country, and by definition was reserved for national children only. It led to adoption of common values and behaviours, but also to expansion of new sociability networks between individuals without previous opportunities of relationship.[7] Similarly, tribal differences became less important, whereas the generational gap was reinforced, also being widened by the tremendous post-1970 material and technical development. Religious and secular knowledge was no more the monopoly of elders, but was acquired in contact with peers. The entire cultural foundation of local groups—family narration, empirical knowledge of geography and nature, local dialects—was to be delegitimised or even denigrated in favour of "official knowledge" acquired under the aegis of the Ministry of Education.

This nationalisation of each individual involved, for adults, mechanisms of strong differentiation from foreigners settled in Oman, whether Arab, Western or from the Indian subcontinent, in order to strengthen awareness of belonging to an immediately and concretely identifiable community. All national civil servants have to wear a white *dishdasha* at work. Similarly, the spread of the *kumma*, an embroidered multicoloured round cap around which a *masar* (cashmere scarf) is wrapped for official ceremonies, is an additional means to distinguish symbolically what is "inside" and "outside" Oman; it helps to make concrete the new national community everybody has the duty to belong to with pride. These external signs of belonging/exclusion automatically encourage different sets of social practices and behaviour, depending on whether one is dealing with an Omani or an expatriate.

The effects of the oil rent on the family model. As a consequence of bureaucratisation of jobs and ways of life, post-1970 Oman has been characterised by internal migration on a scale unknown before. Moving out of the community area was reserved in former times to "intermediate powers" (*walis*, *qadis* and tribal *sheikhs*), but it suddenly extended to all social strata. Recruitment for jobs, by government departments at a national level, led individuals to acquire financial autonomy and sometimes to start a family far away from their clan. The Muscat urban area, which grew from 40,000 inhabitants in 1970 to 600,000 within twenty years and to 1.2 million in 2013, best illustrates the resulting drift from the land. This kind of work-induced migration represented certainly the most powerful vector for language standardisation at a national level, but also for changes in cultural customs, with fast adoption of a nuclear family model—especially since, in many cases, it was stipulated in a marriage agreement that the couple had to settle independently as soon as possible, as young women usually refuse to live under the same roof as the husband's family. State distribution of lands on an individual basis consolidated autonomy from the clan.

The social activities of tribesmen, formerly restricted to the village and its vicinity, broadened into larger networks, such as work colleagues, new neighbours, parents of children going to the same schools. This helped to marginalise the influence of old solidarity groups on daily life and favoured a slow homogenisation of references within a national framework which imposed itself on everybody. In addition the national armed forces served as a means of inclusion in the national community for many Omanis. This process took place in different ways, the most obvious one being literacy classes teaching citizenship and patriotic values to soldiers. More informally, a new serviceman set himself up as mediator of his village or his group with the state; acting as a go-between to deal with the needs of his community as well as the administration's requests, he helped gradual adjustment of the state and local communities' agendas, and thus the encapsulation of local references into state-national ones.

In a very different chapter of family life, the rentier-model economy has influenced the role of children in the family. The Omani authorities have only recently become aware of the consequences of the massive presence of Arab and Asian expatriates in all fields of social life—and in particular, in the educational and para-educational sectors. Since their infancy, the closest human environment for middle- and high-class Omani children, in addition to their Omani peers, is made up of foreigners: Egyptian or Tunisian school-teachers, Indian drivers, Indonesian or Philippine nurses (*nani*), etc. These people often cannot speak Arabic with the children, and can in no case be reference markers to the children for social belonging and values—or only through a mirror effect which merely reinforces children in their superiority feelings. The sociologist Louis Roussel's words about France apply without restriction to the Omani case:

> What characterises nowadays the child's position in the family is the way the adult couple needs him: not any more socially like before, but to consolidate the mutual assent the married couple gave each other. Under these conditions, the adults will ensure that there are no conflicts [...] between them and the child.[8]

As immigrants permanently under the threat of deportation, the people responsible for a child's upbringing cannot exceed their role, without being reminded of their status in one way or another—by the child himself, well aware of his situation. The child spends much of his time with an over-protective *nani* and cannot forge any figure of authority. The upheaval of family structure, following that of the whole social structure, has moreover weakened the parents in their own life. While they cannot find reference markers in the former generations, they try to keep the child away from their own troubles and help reinforce a permissive situation, by anticipating the child's least desires: "His reasonable desires will be filled as much as possible, and for the unreasonable ones—not to work at school, for instance—we will negotiate."[9]

More broadly, "Young couples more and more choose their accommodation according to two criteria: the neighbourhood and its reputation, first; and the school. Information is gathered about the teachers' skills, the fields taught, the quality of the refectory's food, the school transport possibilities... And the parents do not hesitate to change the child from one school to another if they feel that one is not convenient."[10]

Such behaviour illustrates profound changes in Omani society, in which dynamics and decisions do not come any more from the elders, but from the youngest generations.

Expanded contacts among people. A concomitant task of the new state was to compile statistics of the country, through maps and surveys, in order to count and classify the territory and its inhabitants. Between September and December 2003, in the second census, the population was fully mobilised, thanks to a huge patriotic consciousness-raising campaign coordinated by the High National Committee for the Census, chaired by Haitham bin Tariq, to encourage everybody to get involved in this national initiative. This campaign assumed various shapes: daily messages to mobile phones and mail addresses,[11] radio and television advertisements, etc. The data collected dealt exclusively with aspects of people's homes (moveable property, room numbers) and other property (vehicles, electric supplies, etc.) and not with the inhabitants themselves. Only the numbers of people, nationality and gender were collected, but nothing about age, level of education or job. Thus the census' main goal was not really to count people; it was part of a movement aimed at enhancing the state's symbolic authority as the driving force for social organisation and development. The census was a means to give a quantifiable evaluation— through data on urbanisation, access to infrastructure, electricity connection rates, etc.—to progress achieved by the country over thirty years, in a kind of national impulse of self-congratulation.

In information and communication services, Oman's gap in 1970 was particularly wide. During the weeks following the coup a temporary radio station, which broadcast two hours a day, was set up in Bait al-Falaj for Sultan Qaboos to have his message spread. In 1976 the Ministry of Information was built in the new district of Madinat al-I'lam and a modern transmission centre was established, with studios for two Omani channels, one transmitting in Arabic 24 hours a day in 1998, the other in English 17 hours a day. Slowly relays were set up in the main towns, but reception is still difficult today, or even impossible, outside towns. In July 2003 a third radio channel dedicated to youth especially (Shabab 'Uman) started to transmit from the same centre. But radio never represented a technical revolution comparable to the European one at the beginning of the twentieth century, as its arrival in Oman almost coincided with television.

The development of television was intimately linked to the ruler's political strategy, as the national channel's transmission began on the National Day in 1974.[12] Initially only 2,000 people from Muscat and the Batina, who had only received Iranian and Pakistani television until then, were involved. Since 1998 implementation of new relays, in addition to democratisation of television, has allowed the national channel to be received all over the country. At the end of 2004 a royal decree allowed the establishment of private radio and television companies. In September 2005 the Ministry of Information approved licenses for two major companies (Sabco, chaired by Sayyid Hamad bin Hamud al-Busa'idi, and OHI) to set up one new television station and three radio stations.[13] At the launching of the second public TV channel in November 2006, which is targeted at the young, a contract of exclusive sponsorship was signed with Reem Zawawi and Sa'ad Bahwan. Opening up the media to the private sector should not disrupt the sector, as the OHI chairman's own words testify: "The Sultanate, under the wise leadership of His Majesty Sultan Qaboos, has given me a lot and I owe a great deal to the country. I consider my involvement with the media as a service to the country."[14]

The government lifted a ban on individual satellite dishes only in 1994; people could then tune in to satellite channels from all over the world. Each family nowadays is used to watching Sultan Qaboos on television, but also to listening to the Mufti of Oman's religious lessons live,[15] and seeing Omani diplomats treat on an equal footing with their foreign counterparts during Arab summits and Islamic conferences. These pictures concretely illustrate the recognition of Oman as a fully-fledged actor in the international arena. Besides, television sets in Oman, as a meeting point for family members, have been a huge means of spreading the standard Omani Arabic language all over the territory. But television has also put all Omanis symbolically in contact with each other. The universalisation of television thus made it possible to focus thousands of "isolated" citizens' attention on one source of information and leisure.

Besides radio and television, Sultan Qaboos' accession to the throne also marked the beginnings of the Omani press. As early as 1970 a daily information sheet was distributed free in the street by the newly created government news service. In 1972 a government daily newspaper (*'Uman*) and an "independent" weekly (*al-Watan*), started in January 1971, coexisted in Muscat. Even though censorship was officially abolished in 1985,[16] the press is still governed by a 1984 law which laid down that all publications and journalists must be registered with the Ministry of Information. The pressure the latter still exerts on the Omani press today explains why it gives no accounts of any social or political controversy and no criticisms of the regime are expressed. The information dealing with the Gonu cyclone which hit the eastern coast of Oman in June 2007 is revealing; while officially around 80 people were reported died or missing at the end of 2007, one top official spoke in private of 200 killed, while it was not unusual to hear expatriates employed in contracting sectors speaking of 500 dead people.[17] The establishment of a non-governmental association of Omani journalists, which was announced by the Ministry of Social Development in 2005, did not change the situation, as is shown by the fact that two intellectuals were declared *persona non grata* for the whole Omani media at the same time (see chapter 6).

At the moment eight national daily newspapers are published, two of them by the Ministry of Information (*'Uman*, in Arabic, and *The Oman Observer*, in English, which was born in 1981), while six are owned privately but funded by government subsidies (*al-Shabiba*, since 1993, and *al-Watan*; *Oman Tribune*, born in 2005; *The Times of Oman*, *al-Ro'ya* and *Muscat Daily* since 2009). These publications mostly use news reports produced by the official press agency, the

Oman News Agency (ONA), which was created in May 1986 and placed under the Ministry of Information's authority in July 2006 by a Sultan's decree. In October 2010, the Public Authority for Radio and Television, under the supervision of the Council of Ministers, was established by Sultan's decree.

Recreating a national identity within the framework of an omnipresent state and unifying cultural and religious references have also occurred in the religious field; the authorities have tried to smooth over doctrinal differences between schools in order to promote an Omani Islam which is impervious to any historical or political takeover.

Promotion of a 'generic'[18] *and consensual Islam.* The selective reading of Oman's history extends to religion, which is used to strengthen a feeling of national unity and hence of the authorities' legitimacy. While Oman's territory has been influenced by both Ibadism and the movements that gave rise to diverse interpretations of Islam, the government soon began to promote a consensual and "generic" Islam that is peculiar to Oman and neglects both controversial past influences and foreign ones, such as the Saudi Wahhabi influence.

Estimates of religious allegiance among the Omani population are not based on official figures, as the Omani authorities have never published data. Article 2 of the Basic Law only establishes that "the religion of the State is Islam and the Islamic sharia is the basis of legislation". A senior Ministry of the Economy official explains that among *imam*s and *qadi*s appointed by ministerial decree every year, he infers their school (Ibadi or Sunni) from their tribal names, the idea being a confessional balance among such appointments.[19]

There have been various estimates by foreign observers. The most commonly mentioned one, by the US Central Intelligence Agency, is that 75% of Omanis are Ibadi while the other quarter can be divided into Sunni, Shi'i and Hindu.[20] For his part, Dale Eickelman considers that "roughly 50–55 percent of its citizen population is Sunni, 40–45 percent is Ibadi and less than 2 percent is Shia".[21] John Peterson gives estimates of 45% Ibadi, 50% Sunni and probably less than 5% Shi'i and Hindu.[22] According to our own calculations, based on the results of the 2003 census, Ibadi Omanis appear to number 48 to 53% of the whole population, Sunnis 45 to 49% and Shi'a 3 to 4%.

For thirty years the Omani religious authorities' policy, led by the Mufti of Oman, Sheikh Ahmad al-Khalili, has sought to dilute the differences between the Ibadi and Sunni schools of Islam, while believers of both pray together. In standard sermons established nationally by the Committee for Friday Sermons,[23] differences of confession (*madhhab*) are never mentioned. This does not mean that both confessions are put on an equal footing, as Ibadism still has a more than symbolic pre-eminence: both Muftis who have been appointed since 1970 are Ibadi, as well as the Ministers of Justice and Religious Affairs and most of the leading personalities and *imam*s in both those departments.

Sultan Qaboos never could and never wanted to make Islam a trump card in his process of legitimacy-building. The authorities consider that they are not protected against the emergence of an opposition movement invoking the Ibadi Imamate legacy—or, more generally, any ideology invoking political Islam—to challenge the regime. Nevertheless the Muslim character of the state and its leader is constantly emphasised. Qaboos has never failed to display his observance of Islamic precepts, by appearing regularly accomplishing his ritual obligations or taking part in Friday prayers on special occasions (inauguration of mosques, Muslim festivals, etc.).

Moreover, while Sultan Qaboos has never claimed any formal religious authority and has left the public monopoly of religious discourse to the Mufti, he has achieved what Malika Zeghal called, speaking about Morocco, "the domestication of men of religion".[24] Not only did the ruler seek at an early stage to "bureaucratise" those men of religion by integrating them into the state apparatus, he also endeavoured to confine them within the Omani field only, through creation of a national Islam. That is why relations with Ibadi communities of Tanzania, Algeria, Tunisia and Libya remained weak after 1970. By confining religious personalities within the national framework, the regime has not only controlled their voice and influence more easily but also involved them personally in the promotion of a national identity.

No official policy has been implemented to preserve the oldest Omani mosques; for instance, the biggest one in Salalah (al-Jami'a in Rawas quarter) was destroyed at the beginning of the 1990s to build a modern one on the same location. In Nakhl, the remains of the old mosque were razed to the ground and replaced by a modern copy of the old *mihrab*.[25] And in the most important towns (Ruwi, Bahla, Sohar, Sur, Salalah, Nizwa, etc.), new Sultan Qaboos mosques, in which Friday sermons are delivered, have supplanted neglected historical ones, in order to promote a modern, asepticised Omani Islam. The best example is the gorgeous Great Mosque which was inaugurated in 2001 in Bawshar; the edge of its inside court is adorned with niches in honour of various Islamic cultures (Iran, Syria, Andalusia, Central Asia, etc.), to recall Oman's belonging to the regional civilisation; Franck Mermier says the Ibadi heritage is "both covered up and glorified".[26]

Nevertheless, while the Omani authorities always endeavoured to place the religious issue in a timeless situation, they were not able to prevent the intrusion of political issues, or the awareness of differences between Islamic schools, into the mosques. It is not without significance that the first faculty of Islamic Law and Sharia, under the aegis of the Ministry of Education, opened in Muscat in 1997, only three years after the 1994 arrests among Islamic circles and the year after promulgation of the first Basic Law. The state relied for long on local religious authorities who were depositaries of traditional Ibadi knowledge; through them, it sought to control religious discourse by isolating it from any foreign influence. Over ten years, the regime became aware that this outdated strategy only contributed to shifting debate away from the mosques and strengthening young people's interest in what the government prohibited, like publications banned by the Ministry of Information.[27]

More broadly, Oman has experienced a major change in daily religious practices, with the emergence of new ones followed by some schools of thought but breaking with the Ibadi tradition, like the building of small mosques by rich individuals in Muscat's most recently urbanised districts (al-Khud, al-Mawaleh) or frequent prayers in the mosque by a growing number of women and children. If these demonstrations of piety were not of course prohibited, Ibadism was not used to them, as Friday prayers by men were not considered compulsory. In addition, it is common to meet young Sunni Omanis wearing big beards without moustaches, as a sign of *Tabligh* membership.[28]

In matters of dress, some young Ibadi have re-adopted the distinctive white turban (*'imma*) joined with a strap under the chin. Independently of religious school (Ibadi or Sunni), a growing proportion of young men wear the *dishdasha* that only reaches the ankles, so as to prevent it touching dust and maintain the purity necessary for prayer. The Omani authorities' tolerance of this religious development was originally based on the idea that someone occupied with religious matters will not question the political regime. But nowadays religious charity associations' aid to the underprivileged and newcomers, the widespread idea that the gap is continually widening between those who have access to the levers of power and others, and finally the lack of public means of expression all give support to the spread of conservative practices in the name of Islam. For instance, debates on music, rejected in the name of the religion by popular *ulama*,[29] take on a very noticeable connotation in Oman, in view of the role of music in the Sultan's life, shown by the Royal Omani Symphonic Orchestra, the only such orchestra in the Gulf. Polemics in 2005 on whether the Muscat Festival was lawful according to Islamic teaching—as songs and folk dances were staged—only revived this issue. The severity of the regulations drawn up by the government to deal with possible troublemakers shows the tension surrounding this issue, seemingly a purely theological one.

a: The historical legacy at the heart of the new national identity

The coincidence of the beginning of oil production in Oman and Qaboos' rise to power is never mentioned in the official historiography. This omission is obviously aimed at downplaying the crucial role of the oil rent upon which the country's development hinges, in favour of an emphasis on the ruler's actions. With 85% of the population never having known any ruler other than Sultan Qaboos, it is easy for the Sultan to portray himself as the embodiment of modern Oman in general and of the 1970 renaissance (*nahda*) ideology in particular—the regime's leitmotiv in any national celebration.

Rewriting Oman history. The town of Nizwa is called "the egg of Islam" (*bayda al-islam*), a reference to its central role in Imamate revivals. Nevertheless, in working to create a new national identity, it was inconceivable for the regime to rely on this long rebellious region, in which the Sultan did not have any ally. In order to take over the Ibadi legacy, Sultan Qaboos held a few personalities, like his own father and Imam Ghalib, fully responsible for the pre-1970 situation, so as to exonerate the whole Inner Oman population, including its tribal leaders. This decision made it possible to draw a veil over all the events and to avoid looking into half a century which had to be effaced from national memory. Besides, it made it possible to present the 1970 coup as a new start and to co-opt former Imamate scholars as intellectual support for this policy.

The pre-1970 period was stigmatised as a tragic parenthesis in Oman's life, like a metaphor of the "chronologically gauged A.D.-style slumber."[30] Nineteenth-century European promoters of nationalism thought that they were living through the "awakening" of a timeless nation which had existed for ages. When he came to power, Sultan Qaboos used a metaphor which spoke for itself: "Yesterday, it was complete darkness and with the help of God, tomorrow will be a new dawn on Muscat, Oman and its people".[31] The book *Oman in History*, published by the Ministry of Information, sketches Oman's history exactly, but skips directly from the Seeb agreement to Qaboos' access to the throne, as if these events were separated by several years only. The new ruler's coming to power appears as the year O of the new nation.

The selectivity of Oman's national memory is well illustrated by the way Omani history is taught in state schools. In the lower grades, especially primary and preparatory ones, ancient history predominates; common themes are Oman's Islamisation, its relations with the Persians, and the Middle Ages until the thirteenth century. These periods' contribution to the building of national pride, which (it is suggested) made it possible for Oman always to remain independent, is stressed. In preparatory grades, the al-Ya'arubi and al-Busa'idi maritime empires are studied in detail. At secondary level, history is only studied in arts sections (*al-qism al-adabi*). In the first year the European Renaissance, the Enlightenment, the American and French revolutions and the First World War are taught, while in the second, historical links between the Christian and Muslim worlds are detailed. Twentieth-century Oman is only skimmed over, leaving a black hole between the imperial nineteenth century and the *nahda*. Besides, it is significant that Ibadism is only referred as an Omani-based "variation" of Islam; its political dimension, especially in modern and contemporary times, is never evoked.

In this way the post-1970 authorities seek to conceal political troubles and actual division of the territory between two political entities, thus promoting political oblivion. The first idea is to obscure the political reality on the ground in the first half of the twentieth century, during which the Sultan derived his power from British protection and stood on equal political terms with the Imam, as the balance was only maintained by a tripartite pact overseen by the British. This veil drawn across Oman's twentieth-century past contributed to the creation after 1970 of a fraternal collective imagination that has to be appreciated in comparison with the former tragedies—which must be forgotten, but which everyone is constantly told to remember so as to reject them absolutely. Benedict Anderson highlighted this paradox in building collective memory: "Having to "have already forgotten" tragedies of which one needs unceasingly to be "reminded" turns out to be a characteristic device in the later construction of national genealogies".[32] This political effacing of the country's memory was well illustrated by a fifty-year-old Omani from Tanuf, dynamited in 1957: he placed the British attack "in my grandparents' time; I did not live it, it happened a century ago".[33] The Jabal Akhdar war was no more than a vague recollection which worked as a powerful repulsive.

The Omani state, under the Sultan's and the Ministry of National Heritage's aegis, holds the monopoly of historical discourse. During our interviews with *sheikh*s from various geographical and tribal origins, to whom we were inevitably directed when dealing with Omani history, the topics mentioned straight away were events prior to the twentieth century (the eighteenth and nineteenth centuries, the constitution and settlement of contemporary tribes, etc.). The twentieth century was discussed only after several meetings, but always with reliable persons and on a confidential basis only. Thus Oman's twentieth century is still thought about in a subversive way, because talking about it means lifting, even partially, the official curtain over this period. The Omani case confirms that "by its subversive and distorting perspective, the mnemonic narration is a power relation, and the gap of its oblivion and silences structures the use of domination".[34]

The Renaissance ideology. The Omani national identity is basically built on the negation of the country's pre-1970 history, any reference to which remains taboo. Regular references in official discourses to a "new era" implant the conviction that History started in 1970. Nevertheless the Omani "Renaissance" (*nahda*) concept, which gave its name in 1990 to the 23 July commemoration of the anniversary of Qaboos' accession to the throne, appeared in 1974 only: "On this immortal landmark day, four years ago, a new sun shone in our beloved land to light the flame of the national spirit and zeal of our citizens, who plunged into building this renaissance [...] Our beloved Oman lives today in the dawn of a great and comprehensive renaissance."[35] This term became definitely predominant in the early 1980s when preparatory school pupils were asked to "strike out the word 'intifada' and to replace it with 'nahda', in schoolbooks describing 1970 events."[36] The word *nahda* is used in many place names in post-1970 urban development: Madina al-Nahda's remote Muscat suburb, which was nicknamed "Chicago" because of social insecurity there in the 1980s, is inhabited by citizens returning from Africa and Baluchi-native Omanis. Similarly the first modern hospital in Muscat, whose construction started under Sa'id, should have been named the Ruwi Hospital, but it opened only after 1970 and was renamed the Nahda Hospital.

The *nahda* metaphor did not stop there in 1970; Sultan Qaboos, as the "brain" of the Omani social body, exhorted his subjects to come back to life properly: "The Government and the people are as one body. If one of its limbs fails to do its duty, the other parts of the body will suffer."[37] The Sultan has followed the metaphor all through his rule, as he showed when he said on the 20th National Day, "For two decades, we have renewed life in all parts of our country".[38] He has constantly reminded everyone that the country started from scratch in 1970: "We are proud of what we have achieved in our country during the past two years [...] We had to start from the foundation and this foundation is the people of Oman and we followed the most difficult road to bring her out of her isolation."[39] Sultan Qaboos has presented himself as the tutelary father of a just-reborn nation which "he conducts in its march towards progress and prosperity".[40]

Sometimes, as an antonym to the long "sleep" before the ruler's coming to the throne, historiography has used the metaphor of a "national awakening" (*sahwa*), to which many monuments refer, like the Muscat "*Burj al-sahwa*" tower on Nizwa road. Its basis is adorned with eight bas-reliefs. Illustrations of past and present are placed side by side, so as to show harmony preserved despite material upheavals: a dhow at sea beside a tanker, a *falaj* running near a modern machine, pupils squatting around a scholar and learning the Koran near a microscope, etc. In the late 1990s, the "awakening" allegory was even the subject of a TV film in which a man who had had an accident that gave him amnesia for thirty years discovered the new Oman when he woke up and could not believe his eyes.[41] This *nahda* ideology has worked all the better for reaching a wide audience among foreign observers, as is shown in titles of books published in the 1970s: *The Reborn Land*,[42] *Dawn over Oman*,[43] or *Oman and its Renaissance*.[44]

Official post-1970 history usually maintained falsehoods about education, health and infrastructure, so as to impose a Manichaean vision of the father's and the son's rules. For instance, official figures dealing with schools in 1970 neglected to count Koranic schools, while they were included in the 1971 figures, to emphasise the break between the father and the son.[45]

Thus, careful silence has been maintained over the speech Sa'id bin Taimur pronounced in January 1968, a few months after oil exploitation started. The ruler explained his desire that "1968 will be the start of a new era for our country [...] We are looking forward to a bright future by which we guarantee raising the standard of living of the inhabitants of the Sultanate and increasing the income of the individual [...] Naturally projects involve much effort and hard work. The progress we see in other countries was not the work of a day, but the result of efforts over long years [...] We shall ensure every benefit and advantage for the populace [...] in consonance with our people's heritage and ancient history. Much as we progress and move forward we must keep before our eyes our true religion on which we place our reliance and traditions which are our heritage. We are humble towards the Almighty [...] whose power brings us success in what is for the good of our Omani people and our country."[46]

The similarity to words Qaboos used on 23 July 1971 is striking: "In the task of raising our people's living standards, we strive from guidance from the Light of the Shariah and humbly beseech the Almighty to bless our endeavours so that all can enjoy their fruits. The community must be aware of the achievements and gains that have been made on behalf of this people and this ancient land during the first year of our new era [...] There is no doubt that the building process is an exacting one, and that much hard work and sacrifice is needed to overcome the obstacles and difficulties before us."[47]

Moreover, it must be said that in the achievements in the 1970s there was usually more sign of continuity with what had been undertaken by Sa'id after 1967 than of a fundamental break with his rule; most of the technical achievements of years 1970–74, like the Muscat-Sohar, Muscat-Nizwa and Muscat-Muttrah roads, Qaboos port, the Ruwi, Salalah and Buraimi hospitals, the Muscat water scheme, etc., had been conceived, and sometimes even started, before July 1970, which explains partially their fast implementation under Qaboos.[48] Thus, it is interesting to note that the perception of Sa'id on the international arena changed from an "enlightened despot [...] with patriarchal wisdom" in the early 1960s to an "anachronistic tyrant" immediately after the coup.[49]

The *nahda* ideology finds its place within the larger conception that the "people is not mature for Western-type democracy"[50]—an argument used by Qaboos to justify the personalisation of his rule, but which recalls once again the way how his father explained the isolation of the country: "The man in the street often doesn't want or know how to deal with foreign governments or defend the country. He trusts me to do it. That is why these areas have been excluded from the *Majlis* debates. In this part of the world, giving too much power too fast can still be exploited. Elections in many countries mean having the army prevent bloodshed. Is this democracy? Are these happy countries? [...] No. They are really just power struggles. I am against creating such situations when people aren't ready for them."[51] The metaphor of a political body which has not yet reached adulthood underlies this.[52]

Using the *nahda* vocabulary is not meaningless in Oman; it refers first and foremost to the Ibadi tradition and to the Imamate's recurring renaissance when the territory is ruled unfairly.[53] By referring to this Oman legacy, the Sultan makes a point of positioning himself within the line of great figures of Omani history who took part in Oman nation-building. It is a way to situate his power within a long and glorious history of which, it is implied, the current ruler is the heir and the reviver—the twentieth century being only a parenthesis. A parallel is sometimes established between Sultan Qaboos and Imam Ahmad, the founder of the al-Busa'idi dynasty in the mid-eighteenth century: "Like his famous ancestor Imam Ahmad [...] an outstanding leader who had ended a turbulent era of civil wars and brought peace and stability to Oman, Sultan Qaboos inherited a stagnant, conflict-ridden country."[54]

In official historiography, then, the ruler is personally associated with the *nahda*, and hence with the economic and social development associated with his accession to the throne. Favours granted by the Sultan fit in with this historiographical and symbolic device: on the occasion of the 15th National Day, every civil service director-general received a royal gift of 50,000 OR;[55] similarly, five years later, on the occasion of the 20th National Day, the state redeemed all the debts of Omani individuals.[56] Because Oman experienced a sharp increase in the cost of living and problems in employment policies in 2005 and 2006, royal benevolence gestures reached unprecedented levels since 1990 in these years (see chapter 7). Sultan Qaboos being the modern Oman builder, the personalisation of the nation around the ruler's tutelary figure is thus justified.

Personalisation of symbolic emblems of the nation. This ambitious national unification policy constitutes the pivotal piece of Sultan Qaboos' political legitimacy. A series of symbolic "founding acts" marked the break with the former regime and the beginning of a new era.

On 30 July 1970, Sultan Qaboos came from Salalah to Muscat to announce his accession to power. After the *bay'a* had been pronounced by Al Sa'id family members who had came back from abroad,[57] he received, like Ottomans Caliphs[58] but also Ibadi Imams, the allegiance of the people, who thus officially recognised his authority. This journey from Salalah to Muscat illustrated a transfer of political decision making and represented another symbolic step indicating the end of a period and the beginning of a new one. Immediate initiatives were taken to liquidate the former regime in people's minds; as early as 27 July Qaboos announced his first act: "immediate abolition of all the unnecessary restrictions",[59] such as prohibitions affecting daily life. He cancelled all taxes, like the Ruwi gate tolls, that Sa'id had imposed on products and people coming from Inner Oman, to promote reunification of the territory. Many political prisoners, who had no fixed sentences, were freed on 30 July.[60]

At the beginning of August 1970, official despatches were sent to tribal chiefs all over Oman in order to announce the ruler's arrival; for ten days, he travelled across the country to receive allegiance from local elites and to show everybody he was taking physical possession of the territory. It was the occasion to increase his personal prestige by distributing presents to local chiefs and banknotes to the people. Everything was done to give the perception of a new ruler as a "reverse mirror" of the former one and to build legitimacy going beyond power circles; by his liberalities, the Sultan was like a divine apparition for one of the world's poorest populations.

As for the new regime's symbols, the "Sultanate of Muscat and Oman" was renamed "Sultanate of Oman" on 9 August, in order to mark the unification of the territory under the single centralised authority of the Sultan. On the same day the former plain red flag, symbol of the Omani empire, was replaced by a new flag, with a red background as a symbol of the struggle of Omanis against foreign invasions. It is adorned with two stripes, white (representing the "faith of Omani people in peace and prosperity") and green (symbol of vegetation and land fertility), with new arms—a dagger (*khanjar*) and two intertwined scimitars. Significantly, the red of the Sultanate retained pre-eminence over the Imamate's white. To replace the Sa'idi rial, the first coins and banknotes of the new currency, the Omani rial, were issued at the beginning of 1971. Sultan Qaboos, whose picture appears on the right of each note, is the only personality to be represented.

Another strong symbol is the National Day, first celebrated on 23 July 1971, but held from the following year on 18 November, Qaboos' birthday. This change had the advantage of diverting attention from the conditions in which the ruler accessed to power—malicious observers could have said that was just a putsch and there could have been questioning of the Sultan's legitimacy. More broadly, the change of date personalised the renaissance of the country even more in Omanis' eyes—the "miracle" was necessarily the unified State under Qaboos' paternal authority. The 18 November commemoration represents a desire to exclude any question of succession: how is it possible to conceal that the *nahda* is the work of one man and that his death will be the sign of end of prosperity? Once the ruler passed away, will the Omani people be shielded from return to the former era?

The national anthem was created soon after the regime change and followed the same idea. It is in two parts; first a prayer to God and then an exhortation to the Omani people, it pays homage explicitly to Sultan Qaboos. The ruler is described as the providential man, who came to bring "proud and security" to Oman, with God's blessing. National unity behind the ruler is repeated twice, as an exhortation to God to support him. Finally, the Omanis claim to be ready to pray for his salvation and to "sacrifice their soul" for their ruler.

Slowly, the ruler has become the subject of a real personality cult. Most major contemporary urban achievements bear the Sultan's name: the capital's main highway that connects the city's quarters in a metaphoric hyphen, the main roads of most of the cities (Salalah, Nizwa, Khasab, Sohar, etc.), the Muttrah industrial port, the Muscat and Salalah public hospitals, the private school where the most well-off families' children are registered, the wealthier area of the capital where Western expatriates and the local upper bourgeoisie reside (Madina Qaboos), etc. This omnipresence of the ruler is completed by his portrait in most houses' *majlis* and in every shop. Furthermore, every news bulletin on the radio or TV begins with an announcement of the decrees issued, the visits made, and the telegrams received and sent by Qaboos, and the night-time programmes end with the national anthem in his praise. Any mention of his name in the media is followed by: "the Great, God protect him and take care of him" (*al-jalala al-sultan Qabus bin Sa'id al-mu'azzam, yahfa-zuhu Allah wa yar'ahu*). Each year, during the whole month of the National Day, the street lamps of the major avenues are decorated with his portrait and Omani flags. As John Townsend was already noting in 1977, "these photographs show a good looking man with an air of undoubted authority, [...] a man who knows what he has done, knows that he proved to the world that he was not the tool of his British advisers [...] Indeed, one of the most striking developments in Oman over the six years since July 1970 has been the growth of the Sultan's self-confidence."[61]

Thus, the extreme personalisation of Oman's external signs of sovereignty is an integral part of a modern national-identity building process, to assert Sultan Qaboos' legitimacy and to link both the institution he embodies and his own person to the "renaissance" of the country. But it is also necessary for the members of the new community to reappropriate the territory's legacy. The nation must be the subject of representations, it must be symbolised, illustrated, in a word: staged.

The staged national heritage

Various heritages of the past in contemporary Oman—in architecture, environment or customs—play an important role in anchoring the new nation in its "long" history. They have been stressed by the new regime not only to illustrate Oman's special place in the international arena, but also to consolidate every individual's attachment to a mythicised past of which Sultan Qaboos is the worthy successor, and on which he has relied to lead Oman: "It is the duty of all of us to continuously bear in mind that the development we look forward to implementing must be based on the strong foundations of our ancient heritage [...] inherited traditions and customs."[62]

The leading role of the Ministry of National Heritage. As Gérard Lenclud stated, "in every society, the criterion of "authentic" tradition is not only its content, which has been hypothetically conserved as it was, but the social authority of those who were commissioned [...] to take care of it, that is to use it."[63] The tradition that historiography portrays is the result of social and political arbitrations fulfilling contemporary political requirements.

In Oman, this mission is entrusted to the Ministry of Heritage and Culture. The calibre of the only two people who have held the post (Sayyid Faisal from the Ministry's creation in 1975 until March 2002, and Sayyid Haitham bin Tariq, one of the possible successors to the throne, since then) gives an idea of its central role within the state institutions; so does Sayyid Haitham's third position in government protocol, the ruler apart. The Ministry is entrusted with collecting all records of national and local memory, whether written or oral, in order to become the main source of historical discourse in contemporary Oman and to propose a symbolic alternative to coercion in the process of creating allegiance to the current regime.

One of the main trends of the Ministry's policy is to co-opt the old intellectual elites, like holders of local knowledge and Omani history and Islamic law specialists. Many positions of advisers and experts, most of the time devoid of any real mission, were created in Muscat in the 1970s for these notables who could have served as rallying points for any "intellectual" opposition to the Sultan. In addition, over the last twenty years, the Ministry has collected Omani manuscripts dealing with all social and political subjects. Emigrant Omanis explain how, when they came back from Africa, the authorities asked them if they had with them old books or historical documents;[64] the Ministry's library of manuscripts contains the largest collection of such documents in Oman. By publishing some of them, the Ministry has become the first Omani publisher. As any author has to submit to its censorship to be published in the country, the Ministry enjoys a hegemony over the literature and arts sector.[65] The same policy applies to music, with collection and registration of thousands of hours of songs and folk dances.

Within the Ministry or in partnership with it, several official organisations and cultural associations have been set up, such as the Historical Association of Oman; it holds frequent conferences on Omani history and aims to collect legends and disappearing customs. It is interesting to note that British expatriates are intensively involved in this quest for "picturesqueness" and "authentic" elements.

In April 2004, under the aegis of the Ministry, an International Symposium on Magan was held to summarise all current knowledge about this civilisation which had its apogee around 2,500 BC. But the main goal was a political one, because this conference aimed at reasserting Oman's descent from Magan; the official booklet started with these words: "The archeological discoveries always provided the evidence that "Magan" is Oman."[66] As the pages go by, names of "Magan" and "Oman" become interchangeable: "Archeological discoveries [...] proved unquestionably the existence of trade relations between former Omani people, and Indian, Mesopotamian and African centers of civilization. It is obvious that Omani traders sailed on oceans [...] during the third millennium before Jesus Christ." Magan's inhabitants already possessed the Omani national spirit (sailing, commerce, etc.) and prefigured then the glorious fate of the maritime empire three millennia later!

The grip of the Ministry of Heritage on "official culture" is found also in museums, which are the symbols of the nation's human and material treasures. There are around ten Omani government museums, seven of them in Muscat. Two "national" museums in Muscat are devoted to cultural heritage (like those in Salalah and Sohar), one more especially to Omani natural history (within the Ministry of Heritage building), one to Muscat town itself and one to the Sultan's armed forces, at the Bait al-Falaj headquarters.

Among the few private museums, the most interesting one is without doubt the collection Muhammad bin Zubair gathered. The Bait al-Zubair museum presents many items illustrating twentieth-century Omani daily life, old and new photographs showing the changes over thirty years, and reconstruction of "traditional" villages, inspired particularly by Inner Oman. This assimilation of "authentic Oman" with the Nizwa region is in line with a policy devoted to recreate a "patrimonially correct" tradition there, as was illustrated in 1994 by the decision to organise in Nizwa the opening national celebration of the "Year for Omani Heritage". The Bait al-Zubair Foundation is especially involved in this promotion of national heritage and has already published five books since 2002. The founder of the museum himself published in 2003 an impressive volume of photos entitled *Oman, My Beautiful Country*, and in 2004 a bilingual historical book whose purpose is to "create, within the Omani population, a deeper feeling of pride for their fascinating past."[67]

Rediscovering 'forgotten' customs and traditions. In March 2003 the creation of a Public Authority for Craft Industries, headed by 'A'isha al-Siyabiyya, the first woman to hold ministerial rank, confirmed the key role of "traditions" (*taqalid*) in the strategy of legitimisation of power. The ministry has established standards of authenticity (*asala*) certifying the work's conformity to traditional know-how, to develop Omani craft products' exports. The best hotels of the country have their own craft shops in which typical objects of Omani handicrafts (jewels, clothes, frankincense equipment, etc.) are available. At the al-Bustan hotel, the doorman greets the visitor in ceremonial dress and invites him to seat on carpets to taste coffee with cardamom and dates, surrounded by frankincense exhalations. The slogan the Ministry of Tourism has publicised for the past few years is "Oman, Arabia's authenticity" (*'uman... ruh al-asala al-'arabiyya*). Thus, it is possible to note in Oman what Eric Hobsbawm and Terence Ranger described as an "invention of tradition", that is "a set of practices [...] of ritual and symbolic nature which seek to inculcate certain values and norms of behaviour by repetition. They normally attempt to establish continuity with a suitable historic past."[68]

Within this framework, the maritime empire has received special attention from the regime. In 1981, the *Sohar*, a boat built according to the tenth-century methods, bearing the Omani arms on its sails, started an eight-month voyage to China to "transform the Sindbad legend into reality".[69] Nine years later, Sultan Qaboos, who wanted to emphasise Oman's role in historic world trade, made his own yacht available to researchers, for an international study of the historic trade with China; the *Fulk al-Salama* (boat of peace) took the old sea route from Venice to Osaka, stopping in Salalah and Muscat to participate in the 20th National Day celebrations.

Other craft sectors are involved in this national quest for heritage, such as textiles, silverwork and basketry. In March 2004 a project initiated by Sayyid Shihab bin Tariq in 1996, the Omani Craft Heritage Documentation Project, was crowned by the publication of a two-volume book[70] whose aim was to list and collect all types of Omani crafts. This "re-found" past is staged especially for increasingly frequent "heritage village" festivals (*hara al-turath*), during which old life is recreated, as in "national pavilions" in Universal Exhibitions. People are engaged there in craft and domestic activities typical of life in the old days (*min zaman*), while visitors can buy "traditional" dishes (*halwa*,[71] bread, etc.) and daily-life products made under their eyes.

The best examples of such heritage glorification are the Monsoon Festival, in Salalah between 15 July and 31 August, and the Muscat Festival, which takes place every year for three weeks after 'Aid al-Adha. These events are organised in two parts: a purely commercial one, run by Indian and Egyptian traders and devoted to entertainment; and a cultural one, named "Heritage Festival" (*mahrajan al-turath*), with reconstitution of daily life scenes of a past which is all the more mythical for being timeless. These exhibitions, which are aimed at nationals who are expected to already know, are an occasion to highlight national folklore, through the presentation of "traditional" songs, dances and music. The underlying idea is that there is no modern Omani art movement, only variations of an unchanging core which constitutes the national spirit: "Modern Omani music—or Omani music in its modernised form—is but a single strand of the country's musical heritage."[72] National culture can bear various forms, but is and remains basically one. Finally, several organisations for conservation of folklore were created, like the Omani Centre for Traditional Music, founded in 1984. It compiles and archives material relating to national folk music.

All this is in the context of a collective celebration of an idealised past, retranscribed today in a festive way. These events conjure up excessively picturesque images of this "popular heritage" (*al-turath al-sha'abi*), which evokes nothing to the younger generation but a reinforcement of the amused condescension they feel for their parents' and grandparents' times. In a nutshell, the diversity of the country and its heritage (from the desert or the mountains, from Baluchistan or Africa) is thus merged into a uniform popular culture (*al-thaqafa al-sha'abiyya*). Thus, there is a reification of Omani customs; the latter are displayed as timeless practices, without any reference to region, time or ethnic origin.

Where plant and animal resources are concerned, Oman has been the first Arab state to establish, since 1984, a ministry in charge of Environment Issues; since 1989, a "Sultan Qaboos" award for protection of the environment is granted every two years in partnership with UNESCO. Moreover, a National Environment Day is observed every year in January, and the years 2001 and 2002 were declared "Environment Years" by the ruler. Concretely, several natural reserves have been established, such as a sanctuary—registered on UNESCO's World Heritage List—for the Arabian oryx, which had been reintroduced in 1980,[73] and two reserves for protection of sand gazelles and mountain goats. It is strictly forbidden to hunt wild animals in the whole territory. To preserve nature has been declared a patriotic duty, as infringement of the environment is considered officially an infringement of the nation itself.

Moreover the Omani government has established strict rules in the building and public works sector. White and beige are the only approved colours for outside walls of new building, whose height rarely goes above five storeys. This uniform model legislation requires owners of roof water tanks to hide each one inside a crenellated white cylinder, displaying the Inner Oman forts' architecture, so as not to clash with the harmony sought. Similarly, air-conditioners on buildings' facades have to be encapsulated into an open-work box symbolising a *musharabieh*. Since the early 2000s, unfortunately, these principles have not stood up to economic interests, as in 2000 when the construction of a slip road on the Qurum beach crossed right through one of the last mangroves in northern Oman, or in the implementation of high-class tourism projects on beaches in Muscat suburbs (see chapter 7).

The folklorising[74] *of heritage.* As with the historiographic treatment of Omani culture, the regime's conception of architecture and the environment serves two strategic requirements. First, it must appear as consensual and leave no room for political claims; moreover, this process stages a bygone past that is all the more difficult to appropriate since it appears excessively archaic and will not be able to serve as political counter-model.

The forts of Muttrah and Inner Oman, like Bahla, Rustaq, Sohar, Nakhl and Nizwa, best exemplify this policy. They are subject of the same instrumentalisation of memory, as they have been recently done up to look new. Just as the European nineteenth century did not like crumbling old buildings and made a nice whole, clean and accomplished through imagination of what existed before, the post-1970 Sultanate of Oman prefers rehabilitated monuments in accordance with contemporary political requirements rather than historical plausibility. These replicas of the glorious Omani Imamate are now supposedly rebuilt with the aim of cutting off their connection with the past and silencing their historical testimony to the younger generations. One notable exception is the former tribal fiefs of the Jebel Akhdar that were dynamited on the Sultan's orders (Tanuf) or were the site of fierce fighting in the 1950s (al-Ghafat). As manifest evidence of the almost divine punishment that swoops down on anyone who disobeys the sultan's orders, these villages have been left carefully untouched.

The folklorising of heritage is emphasised by "cardboard" representations, such as multiple terracotta and porcelain figurines, placed at the main cities' entrances and along Sultan Qaboos Street in the Muscat urban area, and representing animals or traditional daily-life objects (oryx, turtles, daggers, coffeepots, frankincense burners, etc.). Trivialising of heritage reaches an extreme in what Benedict Anderson called its "logoization",[75] that is the transformation of monuments or other symbols of nation into stereotyped decorations of daily life objects, such as stamps or banknotes. Omantel phone cards are a nice illustration of this conversion of heritage treasures into logos: themes of phone card illustrations can be traditional domestic objects (frankincense burners, *khanjar*, etc.), monuments (Qalhat, Jabrin) or even roundabouts symbolising the *nahda* in Salalah, Sohar, Burj-al-Sahwa.[76]

The encounter between state modernity, symbolised by administrative redrawing of boundaries in the early 1990s, and tradition led to overshadowing of old provinces and solidarity groups' fiefdoms. The new regions are displayed as culturally differentiated and homogeneous entities. Thus the Committee for the Omani Costumes Festival, which comes under the Ministry of Heritage and organises a yearly meeting of traditional dance costumes, bases its classification on current regions, such as "Batina" or "Dhofar". Yet the costume originally displayed "for Batina" shows a strong Baluchi influence, without any such regional precision; similarly, the "Dhofari"-displayed costume illustrates a region whose extreme demographic diversity can hardly be summed in one item only. The heritage peculiarities of the various groups have been merged into a wider regional "cultural identity" so as to adapt to new administrative boundaries; in this way the nation itself can be defined as a sum of cultures geographically delimited, but without any group being able to identify with it.

Heritage (*turath*) thus holds a basic position in Sultan Qaboos' legitimisation process. By recreating a national identity within the framework of an omnipresent state and by unifying cultural and religious references, Qaboos, who has become the subject of a genuine personality cult and daily embodies the nation, has legitimised his paternalistic authority. Thanks to the promotion of this national identity, the goal is to "naturalise" the untouchable triptych encompassing Oman's renaissance, the state apparatus, and its supreme figure, the ruler.

Nevertheless, far from working for the disappearance of infra-national allegiances and so-called "traditional" socio-political structures, as the development of a state apparatus and a nation could have led one to believe, the Sultanate under Qaboos displays their integration—unofficially, of course—into the state apparatus. More broadly, the regime has sought to counterbalance excessive modernity—both institutional and technological—by wrapping itself in a political "tradition" of government which is supposed to be authentic, and in the continuation of a magnified and reinvented past.

6

THE REINVENTED POLITICAL TRADITION

In the 1990s, it was still generally accepted that the Omani tribes and clans, under the blows of urbanisation and technological modernisation, were slowly disappearing. This perception was reinforced by the omnipresent official discourse emphasising national unity feeling behind the authority of Sultan Qaboos. However, while the tribe has not had any visibility in the political arena since 1970, it is still there as a network of sociability that the decades following the *nahda* have been far from calling into question.

The national identity the authorities have promoted has imposed itself as the basis of the new regime's legitimacy, as an arbiter above infra-national allegiances, which the official discourse has not failed to present as obsolete. Nevertheless, in order to avoid falling into moral breakdown or inviting criticism of a "loss of values" to the benefit of badly-digested modernisation, the authorities had to refer to "reassuring" political and social categories. This involved perpetuation of political legacies which were sometimes only readapted to fit the current context, sometimes truly "recreated" from a framework which makes sense for the individuals meant to appropriate it. The recourse to these political references which are given the appearance of tradition is part of a determination to fill the ideological gap between social infranational structures and the state, and thus to facilitate acceptance of the new official order by individuals.

This chapter will develop the strategies the Omani regime implemented in order to take over infra-national legitimacies to serve its own interests, by integrating them into the new political order and using them to consolidate its authority. Far from erasing them from the socio-political map, the advent of a modern state has articulated itself with them, to include them better and use them for its advantage.

The encapsulation of local legitimacies into the state

Since 1970, one of the guidelines of the Sultan's strategy of legitimisation has been "de-autonomising" local solidarities (ethno-linguistic tribes, groups, etc.), that is, neutralising their impact by subordinating them to the state and making them more and more dependent on a game which the regime controls, where it lays down the rules—as Clifford Geertz stated:

"What the new States—or their leaders—must somehow contrive to do as far as primordial attachments are concerned is not, as they have so often tried to do, wish them out of existence by belittling them or even denying their reality, but domesticate them. They must reconcile them with the unfolding civil order by divesting them of their legitimizing force with respect to governmental authority."[1]

This process takes place *within* the state, in the state (in the political arena it represents) and for the state (to create or consolidate powerful positions within it). Far from being the negation of the state, the solidarity group (*'asabiyya*) cannot be understood apart from the state, which gives it its raison d'être and recomposes it.

The state and 'solidarity groups'. The central political authority seeks to act on the *'asabiyya* in order to remodel it and insert it into its own framework of political legitimisation. During this process, the regime tries to monopolise the "tribal", "ethnic" and religious references for the state's advantage. Its political practices claim a link with a local "tradition" of rule which is able to place the sovereign in continuity with great national personalities. Another process is the encapsulation of infra-national allegiances into the state apparatus in order to strengthen the latter's legitimacy.

But this process is not unilateral; just as the state handles *'asabiyyat*, *'asabiyyat* handle the state: "The solidarity groups are recomposed by the state and have need of it [...] in order to affirm their power and their difference, to obtain the material or symbolic goods which will animate by their circulation the networks constituting them. What is concerned is the hierarchy between the solidarity groups."[2]

This hierarchy can only be established within the state, as it is both the arena where the various collective interests interact and the issue at stake in the competition. In Oman, the state is indeed the ground on which the competition for power and wealth takes place, since it has been the political framework for all private interests since 1970. But as the sole depositary of the oil rent, it is also the object of all covetousness, the stake for which all actors' strategies contest. By being used as intermediary between insiders and outsiders, it is captured by those who act on its behalf and make it work to their own profit.[3] Through jobs and powerful positions that the state grants, through material and symbolic resources that it distributes directly or indirectly to its agents, the state is the final object of the socio-political strategies of each of the solidarity groups. The local political arena thus loses its interest by comparison with the opportunities offered by the national one, the state.[4] Thus it appears like a set of public agencies to be conquered and made to prosper, not sucked dry.

Whether tribal or ethnic, based on regionalism or factionalism, the solidarity group, although officially repressed by postcolonial governments in the name of national integration, is concretely recognised as one of the main means to enter the political arena and to access the opportunities offered by the state. If it is led to defy the modern state, this is not to challenge allegiance, but on the contrary to strengthen its position in the state. In the end, one does not fight against the state but for it, to take over control of it, wholly or partly.

Tribal references subsumed by the state. No national debate on the role of tribes in the modern nation-State building has been started in Oman. In the promotion of a national identity, the official historiography has constantly done its best to present the state or the Sultan himself as the Omani citizens' only interlocutor. In 1974, for example, the Sovereign said very clearly: "Oman loves her sons equally and the Omanis all are sons of their merciful Motherland. She expects them to be loyal and obedient to her cause, but the love of country differs from one citizen to another, but Oman loves all her sons, and the principle we have declared is to forget the past. We shall adhere to this code".[5]

The tribe was never recognised as an official political entity or a level of the administrative division. Except for some administrative acts to which we shall return later, there is no institutional intermediary between the state and the individual.

Nowadays, the taboo on the question of local groups' role in the state remains strict, as is shown by the fury of a Sultan Qaboos University professor when the word "*qabila*" was pronounced in his office: "Do not try to make tribes and communities grew artificially in Oman like plants [...] There are no more tribes and communities since 1970 [...] What did the English do in Oman before 1970? Nothing for the development of this country, no school, no hospital, no road, nothing! They did everything to divide us!"[6]

Here, mention of tribes refers without ambiguity to division of the nation, through the presupposed idea that the individual cannot claim several collective allegiances at the same time—one necessarily excludes the other. Reference to tribes also evokes regression, characteristic of the pre-1970 period.

Despite the official discourse, the tribal issue has remained a major concern of the authorities since 1970. Far from eradicating them, the regime has worked to co-opt them while depriving them of their supposed harmful potential so that they contribute to strengthening of the state.

According to Gregory Gause, "the successful monarchies are those which tamed tribalism [...] All the monarchies of the [Arabian] Peninsula favoured the survival of tribalism as a personal marker of identity. They brought financial support and a recognized social position to tribal *sheikh*s. They celebrated tribalism during official representations of national culture. But they also achieved with success what their predecessors failed: to deny the tribes any autonomous political and military role in their societies."[7] In Saudi Arabia, Bahrain and Oman, Khaldun al-Naqeeb considers that it is possible to talk about "semi-official tribal corporations".[8]

As for Oman, Sultan Qaboos hastened to proclaim a general amnesty for former political opponents. While the latter were offered top positions and economic opportunities, these personalities had no other choice to accepting the Sovereign's proposal and support the new authority. This skilful co-optation manoeuvre prevented the respected notables from feeling humiliated and opposing the new regime. Many positions of advisers and senior government officials were created in the 1970s for co-opted former local elites. For instance, a former governor from the interior was transferred in a few weeks from his office in a village fort to a modern residence in Muscat offered by the authorities, with a private limousine.[9] As a consequence, these notables were cut off from their traditional power basis, which greatly weakened their political and social influence.

The most obvious example is the noble branch of the Khalili family, heir to a prestigious lineage of Ibadi *imam*s (see figure 10); one of these—from a related branch—who came back from Africa after the Zanzibar revolution, Sheikh Ahmad bin Hamad, has been the Mufti of Oman since 1975. Sheikh Sa'ud bin 'Ali was co-opted at an early date by the new regime; as a former

Ambassador in Egypt and nephew of the last Imam of Oman, Sheikh Muhammad bin 'Abd Allah (1920–54), he became one of the four members of the very first Cabinet appointed on 15 August 1970. In addition Sheikh Sa'ud owns the powerful business group Al Taher that he founded in 1973, active in contracting (Caterpillar), food and drink (Sprite, Coke, the Al Sarooj supermarkets), industrial fisheries and distribution of Shell products.

The course followed by his brother, Sheikh Hilal, is even more curious. *Wali* of Bawshar under Sultan Sa'id since 1943, he was thought likely to succeed his uncle as Imam, but tribal balance was not favourable to him. He took the Imam's side in the conflict and was named the Imamate's Ambassador in Riyadh in 1954. Benefiting from the 1970 amnesty, he was immediately appointed Sultan Qaboos' Ambassador to Saudi Arabia. His son, Sheikh Salim, currently a State Council member, was minister of Agriculture and Fisheries between 2001 and 2011, while his grandson, Qais, chairs the family business group, Al Khalili Group. Salim's cousin, 'Abd al-Malik bin 'Abd Allah—previously both the executive chairman of the Royal Court Pension Fund, the chairman of the first Omani banking group, Bank Muscat, and Minister of Tourism (2011–2012)—was appointed Minister of Justice in February 2012.

Other prominent Imamate families were also gradually co-opted by the regime. This is the case of Sheikh Sulaiman bin Himyar Al-Nabhani's children: Sheikh Sa'ud, a former under-secretary for Communications, became state adviser with ministerial rank in April 2008, while Sheikha Zahra has been a member of the State Council since 2003. Their cousin, Lieutenant-General Ahmad al-Nabhani, is the current chief of staff of the Sultan's Armed Forces.

Another illustration of this "deal" with the authorities is given by the descendants of 'Abd Allah al-Salimi, one of the principal instigators of the Imamate's renaissance at the beginning of the twentieth century. While his son Muhammad had a leading role within the Imamate's political authorities in exile, his grandson, Sheikh 'Abd Allah bin Muhammad, has been Oman's Minister for Religious Affairs since 1997. Several of his relatives occupy crucial positions within the ministry. The minister's cousin, 'Abd Allah bin Salim, previously chairman of the Muscat Securities Market (2002–08), is the executive president of Capital Market Authority. Lastly, Major-General Sa'id bin Nasir al-Salimi was Commander of the Royal Army of Oman until 2013.

Similarly, Sultan Qaboos has shown skill in using the offers of reconciliation to former leaders of the Dhofar rebellion to interest them in a personal way in development of the country and thus neutralise their nuisance capacity.

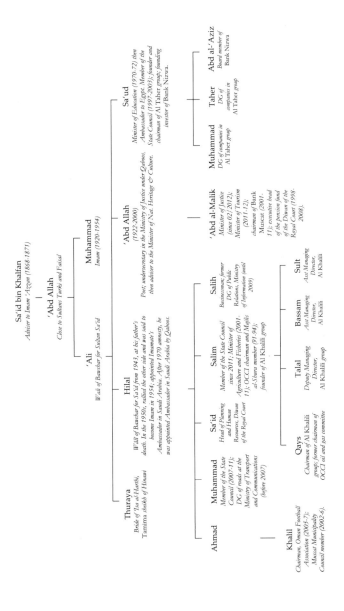

Figure 10: Family tree of al-Khalili noble branch

One of the best examples is Yusef bin 'Alawi, one of the Dhofar Liberation Front's leaders before it split in 1968, who has been Minister responsible for Foreign Affairs since 1982. Yusef bin 'Alawi is represented, via his sons Shihab, Ahmad and Muhammad, on numerous boards of directors of companies listed on the Muscat Stock Exchange. Moreover, Sheikh 'Abd al-'Aziz al-Rawas, who was Minister of Information between 1979 and 2001, had been a DLF member in the 1960s. Salim al-Ghazali, son of one of the founders of the Dhofar rebel movement in the early 1960s, was secretary of the Council of Ministers in the 1970s, then under-secretary in the Ministry of Defence between 1980 and 1982.[10] Between 1982 and 1991 he was Minister of Trade and Industry, then he served as Minister of Communications until January 2000, when he was appointed as Special Adviser to the Sultan. His brother Ahmad was Minister for Land Affairs and Municipalities in the late 1970s.

The new state also hastened to being lesser notables into the bureaucratic hierarchy. In this policy, the Ministry of Interior—and, within it, the Directorate of "Tribal Affairs"—has played a decisive role. In 1979 a *General Directory of Wilayas and Tribes of Oman*,[11] which details the tribal composition of all the communes, classified by *wilaya*, was printed but not put on sale.

The tribal hierarchy was, definitely, not destroyed but rather subsumed within the state apparatus. The most influential authorities commanding such local loyalties, the ones most likely to challenge the established order, especially in Inner Oman and Dhofar, have been regularly granted by the Diwan gifts in cash and in kind (cars, houses, etc.) so as to ensure their loyalty to the regime. Subsidies could reach OR 30,000 per year.[12] Moreover, the *sheikh rashid*, who is paid as a state employee between OR 250 and 500 a month, acts as intermediary between individuals and the public administration. Usually descended from a "noble" family, he officiates in a geographical district (*hara* or *hilla*) and no longer according to tribal or family criteria.[13] He deals with multiple daily acts aiming at facilitating relations between individuals and the state apparatus, such as certifying a person's lineage in order to deliver a passport,[14] and the solution of smaller disputes. The *sheikh rashid* has to give regular accounts of his acts to the *wali*, especially in the most sensitive cases. His role is then crucial in the articulation of society and the state apparatus, since he personifies the myth of a traditional direct democracy, in which everyone has access to the representative of his community: while representing society for the state, he embodies direct access to the state for citizens. When the district *sheikh* dies, the choice of his successor is decided within the framework of the Ministry, in the presence of the notables of the district and with their approval.[15] 1970 did not mark the extinction of tribal *sheikhs*. The Directorate of Tribal Affairs of the Ministry of Interior lays down an exhaustive list of tribes, as well as their respective *sheikhs*. This determines the individuals officially allowed to hold the title of *sheikh*. Thus no social recognition remains besides that granted by the state, which has appropriated the symbolic spaces that local authorities controlled before 1970. The Ministry of the Interior has thus made a double takeover of the symbolic system of traditional local leaders to consolidate its own local anchoring.

Moreover, the Omani authorities decided in 1980 to establish *sheikhs qabila* for the Baharina and Lawatiyya communities of Muscat, comparable to those in the Inner Oman tribes. These *sheikhs* act as intermediaries between the members of the community and the administration. While this process was not unanimously approved, the government wished, just after the Iranian revolution, to preserve Oman from any external religious influence, and to emphasise the anchoring of Oman's Shi'a into the nation by "tribalising" one of the non-Ibadi groups. As for the Banyans, they have been represented by a *sheikh* in the Ministry of the Interior since 1979.

Another illustration of the way the former order's references have been encapsulated into the modern state is the official decision, in 1981, to give every citizen a patronym referring to his native tribe. This decision focused on the groups which cannot claim Arab tribal descent, like client groups of the noble tribes, and the Lawatiyya, the Baharina and Baluchi-native Omanis. For these last three groups, it was decided to give them the patronyms of "al-Lawati", "al-Bahrani" and "al-Balushi". While Baluchi-native Omanis thus acquired legitimacy to regard themselves as the most numerous tribe in Oman (see chapter 8), many Lawatiyya still refuse to use this patronym, so as not to be compared to "nomadic tribe"[16] and not to reinforce stigmatisation to which they are still subjected by some Omanis of the Interior.

As for the interior, a good deal of bargaining about identity started at that time, in order to rebuild forgotten genealogies. One person we interviewed[17] holds a passport with the "al-Harthi" family name, but he belongs to a small tribe which was historically a client of that confederation. In the 1960s the issuing of passports, which required the signature of one of the most powerful *sheikhs*, was a means to evaluate the demographic, and thus political, power of the groups headed by these local notables. This explains why this man's father had to register himself under another name than that under which his group was known. In 1981, the Sultan proposed that such people should revert to their native names. However, changing one's name meant losing the support of the influential notables of a recognised tribe like the Hirth and thus destabilising one's own social and professional position. If some seized the occasion to return to an ancestor's name, this man chose not to change his name, since the tribal name is the means par excellence through which individuals are classified compared to other Omani social groups.

This instrumentalising of tribal membership by the regime has gone so far as adoption of the often malevolent tribal nicknames (*laqab*) inherited from the oral tradition. A clanic or tribal nickname is thus officially required on the forms to be completed in the Ministry of Manpower when looking for employment. The Diwan produced, for strictly internal use, a collection of the nicknames of the Omani tribes.[18]

While lying within a general political scope of weakening the social and political cohesion of the infra-national groups, this method of government has worked to strengthen individuals' primordial identification. In social interaction within the new Omani state, it is not possible for the citizen to escape from his name, his geographical origin or his ethno-linguistic group.

Bureaucratic nepotism tolerated by the regime. In a speech to senior state officials in 1978, the Sultan took care to stress that: "An official position is a duty and a responsibility rather than a means of acquiring power and influence [...] Officials must put the interests of the state above all other interests [...] All Omanis are brothers and sons, and we do not like to hear of cases in which jobs have been given, favours granted or discrimination practised on any basis other than competence."[19]

Nevertheless, in the 1980s and 90s, a semi-official, but universally recognised, distribution of employment in various economic sectors and in government departments on tribal and ethnic bases was operated. Several phenomena must be distinguished, the first being the consolidation of the old hegemonic positions. For instance, the high proportion of Baluchi-native Omanis in the security forces, like that of tribes historically allied to the sultan (the Hawasina, Ma'amari, Bani Kalban, etc.), has never been put in doubt. Swahili-speaking Omanis have known how to benefit from their skills in the English language and their supposed non-involvement in internal political issues to become essential in sensitive sectors like intelligence and security.

Besides, senior office holders have tacitly been allowed to reconstitute their client networks, by recruiting individuals from the same group or the same area for positions in the sectors they control. This phenomenon works at all levels of administration and comes from the need for everybody to reposition

141

himself socially, when old solidarities no longer play their traditional roles and seem to be diluted by inter-regional migrations. It makes it possible to find a peaceful and non-political solution to the potential social strains. Moreover, until the end of the 1990s, the lack of institutional procedures for finding work for job seekers led recruiters to use the old social networks in which they themselves were included. For instance, Baluchi-native Omanis prevail in the semi-public telephone company, Omantel, the responsible Minister having for long been one of them; the Dhofar-native Shanfari tribe was over-represented in the Ministry of Oil and Gas, as the Minister was for fifteen years Sheikh Sa'id al-Shanfari; in Sultan Qaboos University, and in the Ministries of the Interior, of Religious Affairs, of National Heritage and of Justice, Ibadi Omanis still hold the majority of positions. Lastly, the combination of both factors we just mentioned—skills acquired before 1970 and corporatism—explains that Lawatiyya are over-represented in health-sector jobs.

The encapsulation of these primordial solidarities structures in the state apparatus since 1970 is evidence of the regime's determination to reappropriate their legitimacy to place the new regime in continuity with a mythified political tradition.

The Council of Oman (Majlis 'Uman)

As we saw in chapter 2, the *shura* (consultation) principle had a crucial role in the Ibadi Imamate's legitimisation. This reference was appropriated by Qaboos in order to place the institutions of the contemporary state in continuity with that Omani "democratic tradition" and, consequently, to naturalise his authority in the eyes of his subjects.

Liberalisation spread over twenty-five years. The first top-down initiative for consulting Omani's civil society was launched in April 1979, with the creation of the Council of Agriculture, Fisheries and Industry. Composed of twelve appointed members, its competence was limited to giving recommendations on well-defined subjects and projects. Dissolved in 1981, it handed its duties over to the State Consultative Council (SCC), which, as its name implies, had no legislative power. The duty of the new chamber was to "formulate opinions and advice" about the economic and social development of the country. These were to be communicated to the Sultan by its president; the ruler could then take them into account if he wished to. Like its predecessor, the SCC was officially intended "to allow a larger measure of participation for the citizens

[...] [in order to] take into consideration their wishes in forming our national policy in the economic and social fields".[20] Members were allowed to question different government officials, except those from ministries linked to national sovereignty (Foreign Affairs, Defence, Finance, Interior): questioning them would indirectly implicate the authority of the ruler. Royal decree no. 86/81 guaranteed freedom of speech to its members during debates, insofar as they respect the agenda and the law.

The State Consultative Council was originally composed of 45 members appointed for two years: 17 belonged to the government, 11 to the private sector—their names were proposed by the Chamber of Commerce—and 17 were proposed by the *walis*. In 1983 a royal decree enlarged the Council to 55 members. Dale Eickelman's study of the 1981–83 State Consultative Council members shed light on what he called "shaykhocracy":[21] 15 of the 18 Interior-native members belonged to tribal *sheikhs*' lineage; 64% of the members had not lived in Oman at the end of the 1960s, for either political (21%) or economic reasons (43%). Even though the debates have been broadcast live on television since 1983, the SCC never questioned Oman's balance of power in decision making. One of the delegates compared the SCC to "a child just out of its womb, which soon will walk, speak and eventually, with His Majesty's guidance, act on its own". Another explained that the consultative process was similar to the relationship "between father and small children. The Sultan is our father and tells us what to do. That is consultation."[22]

Nine years after creation of the SCC, the Sultan announced the replacement of the SCC by the *Majlis al-Shura* (Consultative Council, CC) from 1991. The new assembly was composed of 59 members—who individually represent each *wilaya* of the country—and a president, appointed by the Sultan. Within each constituency, 500 people whose opinions and experience were valued were gathered to elect three candidates. From these three, one was chosen by Sayyid Fahd, Deputy Prime Minister for Legal Affairs. The final decision was taken by the ruler himself. The members were appointed for three years, without any limit to the number of terms.[23]

The structures and the functions of the Majlis al-Shura were not to be modified until 2011. The then appointed president—'Abd Allah al-Qatabi, between 1991 and 2007; Ahmad al-'Isa'i between 2007 and 2011—was assisted by two vice-presidents. A Majlis executive bureau—which included, in addition to the three people just mentioned, five other elected members—had the tasks of planning the plenary sessions' agenda, managing business between the four sessions of the year and supervising the activity of the five permanent expert committees, on the economy, local communities, health, legal affairs, and education and culture. These committees could ask for a minister or any official to come to explain himself in front of them, but the latter was not compelled to obey. Unless the Council of Ministers explicitly wished to pass it on directly to the ruler, any proposed law in the economic and social sectors had to be presented to the Majlis to be discussed and, if necessary, amended. The bill was then voted upon by the assembly and returned to the ministry. Afterwards, the ruler ratified the bill, choosing whether or not to take into account the recommendations introduced.

In addition, the Majlis had to submit proposals to the Council of Ministers for legislation in the economic, social and environmental fields; to give its opinion on the government's policy in these fields; to contribute to preparation and implementation of the development plans as well as of the national budget; and finally to help deepen citizens' involvement in the country's development. The so-called "service" ministers had to appear in front of the Majlis twice a year to answer the members' questions and to send them an annual report on their activities. The members had total freedom in the Majlis building.

There were several changes in Oman's Majlis al-Shura by 2003. After the first census was completed in 1993, the authorities decided that *wilaya*s whose population exceeded 30,000 inhabitants could elect two delegates, and smaller *wilaya*s just one. Furthermore, the selection and appointment process was for the first time open to women in the Muscat governorate; two women, chosen by the electors of Seeb and Muscat, were confirmed by the Sultan. In 1997 the electorate amounted to 51,000 people (one for every 15 adults), 10% of whom were women. In that year, women were also given the right to vote and to stand for election all over Oman.

In the following elections, in September 2000, 175,000 electors (i.e. one adult in four; 30% of them women) were called upon to choose from among 540 candidates (including 21 women) for 83 seats. Decree no. 128/97 of the Ministry of Interior established that any Omani who was over 21 and who was either a *sheikh* or a dignitary or holder of a high school or university degree, or a businessman, could vote. 114,500 people (65%) finally registered to vote, and 87% of the latter actually voted. The candidates with the highest numbers of votes were automatically elected, and the Sultan no longer intervened in a discretionary second round. In Muscat and Bawshar, two women were elected. In October 2003, the delegates' term was increased from three to four years. But the real innovation was the introduction of universal suffrage.

The 2003 and 2007 elections.[24] The introduction of universal suffrage for Majlis al-Shura elections[25] has to be studied within the Omani political context. Alain Rouquié reminds us that "The election is part of a justifying—usually legitimizing—discourse of those who organize it. It is possible to evaluate its sense, its value, its function only as a piece or a mechanism within a normative framework."[26]

While freedom of association is very strictly limited by article 33 of the Basic Law, the establishment of political parties is simply prohibited in Oman. Article 10 of 1 March 2003 law dealing with organisation of elections states that any citizen has the right to stand, provided that he is a native Omani (*bi-l-asl*) who has reached the age of 30 on the election day, is a "son of the *wilaya*" (*min abna' al-wilaya*) in which he is a candidate or owns a residence there, and finally holds a "fair (*maqbul*) level of culture and professional experience".

In 2003 and 2007 elections it was forbidden to tackle any general topic (like the role of the religion in present society, or that of the assembly in the division of powers) or to present public promises or campaign together with a candidate from another *wilaya*. These limits prevented the elaboration of political strategies. Candidates therefore stood in their own names only. Campaigning remained very restricted as public gatherings were explicitly forbidden. It took place largely in the *majlis* of the tribal *sheikh*s, but also through door-to-door and personal networks. Women have used the women's associations recognised by the government to make their ideas known.[27] There was a notable development between 2003 and 2007 in respect of posters and advertisements on TV and in the newspapers; while all were forbidden in 2003, they were allowed four years later, so that roundabouts and public places were decorated with banners, portraits and slogans of candidates during the weeks before the elections, and newspapers were flooded with advertisements. Pamphlets produced by the candidates to promote their names were much more sophisticated than in 2003, usually presenting the family, educational and professional background as well as the candidate's credentials. Except for these small steps forward, it must be admitted that 2007 elections were broadly only a "repetition of the previous elections."[28]

If the media stressed the importance of this event, two aspects were given special attention. The first was the role of women; through interviews with prominent personalities and in other ways, the authorities emphasised the need for women to take part in the poll and highlighted the extra quality women's presence in the Majlis' debates would not fail to bring. The second axis was the qualities a good candidate should have, and therefore the criteria which must govern the voters' choice:[29] rational selection criteria (honesty, desire to promote the general interest, etc.) must prevail over kinship and clientelism.

In practice, in 2003 as well as in 2007, all candidacies had to be registered at the *wali*'s office and receive the agreement of the official elections committee. Voters residing in the capital were strongly encouraged to vote in their native *wilaya*s through indirect measures: the organisation of the voting on a working day, and the granting of an additional holiday without loss of pay the next day on presentation of a stamped voter's card. Moreover, the authorities worked to depoliticise the elections and reduce them to local and personal issues. The organisation of voting on a local basis tended in this direction. Similarly revealing was the absence of any members of the royal family, noble lineages of the al-Busa'idi tribe, or leading merchant families among the candidates.[30] This was due both to reluctance to involve the royal name in a "vulgar" electoral game with popular voting and to the regime's unwillingness to face the implications of symbolic over-investment in such candidatures: voters and observers would be tempted to interpret the results as a referendum on the authorities' general policies, and that would be inconceivable for Sultan Qaboos. These elections do not, in any case, question the legitimacy of the ruler, but that of all the old local political actors.

Thus it is not very surprising that the criteria of choice most commonly used by electors have related to primordial solidarities, especially in rural areas where choice mainly follows lines of tribal belonging. Insofar as electors have no rational way of making a choice between different candidates, they will logically resort to "natural" criteria. The candidate's name itself conveys his programme and defines by itself the social and political symbol the candidate embodies. Besides the candidate's personal wealth, which allows him to "convince" electors,[31] clientelism (*al-mahsubiyya*) and personal relations (*al-ma'arif al-shakhsiyya*), but also the *sheikh*s' support for this or that candidate, rank among the fundamental elements in the choice. One example demonstrates the importance of the *sheikh*s' influence in elections in rural *wilaya*s.

At Bahla in 2003, where two seats were contested, five out of 16 candidates were tribal *sheikh*s themselves, or very close relatives of the *sheikh*s: Ibrahim al-Hina'i, the son of the last Imam of Oman's cousin, Ghalib bin 'Ali; Hamud al-Khalili, the mufti of Oman's brother; Fadl al-Shukayli, the *sheikh*'s nephew of the tribe of that name; Muhammad al-Sha'ili, descended from a noble lineage and the only candidate from the tribe; and Hamud al-Ma'ani, the *sheikh*'s son. The symbolic perception of these candidates allowed electors to identify them immediately as having inherited a political heritage from several historically distinguished lineages. Significantly most of the other candidates were not taken into account, and their claim to represent the community had no credibility: on such a territory over-charged with references, eligibility is only conferred to a minority, like a natural attribute of the individual. The winning candidates, Fadl al-Shukayli and Muhammad al-Sha'ili, benefited from better group cohesion, knowing how to weld the whole group around their names. The patronymic prestige of the Hina'i and Khalili families, less established in the *wilaya*, was not enough to challenge the strength of solidarity groups. They had their national prestige but were not able to articulate it with issues at stake in the local game.

Nevertheless, it would be misleading to reduce the introduction of universal suffrage for Majlis elections to simple political retribalisation. Clientelism is an inescapable variable of the current Omani political process and can be perceived in other forms, particularly in the capital, where old solidarities seem weaker. Considering that most individuals connected with interior tribes voted in their native regions, the Muscat election led to polarisation on new grounds. These were no longer just tribal or clan-based, but also ethnic, linguistic, or based on professional or generational networks. We can thus note the far-reaching capacity of mobilisation displayed by candidates of Baluchi origin, not only in the governorate of Muscat (where they won three seats out of twelve, two of them by very large margins in 2003 and 2007) but also in the Batina region.

But what we would like to focus on is the lack of enthusiasm shown by Omani citizens in these consultations. Despite an intense government media campaign urging citizens to "exercise their right to vote,"[32] despite formally competitive elections, despite the pressure by shareholders upon company managers to check if their national employees were effectively registered as voters,[33] only 262,000 people, i.e. 32% of the population above 21 years of age (36% of whom were women) registered to vote to choose among the 585 candidates (16 of them women) in 2003. In 2007, boosting turnout was once again the major topic of the Ministry of the Interior and 389,000 citizens, i.e. 45% of Omanis eligible to do so, registered to vote for one of the 632 candidates—20 of them women.

Thereafter, while the authorities published official figures for turnout at the national level in 2007 only, they did not do it for turnout in each *wilaya* either in 2003 or in 2007. Only the number of votes the elected candidates obtained was given. Never were the votes cast for the other candidates or the order in which they were placed mentioned, nor even the *wilayas'* total number of voters. Clearly, the authorities wished to abstain from arousing resentment by establishing a hierarchy among individuals, or among the groups they belonged to. Some local observers estimated in 2003 that only 70–75% of registered citizens went to vote;[34] thus only 22–24% of citizens old enough to vote actually did so. In 2007, the government announced that 62.7% of registered citizens actually cast their votes,[35] which meant that only 28% of eligible people went to vote. The turnout was higher in the rural regions, where solidarity and patronage networks are still strong, and among women and old people. Turnout rates appear to be more disappointing in the capital and in other urban areas, among men in general, and particularly among the younger generation, state employees, and the educated.[36] In Muscat, there was a profound lack of interest in a vote based on kinship in which individuals without tribal affiliations did not participate; only 30% of registered voters went to the polls in al-ʿAmrat *wilaya*, an area of rapid urbanisation and low living standards.[37]

In the discussions we collected, it is easy to spot a cynical attitude (especially among younger generations) towards a process whose failings people already seem to notice. Very few young people believe that the elected members have the capacity to improve their daily lives. In their view, the representatives' impotence is reinforced by the fact that creating groups based on ideological or origin criteria in the Council is prohibited. So an election is usually an occasion to seek immediate profit through the ballot, on this sort of reasoning: "As he will be elected and benefit from a lot of material privileges thanks to me, it is normal that he has to make me benefit from it right now". Many reports attest the existence of bribes; it can be cash (up to 100 OR for a person's vote; or up to 1,000 OR for a tribal sheikh to gain his support in Batina[38]) or gifts (air-conditioners offered to several houses of a *wilaya's* remote village, cell phones, etc.) in order to attract undecided voters: according to a top official of the Ministry of Interior, "the government is not interested in it, or rather it lets it happen, it closes the eyes..."[39]

The mass abstention illustrates, more than anything else, refusal to endorse a political institution without real power, which citizens consider a caricature of democracy: "People do not vote because they know it is useless. The Majlis al-Shura is only a 'discussion forum' between friends. Certainly, the ministers can be interrogated. But when they come, they know that they will spend a good afternoon because they will not be asked about the most important issues."[40]

This harsh opinion reflects the sentiment of a large fringe of Muscat youth. The good representative is the one who gives services to his electors. And maybe the representative's inability to satisfy his electors' requests, i.e. to make enough of his status and his redistributive acts—mainly because of the weakness of prerogatives granted to the Majlis and, therefore, of material and symbolic resources to offer—could explain the disenchantment of citizens. The October 2007 polls perhaps contributed to revealing one of the main limitations of the Majlis al-Shura as it works at the moment: only 38 out of 64 candidates seeking re-election secured seats. But the hardest blow for the authorities was that no female candidate was elected this time, while the presence of women in the Majlis was one of the main criteria to rely on for promotion of "Omani democracy" abroad. Moreover the rule according to which a candidate has to resign completely from his civil service position in case of election means that many well-educated people were reluctant to enter such a competition, as they know that they will lose financially in the long run, if they are not be re-elected in the next election.

Despite the lucid way many Omanis view this institution, we can note that successive Majlis al-Shura reforms have turned it into a new tool for mediation between the population and the authorities. Citizens have begun to appropriate this chamber to recreate systems of allocation, with the Majlis delegate playing a role complementary to that of the tribal *sheikh*. A 30-year-old state employee explained the reasons for his vote thus:

"M. has been elected because he is young and popular, he is not a snob, he is always cheerful, while you 'count the steps' when you are going to see the *sheikh*... There are many people who come to see the *sheikh* and ask him for services; he is usually very busy... With M., it is not complicated, he is a mate, and you can speak frankly with him. He understands your problems, he understands what you want, he is like you and me..."[41]

The Majlis representative conceives himself here in the most practical way, i.e. as a citizen like others; he is the messenger of his district and its interests, not just a full member of a decision-making authority—a conception the voters have no illusions about. These words reveal also a change since 2000, regarding the entry of new social categories into the Majlis. New members are more educated, better placed to engage in the technical work of considering the files submitted to them, and more inclined to call into question a distribution of political roles that has gone unchallenged since 1970. It is still too early to measure both the political and social consequences of this still marginal development, *a fortiori* as no sociological data about Majlis members are available. Despite the ban on "parliamentary groups", we can see lobbies based on shared interests (like justice, education, and health matters) being formed. Whereas the ability of these *lubi* to influence major national policy orientations remains weak, their very existence illustrates a qualitative evolution in the perception that some delegates have of their responsibilities and positions in the general balance of powers.

Nevertheless, whereas the old *sheikh*s have grown fewer and fewer in the Majlis, their sons and nephews have occupied numerous seats in the assembly elected in 2003 and 2007, especially among the deputies from the interior (Dakhliyya, Dhahira) and from Musandam and Dhofar. Moreover, despite the readjustment of constituencies to the benefit to the most populated *wilaya*s, the 30,000-inhabitant threshold which separates the one- and two-seat *wilaya*s remains very low. Thus, *wilaya*s like Seeb (205,000 Omanis in 2013) and Izki (40,000) send the same number of delegates each: two. The Wusta (21,000) and Musandam (24,000) provinces are represented by four delegates each, twice as many as the *wilaya* of Seeb, which is eight to ten times more populated. Without doubt, the Majlis al-Shura remains a chamber where rural regions are over-represented because of the way its members are chosen. The clearest example is the Dhofar governorate (182,000 nationals), where nine out of eleven delegates are elected outside the capital, Salalah, which has more than two-thirds of the total population of the region.

The State Council. In spite of the pre-eminence of conservative and rural forces within the Majlis al-Shura, Sultan Qaboos decided in 1996 to set up another chamber. The fifth part of the Basic Law created the Council of Oman, composed of the Consultative Council (Majlis al-Shura) and the State Council (*Majlis al-Dawla*), a completely new institution. In a speech at the State Council's inauguration in December 1997, Sultan Qaboos explained that both organs had to work to establish "solid foundations for a genuine consultative process based on the nation's heritage, values and Islamic Shariah".[42] State Council members are appointed by the Sultan for four years renewable, in order to coincide with the Majlis al-Shura; they are recruited from among former ministers and undersecretaries, former ambassadors, senior retired officers and judges, businessmen, and individuals who have rendered services to the nation or who are acknowledged for their skills, as well as "any person His Majesty the Sultan may deem fit".[43]

Until 2011 the prerogatives of this assembly included identifying problems in the economic, administrative and social fields, looking for solutions, revising—after Majlis Al-Shura sessions and before promulgation—laws which were not transmitted directly to the ruler by the Council of Ministers, and submitting proposals to encourage investment and to improve Oman's human resources management. More generally, the Council's mission was to take part in "implementing the overall development strategy and contributing in deepening the roots of the values of the Omani society, maintaining their achievements and ascertaining the principles of the Basic Law".[44] Three special committees (economic, social and legal) worked in parallel with the plenary debates. In 2000, 2003 and 2007, the State Council's membership was enlarged successively from 54 members (including five women) to 61 (including nine women) and then to 70 (14 women).

The extreme caution with which Sultan Qaboos has composed this assembly for every new term reflects its underlying political instrumentalisation. Appointed by royal decree one week after the elections to the Majlis al-Shura, the State Council allows the government to establish closer links with key figures at very little cost. Moreover, it offers a second chance for groups whose members have been beaten in the Majlis al-Shura elections. In 'Ibri *wilaya* for instance, the major tribe, the Ya'aqubi, was divided in 2003 among several candidates, one of them being Sheikh Sa'id bin Rashid, from the noble lineage. The failure to reach an agreement in order to group all the *'asabiyya* forces around a single name led to the defeat of the tribe. Fortunately for them, the Sultan appointed Sheikh Sultan al-Ya'aqubi to the State Council to compensate for it. The same situation arose in Muttrah, where the candidature of two Lawatiyya notables led to the splitting of the community's vote, the result being that there were no Lawatiyya Majlis members. After the Sultan appointed two Lawatiyya to the State Council in the following days, the Lawatiyya remembered the lessons of 2003, as they organised "primary" elections within the community four years later in order to present only one candidate. In 2007 the appointment of 14 women (20% of the members) to the State Council was also a striking way to compensate for the lack of women in the Majlis al-Shura, and above all a strong signal to the country and to the international community of Qaboos' personal endeavour for women's role in the country.

Thus, the Council formalises the integration of infra-national socio-political forces (tribes, leading merchants, etc.) into the state apparatus. For instance, a strong representation of the Imamate's historical influential families is noted, in particular the presence since 2011 of the last Imam's son, Sheikh al-Khattab bin Ghalib al-Hina'i, and since 2003, of Sheikha Zahra al-Nabhani, daughter of one of the Imamate's most powerful personalities. The Council therefore contributes to the central power's legitimisation through a redistribution of both material and symbolic powers. The de-politicisation process reaches its climax here, with the co-optation of traditional elites. By integrating them into the State Council, these elites will finally use their own social legitimacy, which has been independent of that of the nation-state built around the Sultan, in his favour.

The establishment of the State Council is the answer to the ruler's suspicion of any excessive political freedom being granted to an institution based on popular suffrage, like the Majlis al-Shura. While both assemblies are officially given comparable prerogatives, in practice the job of the State Council is to counterbalance the Majlis al-Shura, as the latter's legitimacy, which comes from elections, seems broader and "independent" of the ruler's will. As Hamud al-Harthi, former president of the State Council, explains, the assembly he presided over takes action after the Majlis al-Shura to revise the latter's work and prevent any disturbance of the balance of powers: "The Majlis al-Shura studies the needs of the population and makes recommendations on this basis. The role of the Majlis al-Dawla starts from there."[45] The way the members are appointed and the social composition of the assembly prevent the emergence of any radical political proposals and ensure the unfailing loyalty of State Council members to the Sultan. Has the Sultan not chosen them personally one by one for his trust in them? Naturally, their mission consists in serving him in a proper way, in the face of potential disturbers of the established order, the Majlis al-Shura members.

Legislative liberalisation started 35 years ago as a means for the ruler to neutralise emerging socio-political forces (including religious figures and technocrats) by co-opting them into a game he controls, thereby recognising their existence without taking any political risks. Furthermore, it allows dilution of responsibility for unpopular decisions. A broader spectrum of political actors is now responsible, and no longer consists solely of the ministers of the Sultan's court. On the other hand, this opening up allows the possibility (or the illusion of a possibility) for citizens to choose directly who will represent them and who will bring their message to the top, while simultaneously giving them a new channel for defusing social conflicts.

Last but not least, this political process is the means of establishing a clear distinction between the royal family and prominent members of the state (merchant families, power allies, etc.) on one hand, and the other citizens (including local elites) on the other. The latter group has been ordered to bring its social or traditional prestige into play. If a local elite group wins an election, its power is theoretically strengthened—but to the benefit of the central state as the group become an intermediary between state and society. If the group is defeated, its fate lies in the hands of the Sultan, whose paternal benevolence can grant it a seat in the State Council, which will allow it to keep a bit of "social visibility". Thus its dependence upon royal goodwill is total.

A sultanistic regime?

Max Weber defines patriarchalism as "the situation where, within a group (household) which is usually organized on both an economic and a kinship basis, a particular individual governs who is designated by a definite rule of inheritance".[46] With the apogee of the ruler's personal power Weber introduces the notion of "sultanism":

"Where domination is primarily traditional, even though it is exercised by virtue of the ruler's personal autonomy, it will be called patrimonial authority; where it indeed operates primarily on the basis of discretion, it will be called sultanism. The transition is definitely continuous [...] Sometimes it appears that sultanism is completely understrained by tradition, but this is never in fact the case. The non-traditional element is not, however, rationalised in impersonal terms, but consists only in an extreme development of the ruler's discretion."[47]

H.E. Chehabi and Juan Linz took over this distinction and introduced the notion of "neo-sultanism": "[Such a regime] is based on a personal rulership, but loyalty to the ruler is motivated not by his embodying or articulating an ideology [...] but by a mixture of fear and rewards to his collaborators. The ruler exercises his power without restraint, at his own discretion. [...] The binding norms [...] are constantly subverted by arbitrary political decisions of the ruler, which he does not feel constrained to justify in ideological terms."[48] The use of Omani political "tradition"—or what is seen as such—by Sultan Qaboos directly contributes to consolidation of the regime's legitimacy.

The 'open parliament'. The political architecture Sultan Qaboos has established since 1970 is the most elaborate personalisation of all the area's monarchies. The personal authority is displayed in the public sphere according to a mode which explicitly refers to an inherited past, while mingling royal arbitrary power and the use of an exhumed or in fact re-created "tradition".

Sultan Qaboos intended from an early stage to distinguish the royal family from Omani society as a whole, including the other branches of the al-Busaʻidi tribe; the lineage Qaboos comes from is separated from the others, as if it were outside Omani tribal divisions and remained exterior to the conflicts of interests occurring in society as a whole. The fact that no royal family member participated in Majlis elections highlights this claimed neutrality. As for protocol, the royal family is distinguished from the al-Busaʻidi tribe's other branches in particular and society in general. While the Sultan is the only person to have the "Majesty" (*jalala*) title, the other Al Saʻid family members' names, whatever their professional positions, must be preceded by "*sumuh al-sayyid* (or *sayyida*)", His (Her) Highness Mister (or Madam)...; "*sayyid*" is reserved to the royal family members as well as some major connected personalities from the al-Busa'idi tribe. Finally, the title "*sa'ada*" (Excellency) is given to the other ministers or members of the Council of Oman and other major personalities not related to the Sultan. Even more concretely, the Al Sa'ids are distinguished physically by wearing of special clothes: the official *sa'idi* dagger bears a handle shaping a cross. They wear a turban (*al-'imama al-sa'idiyya*) with special designs—predominantly red, blue and gold—which they roll up in a specific manner.

It is certainly from the Jordanian method of rule, and of its longevity, that the Omani ruler got the most important lessons. As early as October 1970, comparisons between Sultan Qaboos and King Husain were established by observers.[49] They did not fail to emphasise the similar conditions of accession to the throne of both rulers, but also those rulers' weak chances of survival due to almost total lack of legitimacy at the outset. In a way similar to King Husain of Jordan's practices, Sultan Qaboos appears as a *sheikh al-mashayikh* (sheikh of the sheikhs), standing above mundane political debate. Until recently, ministers and Majlis al-Shura members deflected popular criticisms to themselves and served to preserve the ruler from any verbal attack. The ruler's government reshuffles are strongly approved by the Omanis: it is thought, for instance, that the Sultan leaves too much freedom to manoeuvre to his advisers and ministers, who only defend their particular interests and neglect those of the nation, and hide the real situation from the ruler. The ruler's prestige is only strengthened by the Omani propensity, already noticed twenty years ago by Dale Eickelman,[50] to consider that the Sultan does not rule enough and delegates too much to his ministers.

Besides, throughout his rule, Qaboos has tried to embody the role of the nation's tribal *sheikh*; he has thus taken care to spread the idea that there is an unofficial way available to address complaints or requests directly to him, bypassing the "modern" administrative ways. Which Omani has not heard about a friend of a friend who remained in front of the royal palace's entrance while waiting until the Sultan stopped and he could tell him his problems, which would be solved on the ruler's single word to grant the complainant a cheque or the signing of a letter of approval? More generally, the Sultan is the ultimate legal authority when institutional procedures are exhausted; after the Court of Appeal, it is possible to go back to the ruler to obtain the quashing of a judgment or an amnesty for a relative.

Despite this apparent attentiveness to the more mundane concerns of his subjects, combined with the Sultan's symbolic omnipresence in everyday life, the ruler talks little, and most of the political decisions and official visits are usually orchestrated by a minister or his special representative. By this paradoxical double game, which makes him very familiar to every Omani while keeping an extraordinary aura, the ruler gives his reign a strong paternal seal which it is difficult to resist. Discretion in the media gives his personality an air of mystery which is dissipated only in exceptional carefully-orchestrated occasions. The most important is the Sultan's annual journey across the country (al-jawla al-sanawiyya), also known as the "open parliament" (barlaman maftuh).

Performed by the ruler since 1975, this one-month tour is supposed to revive the customary practice of Muslim princes visiting their territory and meeting the people (al-iltaqa' bi-abna' sha'abuh). Its dual function is to situate the regime within longer history, in order to give it an un-temporal image, but also to renew local notables' allegiances to Qaboos. However, this "tradition" is merely reinvented and was never practised before Qaboos.

Thousands of people prepare for this event weeks in advance and line up along the route of the royal cortege, waving Omani flags. With dances, songs and enthusiastic demonstrations, many groups vie with each other for testimonies of allegiance to the regime in order to bring the procession to a halt and receive the greeting of the Sultan. At regular intervals the sovereign stops and crouches on a carpet, his ministers behind him, to listen to the complaints of his subjects. The local nobility is arranged in a semicircle facing the *sheikh al-mashayikh*.

A personal face-to-face discussion with the Sultan is a privilege which gives those who have it huge prestige; photographs of this meeting, copies of which are presented to the *sheikh*'s children and nephews, have a place of honour in the local *majlis*. For a few years, however, protocol has been considerably reinforced, and under the apparent cover of spontaneousness, the tour does not allow for anyone who has not been strictly selected beforehand to approach the ruler.

Through this regular tour, Qaboos is able to pass over the tribal chiefs' heads by granting theoretically the possibility to talk to the humblest of his citizens. Qaboos himself referred to this Omani "direct democracy" to legitimate his power in the eyes of the international community:

"As for the Sultan, he is already elected, but not in the way you know. In Oman, you have to earn kingship [...] I was only *sayyid*, that is, roughly, lord, until key members of my family and the other leading tribes approved me."[51]

For the local notables participation in the ceremony ratifies the direct allegiance of citizens and the local elite to Qaboos, who is "a focal point without whom the community would have no real existence".[52] Moreover, it helps the Sultan to maintain a certain degree of uncertainty regarding the informal hierarchy of the different local groups. The result is a competition that no group can escape, whose material expression is the competing declarations of loyalty to the Sultan by private companies or ethnic/tribal groups in the newspapers.

This is also the reason why Qaboos chooses this tour as the setting for long-awaited political announcements (especially on local development), which are then presented as discretionary decisions, that is, favours granted at the Sultan's pleasure. Similarly Linda Layne says about Jordan, "Whereas the nineteenth-century Moroccan kings accomplished sovereignty by travelling with their armies and collecting tribute, Hussein travels with bureaucrats and dispenses the fruits of economic development."[53] In 2007, the amount of local development projects to be implemented after the Sultan's tour in Dakhliyya, Wusta and Sharqiyya regions rose to OR 83 millions, that is almost 8% of Oman's total investment expenditure.[54]

Last but not least, this "open parliament" is one of the rare opportunities for citizens and local elites to challenge ministers' absolute discretion over the execution of the country's policies. Consequently, such instances of "direct democracy, represented by the direct meeting between the chief and his people"[55] are taken badly by those office holders, who are forced to face the people's criticisms for several weeks. Qaboos' legitimacy is fundamentally rooted in making himself indispensable as a mediator between the respective interests of the various socio-political forces (such as local and central elites or the people and the government). Lastly, this combination of arbitrariness and tradition breeds a feeling of distance from and fear of the Sultan, both of which are prerequisites for obedience.

Sultanistic arbitrary power. Sultan Qaboos has always displayed strong aversion to using physical coercion towards his subjects; intelligence soon replaced direct confrontation with opponents or counter-powers. This does not mean that force has never been used in Omani territory for thirty years, but it has been generally used as a last resort.

The major exception to this principle was obviously the Dhofar war, during which the Sultan hardly showed pity for those who were charged with plotting. One example of expeditious justice occurred when a PFLOAG network was dismantled in Muttrah in December 1972, after one of the rebellion's leaders had been recognised by a defector; 76 people were tried and sentenced to death; 10 were executed the next day, while the others' sentences were commuted to life imprisonment.[56] Until the early 1980s the death penalty, arising from summary trials supervised by the state, was regularly applied, as was explained by a British former director of Salalah prison, who held the post until 1981: "In my experience, if terrorists were caught who were found out to have killed British personnel out in Oman, they were put on trial and executed. That was standard practice."[57] Similarly, torture and imprisonment without trial were applied regularly.[58]

The memory of this pitiless political repression has been used thereafter as a warning to anybody tempted to question the regime: in exchange for restricted use of coercion—replaced in everyday life by co-optation and financial gratification—Qaboos has required his subjects not to interfere in political matters. Public expression of any opinion calling into question the main political orientations of the country has been basically excluded. When this tacit pact is broken and an individual expresses even the slightest doubt about the government's political choices, or transgresses the limits imposed by the official censorship, the authorities' response comes quickly. In the summer of 2004 two intellectuals were declared *persona non grata* by the regime over the entire Omani media, after expressing doubt on the Iranian channel al-Alam about the government's commitment to political reform.[59] Another intellectual was denied, in the spring of 2004, the access to the newspaper where he was accustomed to publish articles, on instructions from above. The reason was said to be that he had spoken in a former newspaper about the economic and social problems the country had to face.[60] According to a top civil servant, "There are no Omani journalists. There are only people who work in the journalism field [...] None of them is ready to assume the consequences of truths everybody thinks about without expressing."[61]

On the other hand, Qaboos has had a magnanimous attitude towards opponents who showed themselves ready to return to the fold; this took concrete form with the general amnesty shortly after the coup d'état. The Sultan thus appears generally, for all the state office holders, as the personal guarantor of their position, as if an individualised bond attached each office holder to the Sultan himself. Later, sultanistic benevolence was displayed on every National Day, the occasion of releases of prisoners (see chapter 7, for instance). He displays himself as the ultimate depositary of the nation's forgiveness towards lost sheep, the only one able to decide on the reprehensible feature of this or that act; on his goodwill depends the fate of all his subjects, and through his arbitration the most complex situations are resolved, on any occasion.

Max Weber had established as a characteristic of a sultanistic regime the creation of a large army, composed mainly of mercenaries independent from internal political forces. In terms of both funding and equipment, the Omani army has been seen, since 1970, as one of the better-trained in the region. The Dhofar war certainly contributed to this situation; military expenditure amounted to 50% of the total state budget in the mid-1970s. Defence and security expenditures have stabilised at around 30% of total expenditure, that is 11.3% of 2013's GDP[62]—one of the world's highest rates.

Foreign personnel have always occupied a leading role in the Omani security forces. In continuation of the policy of the nineteenth- and twentieth-century sultans, the current ruler has relied both on tribes allied with the Sultans of Muscat for a long time (Hawasina, Bani Kalban, Bani 'Amr, etc.) and on mercenaries from Baluchistan and Britain in particular.

Until the Dhofar rebellion ceased to represent a direct threat for the regime, in the early 1980s, all the high-ranking army officers and the vast majority of sensitive positions in the Security, Immigration, Police and Intelligence departments were held by British staff. In 1985 almost 1,500 British citizens served in the Omani army, 80% of them under hire as contract officers while 20% were British officers on loan to the Sultan's army.[63] In August 1981 Major-General Tim Creasey, a former Commander-in-Chief of United Kingdom Land Forces who was put at the disposal of the Sultanate at the end of the Dhofar war (1972–75), was appointed the SAF's Chief of Staff. At this period British influence on security and intelligence structures was still extremely strong. Among the pre-eminent personalities we can note: Malcolm Dennison, a former head of Intelligence under Sa'id and then under Qaboos, later appointed adviser to the Sultan for Internal Security Affairs (1972–83); Anthony Ashworth, adviser to the Sultan for Intelligence affairs in the 1980s, still influential in the mid-1990s, in the censorship department in the Ministry of Information;[64] Reginald Temple, retired officer of the British intelligence service (MI6), appointed in 1979 Director of the Omani Foreign Intelligence department; and Air Vice-Marshal Eric Bennett, who was Head of the Omani Air Force until 1990.

But the most influential expatriate in Oman was Brigadier-General Timothy Landon, who was in the same promotion as Qaboos at Sandhurst. Known in Oman later by the nickname of the "White Sultan", he has embodied what observers called the "coterie of Britons based in Muscat".[65] He came to Oman around 1965 to serve in the Dhofar war and is said to have been directly involved in the 1970 coup. According to various sources, he is believed to have received a fixed payment for his help, counted in tens of thousands of oil barrels per day.[66] A special member of Qaboos' close circle until his death in August 2007,[67] he was registered as adviser to the Oman Embassy in London in the late 1990s.[68]

The "Omanisation" of commanding positions in the army only started in 1982, with the replacement of British people at the head of several regiments; two years later, Major-General Nasib al-Rawahi succeeded General John Watts as head of land forces. When Major-General Creasey retired in 1985, his assistant General Hamid al-'Aufi replaced him and became the first Omani to be the Army's Chief of Staff. Overall command of the Police was also entrusted to an Omani in the same year, then that of Intelligence (ISS, the Internal Security Service) in 1987.[69] But in 1988, these changes did not mislead observers:

"The Sultan is surrounded by British advisers who, presumably with his concurrence, control all access to him, especially during the six months that he spends in Salalah [...] They are there entirely at the Sultan's pleasure, yet their influence, real or imagined, projects an image of British dependency."[70]

The British influence has been eroded for fifteen years,[71] but it remains—British officers in the Omani security forces were estimated at 500 in the late 1990s.[72] This trust in actors who are not involved in the political and historical balances of the country has never failed. A senior foreign official in Muscat confirmed the existence of an agreement with Pakistan; it apparently allows the Omani army to recruit approximately 2,000 men every year in Baluchistan and to grant them and their families Omani nationality in a short time.[73]

Qaboos' distrust of individuals not fully dependent on his goodwill finds an illustration in the security departments' separation into structures which counterbalance each other, avoiding the concentration of too much power under one authority. Thus, besides the regular army, which itself comes under the Ministry of Defence, several units are attached to the Diwan, like the Royal Guard, which is in charge of protection of the Sultan, the royal family and their property. Within it two structures coexist: the Royal Guard Brigade itself and the Sultan's Special Forces (SSF), which are conceived on the model of the British SAS, as elite units directly connected to the Sultan. No command structure, except Qaboos himself, coordinates the action of the regular army and the Royal Guard.

The Diwan of the Royal Court. In 1975 a law (decree no. 26/75) on "organising the administration" established the distribution of responsibilities. The

Sultan is "the source of all laws" (*masdar al-qawanin*). Until now all Omani legislation has been promulgated through "decrees of the Sultan" (*al-marsum al-sultani al-sami*) including 1996 Basic Law. Only subsidiary legislation is promulgated by the minister in charge of the issue concerned, through "ministerial decrees" (*qarar wazir...*). Unlike most other jurisdictional decisions, there is no possibility of appeal against the ruler's decisions, which explains the persistent popularity nowadays of informal channels of requests to the Sultan. He has no account to give to anybody when he appoints or dismisses any people at any level of the political or administrative organisation (Article 42 of the Basic Law).

But the structure that symbolises best the extreme personalisation of authority is the Diwan of the Royal Court, heir to Sa'id bin Taimur's personal secretariat. Qaboos soon showed his determination to keep control of all matters in the country, while giving the image of a ruler close to his subjects' problems. To reconcile these requirements became technically impossible in a modern, fast-developing state like Oman. In parallel to the formal architecture of powers, Qaboos' need for an office only devoted to his affairs led to the creation of a Diwan of Royal Affairs in 1972, then to its transformation into a Ministry in April 1974, under Hamad bin Hamud al-Busa'idi. This administration has the role of filtering files coming to the ruler, while managing national and private affairs which do not concern any other department but do not require the Sultan's personal intervention.

The Diwan slowly became a kind of super-ministry above all the other Cabinet departments. As with defence and security matters, the Sultan early perceived the need to divide the Diwan services into two independent structures. Hamad bin Hamud kept the post of Minister for Diwan Affairs until 1986; his competences ranged from tribal affairs to the coordination of interministerial actions and to the secretariat of the Council of Ministers. In parallel, in the early 1970s Qaboos appointed Colonel Sa'id al-Wahaibi as chairman of the Diwan of the Royal Court, in charge of the Sultan's personal affairs (properties, personal economic interests, etc). He kept this function until December 1985 when he was replaced by Saif bin Hamad, who became Minister with the same title. When the latter died in October 2002, 'Ali bin Hamud succeeded him as Minister of the Diwan of the Royal Court. When the Ministry for Diwan Affairs was abolished in the mid-1980s, Qaboos created a Ministry of State for the Office of the Palace and entrusted it to one of his closest collaborators, General 'Ali bin Majid al-Ma'amari. 'Ali bin Majid became Minister in October 1989, his title until 2011 being "Minister of

Royal Office". While his tasks were theoretically concentrated on the Sultan's personal affairs, in fact his sphere of activity largely encroached on that of the Ministry of Diwan, as 'Ali bin Majid became one of the key figures of the regime. His influence seemed to have done nothing but grow since Saif bin Hamad's death; this occurred in 2002, after a long tenure of office as Minister of the Diwan of the Royal Court—17 years—which illustrates the enormous role he long occupied.

'Ali bin Majid's rise in influence, but also Qaboos' determination to divide up responsibilities so as to establish a balance of power in his close entourage, was illustrated in the state budget. Until 2002, the "Diwan of the Royal Court" budget line appeared in national accounts. In 2003 a new line, "Royal Court Affairs", appeared. This division of the Court's budget is a way to hide the financial pre-eminence granted to this department in the state's expenditure, after the emergence of popular criticisms on this matter. Indeed, both chapters' current expenditure added together rose to 14.6% of total current civil expenditure. In 2009, it made the Royal Court and the Diwan the second department of the state in terms of expenditure, after education.[74]

Thus political authority developed for more than three decades by Sultan Qaboos shows recourse to the symbolic register of "tradition" combined with arbitrary exercise of power, so that it makes vague the boundaries between the Sultan's person and the sultanistic institution. The different subterfuges used to anchor Qaboos' authority in a political tradition presented as immutable have helped to soften the sudden shift towards a nation-state built around the Sultan and, consequently, have facilitated recognition of his authority in the whole territory. However, if until recently the Omani political model has displayed considerable efficiency in the quest for a stable social order, the question is what margins of operation the ruler has now, in a context in which the recent decades' level of economic welfare came to an end.

7

LABORIOUS RENEWAL OF THE BASIS
OF THE REGIME

Behind the image the authorities have so far succeeded in maintaining, the grace period in the Sultanate that has lasted since 1970 is coming to an end. National oil production, 85% by PDO, experienced a drop of 26% between 2001 and 2007 (on average over the year, 710,400 barrels per day in 2007 against 955,700 in 2001, condensates included). In 2013, total production (condensates included) was 942,000 barrels per day.[1] At the same time, however, the share of oil in public revenue (between 70 and 75% since 2001) has not decreased, because of high crude prices on the world market. In 2012, public revenue derived from oil rose to nearly OR 11.41 billion, compared to 1.87 billion in 2001 and 4.49 billion in 2007. This huge windfall made it possible to conceal temporarily the precursory signs of exhaustion of oil, the core of Oman's social and economic development since 1970.

Moreover, the Omani population is one of the youngest in the world. Indeed, 34.3% of nationals are less than 15 years old and 44.6% less than 20, while only 6.0% of the Omanis are over 60.[2] The decline in the birth rate since the early 2000s explains that the proportion of young people (0 to 10 years old) is decreasing, but the most numerous ten-year segment (10 to 20 years old) will enter the labour market gradually in the years to come.

In this perspective, the mid-1990s were the major turning point in modern Oman's internal history. The first public marks of popular dissatisfaction since the end of the Dhofar war coincided with efforts by the Omani authorities to arouse awareness of the need to replace expatriate manpower by nationals and of the political issues involved in this.

The ambiguities of the political opening up

The double warning signal of the mid-1990s. In 1994–95 two events cast doubt on the idyllic perception of exemplary stability conveyed by the regime. In September 1995 Qais al-Zawawi, Deputy Prime Minister for Finance and Economy, died in a car accident near Salalah, while Sultan Qaboos only suffered some injuries. It was suggested that the two men, who were in the vehicle with 'Umar al-Zawawi and Eric Bennett (both wounded too), had been the target of an assassination attempt, an idea later given credence by waves of arrests. Noting the economic and political influence of the Zawawi brothers, Calvin Allen and Lynn Rigsbee comment that "dissatisfied Omanis wondered if it was not a plot against the Zawawis!"[3]

This incident involving two most prominent personalities of the regime was preceded, in 1994, by an unprecedented wave of arrests.[4] Omani Islamism, as an organised political movement, was in 1994 certainly the least developed in the Arab world. Until the 1990s, the only obvious expression of religious activism in Oman had been linked to the arrival in Muscat in 1974 of Sheikh Hasan al-Saffar, who was close to the Iraqi Shi'i Ayatollah Muhammad al-Shirazi. The young *sheikh*, who remained in Oman until the 1979 Iran Islamic revolution, opened libraries and set up religion courses. His relations with the Omani authorities were fairly good; on several occasions he invited the Mufti of Oman to the Muttrah library. Among the Shi'i population, Hasan al-Saffar found a growing audience among some young Lawatiyya, especially as the majority of the Lawatiyya community, in particular the notables and the *'ulama'*, took a jaundiced view of this young outsider claiming to explain to them how to practise Muslim rites better, and thus destabilising the natural order. After the Iranian revolution and Hasan al-Saffar's departure, the regime decided to close the Shirazi movement libraries. Several Shi'i Omanis working there chose to go into exile or to pursue their studies in Iran. Five of them were arrested when they returned to Oman in 1981, and spent several days in jail. Again, in December 1987, fifteen Lawatiyya, including a senior official of the Ministry of National Heritage and Culture, were arrested, once again because of the activity of a clandestine library supposed to be used as a base for the Shirazi movement in Oman. They were freed a few days later.[5]

The Sultan's political strategies to de-legitimise any alternative discourse and rally potential opponents to his side, and the late access to universal primary education of a society closed to the debates that have agitated the area (Arab nationalism, Islamic reformism, etc.) for most of the twentieth century, plus the difficulty of expressing criticism of a regime which has for long known how to satisfy the majority with socio-economic welfare as compensation for restrictions on personal freedom—all these factors explain the underdevelopment of Omani Islamism. When a leaflet entitled *Diwan al-mazalim* (Office of complaints), denouncing the opening of official diplomatic relations between the Omani government and Israel, began to circulate in Muscat in May 1994, it is very improbable that its authors wanted a direct confrontation with the authorities. Was their ambition to evolve into a political organised movement, even to call into question Qaboos' own legitimacy? It is by no means certain.[6]

The authorities' immediate response therefore appears ruthless and without any idea of conciliation. At the end of May, probably with the help of the Egyptian intelligence services, more than 430[7] people were arrested and questioned by the Omani police in an attempt to uncover a possible network suspected of aiming to overthrow the government. Although no official information emerged before the end of August 1994, when legal proceedings began, these events were nevertheless known to all of Omani society. No details were given of the number and identity of the detainees; the only reliable source remained the families of the suspects. When the authorities finally spoke, they talked about an Islamist secret organisation with international connections (in Egypt and Jordan), whose members were thought to belong to the Muslim Brotherhood. Its goal was, it was suggested, to use religion to divide the country, to overthrow the regime and to put an end to the newly-born experiment of representation through the Majlis al-Shura.[8] A few months later, Sultan Qaboos devoted a big part of his National Day speech to this issue, without referring to it explicitly:

> The duty of every citizen is to be the guardian of all the nation's achievements [...] It is also their duty not to allow alien ideas, masquerading as beneficial promises, to jeopardise the security and stability of this country [...] Extremism, fanaticism of whatever kind, factionalism of whatever persuasion would be hateful poisonous plants in the soil of our country which will be allowed to flourish [...] The Muslims [at the time of the Prophet] proved that Islamic Law was capable of dealing with any situation. Unfortunately, the backwardness of Muslims in recent times rendered them incapable of making use of their inheritance [...] This stagnation resulted in a weakness of the Muslim nation, which, in recent years, has brought

about fanaticism based on a lack of knowledge among the Muslim youth about the correct facts of their religion. This was exploited by some to perpetrate violence.[9]

Between 140 and 160 people were tried before a special State Security Court of seven judges, chaired by Hilal bin Hamad al-Busa'idi, former Minister of Justice.[10] Among the accused were Khamis al-Kiyumi, undersecretary for Industry in the Ministry of Commerce and Industry; Musallam Qatn, undersecretary for Agriculture; Ahmad al-Rasbi, appointed Ambassador to the United States a few months before; and Sa'id al-Ma'ashani, son of the *sheikh* of the Ma'ashani tribe, which Sultan Qaboos' mother belongs to, and a Majlis al-Shura member since 1992. Some prominent businessmen were also arrested, like Salim and Hamid al-Ghazali, members of the board of the Oman Chamber of Commerce and Industry's (OCCI) Salalah branch; and Muhammad al-Ghassani, the OCCI's Salalah branch chairman and cousin of one of the DLF founders in 1965. The trial is said to have failed to prove the preparation of a coup or any violent action,[11] but it led to sentences of between three and 20 years' imprisonment. Three people were sentenced to death, but their sentences were later commuted by royal decree to life imprisonment. A year later, the Sultan announced that he would grant royal pardons to every prisoner.

From the available personal data on 125 detainees,[12] some significant sociological tendencies become clear. Mostly Omani, they were natives of several regions of Oman (Muscat, Sharqiyya, the UAE border), though Salalah, from which more than half of the individuals came, was predominant. A large proportion of the accused was of Sunni confession (69%) while Ibadis made up the other third. Thus religious allegiance was not used as distinctive marker or rallying banner, and neither was regionalism: the movement crossed all the ethnic and regional components of society. It is nevertheless interesting to note that one of the centres around which arrested people were organised in Dhofar in 1994 was the Benevolence Society (*al-jam'iyya al-khayriyya*), named after the first association created in 1962 to help needy people, which had led to the start of a political campaign through the DLF.

Moreover, this movement was characterised by the youth of his members, since more than 77% of them were between 26 and 35. 39% held positions in government or local civil service, 9% in the army or the police force, 28% in the teaching sector. Their high level of education is striking, since more than 84% of them held at least the equivalent of a first degree. Among them, only 14.3% had religious training. Nearly 35% held engineering diplomas, especially in civil engineering, computers or electronics. More than 35% obtained their highest qualifications in Western countries, including 24% in the United States; only 14% were fully educated in Oman.

The individuals arrested thus belonged to a minority fraction of the society that we could describe as an upper middle class, the "product" of the post-1970 economic and social modernisation. These young Omanis have been able to benefit from educational opportunities to get good socio-professional positions. Such a claim was not accepted by the regime, which right away perceived in them intellectuals able to organise themselves in a structured movement and make informed criticisms of ongoing policies, and hence to rally public opinion behind their arguments. This ad hoc alliance of personalities from varied social, cultural and geographical backgrounds gave an idea of the increasing fringe of the population who wanted change and were united by educational and intellectual capital which, in their view, legitimised their involvement in the decision-making process.[13]

With the tacit approval of the international community, the government reacted by jailing and denouncing those who were accused of seeking to destabilise the country and of being related to a foreign Islamist organisation. More broadly, the authorities wished to make everybody understand that they authorised no interference in the decision-making process; no concession other than the ones granted by them was possible. If anyone aimed at something else, the official answer would be immediate and without compromise. The magnanimity towards the prisoners that Sultan Qaboos showed in November 1995 belonged to the same strategy, by emphasising that he was the only depositary of the authority which is exerted over everyone, at all times, but that he was ready to forgive unwise behaviour, provided that it did not happen again.

However, both messages were viewed as harsh warnings and would have consequences on the institutional level.

The 1996 Basic Law. The Basic Law of the State (*al-nizam al-asasi*), promulgated in November 1996 with Royal Decree no. 101/96, emerged from this stormy political context. Announced by the Sultan himself on the occasion of his annual tour, this event was not preceded by any public debate or communication. As with previous political moves in the Sultanate, this first Omani constitutional law can be seen as the Sultan's granting of rights to his subjects, rather than a negotiated concession. The decree promulgating the Law, which begins with the words "We, Qaboos bin Sa'id, Sultan of Oman...," confirms this, and avoids any reference to other entities (like the nation or God).

Several days later, the sovereign presented it as a logical step in Omani nation-building since 1970:

"Crowning the efforts of a quarter of a century of fruitful work, we have issued the Basic Statute of the State, which is the distillation of the experience gained over the past years. This historic document has provided the blueprint for the system of governance, the principles for the direction of policies, public rights and duties, and the responsibilities and authority of the Head of State, the Cabinet and the Judiciary."[14]

The text has seven chapters and 81 articles. The Sultanate is described in Article 1 as an Arab and Islamic state; Articles 2 and 3 establish Islam and Arabic as the religion and the official language of the state, while the *sharia* constitutes the basis of legislation. No explicit mention is made of the Ibadi legacy. All citizens are equal before the law; no discrimination on the basis of sex, origin, colour, language, religion, sect (*madhhab*), residence or social status is allowed (Article 17), while freedom of religious practice is recognised (Article 28). The system of government is described as a "hereditary Sultanate... based on justice, Shura consultation and equality" (Articles 5, 9). The principles and the procedures of succession to the throne are formalised in Articles 5, 6, and 7 (see below).

The second part of the Basic Law deals with the political, economic, social, cultural and security principles behind state politics. Among the political principles, the pre-eminence of the tradition of "consultation" (*shura*) is highlighted: "laying suitable foundations for the establishment of the pillars of genuine Shura consultation, based on the national heritage, its values and its Islamic sharia, and on pride in its history" must be pursued (Article 10, Paragraph 3). While the focus is on the principle of a free economy, the role of the state in development is underlined; all natural resources are the property of the state which draws up economic guidelines through Plans (Article 11). On social matters, the state guarantees justice, equality of opportunity, medical assistance, rights to work and education, while the family is the basis of the society (Article 12).

National pride is stressed on several occasions. Education is supposed to "create a generation strong in body and moral fibre, proud of its nation (*umma*), country (*watan*) and heritage, and committed to safeguarding their achievements" (Art. 13, Paragraph 2). Similarly, it is a duty for everyone to reinforce national unity and to safeguard the country (*ta'ziz al-wahda al-wataniyya wajib*, Article 12, Paragraph 2; Article 14, Paragraph 1; Article 38), while defence of the homeland is a sacred duty (*wajib muqaddas*, Art. 37). Regarding the state, it fosters the national heritage and safeguards it (Article 13, Paragraph 4). As Nikolaus Siegfried noted, the Basic Law closely connects the notions of *umma* and *watan*, which refer to Oman, its unity and indivisibility.[15]

The third part deals with general rights and duties. Deportation, forced exile (Article 16) and torture are banished (Articles 20 and 26). Presumption of innocence and inviolability of dwellings are assured (Articles 22 and 27), as well as freedoms of opinion, assembly and correspondence, but within the limits of the law (Article 29, 30 and 32).[16] Freedom of the press is also guaranteed, provided that it does not lead to public discord (*fitna*) or violate the security of the state; in practice, these restrictions favour self-censorship. Financial and psychological tutelage exerted by the Ministry of Information is total, and is even strengthened by the fact that the majority of journalists are still foreigners (in particular Indians and Egyptians). As for freedom to form associations (Article 33), it is guaranteed insofar as they are constituted "on a national basis for legitimate objectives" and their activities are not "inimical to social order".

The division of political powers is at the heart of the fourth section. The sultan is "the symbol of national unity as well as its guardian and defender" as head of state and supreme commander of the armed forces (Article 41). Article 42 enumerates—although not exhaustively—his powers, especially those of promulgating and ratifying laws. He takes all measures to counter any threat to the safety of the Sultanate, its people, and its territory. Besides his large powers of appointment and dismissal, he can grant pardons and commute sentences. Finally, Article 41 explicitly states that his person is inviolable, that respecting him is a duty, and that his orders must be obeyed.

Articles 44–55 establish that the sovereign will be helped and advised by the Council of Ministers, to which is given the task to implementing general state policies (determined by the Sultan, Article 42); the Council of Ministers may submit recommendations and proposals to the sultan, the latter being free to choose whether or not to follow them (Article 44, Paragraph 1). Article 45 plans for a possible prime minister, who would preside over the Council's sessions; his responsibilities would be specified later by royal decree (Article 48). The main oath of members of the Council of Ministers is an oath of allegiance and loyalty to the ruler and the country (Article 50). The Council is also collectively and personally responsible for the general policy of the state and for the actions of their respective departments (Article 52). Furthermore, Article 53 introduces the notion of a "conflict of interest" between the governmental and economic spheres. It forbids members of the

Council of Ministers to combine their ministerial positions with the chairmanship or membership of the board of any joint stock company. The departments they head cannot deal with issues in which they have direct or indirect interests. Generally, they must not use their official positions to promote a personal interest.

Until 2011, the fifth part briefly dealt with the Council of Oman, whose attributions and structures of which are now laid down by law. The following part deals with the judiciary, whose independence is proclaimed in article 60, while the judges are subjected to no other power than the law (Article 61); except in case of martial law, the military courts are only competent to judge crimes committed by members of the armed forces and the security forces (Article 62). Nevertheless, all judges are appointed by the ruler. Article 70 evokes the possibility of checks on the constitutionality of laws, which would result obviously in restriction of the sultan's arbitrary power. The last part of the Law deals with various general provisions, such as the conformity of ordinary laws to the provisions of the Basic Law (Article 79). Lastly, the Law can only be amended by royal decree (Article 81).

When the Sultanate adopted the Basic Law in 1996, it was unanimously welcomed by the international community, which saw in it a step towards the establishment of a constitutional parliamentary monarchy. The text favoured constitutionalisation of the sultan's prerogatives, which were defined explicitly for the first time. Furthermore, it acknowledged a set of inalienable rights and individual liberties in the judicial, economic, and social spheres. It provides a series of innovations allowing for improvements in political transparency, for instance the creation of the Council of Oman, succession procedures, Article 53 on conflicts of interest between political and economic activity, etc.

However, this last provision did not lead to any real change in governance. Only two businessmen in the Cabinet left their positions in the following months: Sa'id al-Shanfari, replaced in December 1997 by Muhammad al-Romhi, and Muhammad al-Yusef, replaced in late 1997. In contrast other members of merchant families, like Ahmad Makki and Maqbul al-Sultan, and individuals who benefited from the opportunities offered by Qaboos to play in both political and economic fields, like Yusef bin 'Alawi and Salim al-Ma'ashani, are still in the Cabinet in 2017; some of these businessmen even entered the government after the promulgation of the Basic Law, like Juma'a bin 'Ali and Salim al-Khalili (both in 2001). While the successive reshuffles since 1997 allowed younger personalities (often too readily described as "technocrats") to enter, this movement has not led, far from it, to the removal from the Cabinet of families historically powerful in economic activity.

Moreover, this text ratifies a paternalistic conception of a state whose guide is the sultan. He is responsible for the country's development, a symbol of its unity and an embodiment of services upon which Omanis are dependent in their daily lives. This gives him the legitimacy to accord himself the right to control every political, economic, and social system. If the text bears all the attributes of a political and legal modernity commonly understood at the beginning of twenty-first century, it is in keeping with a tradition of clan patriarchs whose authority and role of arbitration must be imposed upon all tribesmen while, in return, their task is to ensure the protection and subsistence of the *'asabiyya* members. The prerogatives of government (Article 50) and advisory bodies (Article 56) are aimed explicitly at limiting those institutions to assisting the ruler, the only master of guidance. The multiple restrictions on individual rights throughout the text (*fi hudud al-qanun*)—in particular on freedom of the press, opinion or assembly—illustrate this situation perfectly: the sultan has all the prerogatives of executive and legislative power in the country.

The different institutional answers to popular dissatisfaction in 1994 and 1995, such as granting a Basic Law or enlarging the Majlis al-Shura electorate, did not stop underground "eruptions". In the autumn of 1997 twelve people, among them the secretary of the Commander of the Omani Navy, Shihab bin Tariq, were arrested for "action against the security of the state", because of sympathy and financial support allegedly given to Ayatollah Shirazi's Islamic Action Organisation; they were accused of transmitting confidential documents to Iran and working to overthrow the government and establish an Islamic regime.[17] They were condemned to jail terms from six months to seven years; contrary to what happened in 1994, they were not amnestied by the Sultan and appear to have served all their sentences.

In early 2002 a cache of weapons was discovered in Muttrah by the Omani police, allegedly on the basis of Egyptian intelligence information.[18] In the same year, a militant of the Indonesian organisation Jemaah Islamiyah was caught in Oman and extradited to Singapore, where he was suspected of being "the brain of a plan for attacks against American and Israeli targets".[19] In August, the London newspaper *al-Sharq al-Awsat* reported the dismantling in Oman of a "cell of the al-Qaida network" whose members were said to have been immediately transferred to the United States; the newspaper's American source welcomed "the efforts of the Omani authorities" in this operation.[20] Without denying the operation itself, Oman immediately informed everyone that "no individual was delivered to the United States, in accordance with the Sultanate's policy".[21] Lastly, several dozen Omanis were said to have entered

Iraq via Syria and Jordan to fight the American forces since 2003.[22] Officially, no Omani has been held in Guantánamo Bay.

Political arrests in 2005. In January 2005, rumours of arrests in Muscat and Inner Oman circulated on local Internet forums. Some weeks later, the *al-Hayat* daily's correspondent in Oman revealed that about three hundred people were being detained for questioning, after weapons were discovered in a truck near the Yemeni border. According to this source, these individuals intended to plan "explosions (*tafjirat*) targeting the Muscat Festival, which was boycotted by Islamists who deem it against the precepts of Islam"; it was also rumoured that explosions were planned for the first days of the Aid al-Adha against shopping malls and an oil complex.[23] The threat was considered so credible by the Omani authorities that Sultan Qaboos failed to attend the Aid prayers—for the first time since 1970—on the occasion of his annual tour.[24] Soon afterwards the Information Minister, Hamad al-Rashdi, acknowledged these arrests, at the same time playing down their extent and refusing to give details.[25]

The trial began on 18 April before the State Security Court, chaired by Sayyid Hilal al-Busa'idi. Among the 31 people finally accused, teachers and students of the Education and Islamic Studies colleges of Sultan Qaboos university were included, as well as the head of the Omani delegation for the pilgrimage and son-in-law of the Mufti, Kahlan al-Kharusi, and the controller of the mosques at the Sultan's palace office, Salih al-Ribkhi. All those arrested belonged to the Ibadi school. It is worth noting that the authorities were forced to take into consideration the heightened international sensitivities towards violence against political competitors or challengers. Contrary to the practices in force in Oman until then, the regime had to ensure transparency and to justify its actions. For the first time in comparable events, the accused were allowed defence counsel, while a local press journalist, and the defendants' family members and representatives of the Majlis al-Shura and the State Council, were permitted to attend the trial.

The verdict was delivered on 2 May; six defendants, convicted of having leading positions in the organisation, were sentenced to twenty years' imprisonment, twelve to ten-year terms, twelve others were given seven years and one was jailed for one year. They could not appeal against the verdict, but only ask for the Sultan's pardon. The public prosecution accused them of having belonged to a banned secret organisation, which was established in all the *wilaya*s of the north of Oman; there may have been a public arm which organised youth summer camps, and an underground wing that attempted to overthrow the current regime by force to establish an Ibadi imamate.[26] Defence counsel for the accused always denied the political dimension of the organisation, but focused on its religious character and on the shared desire of all of them to "defend the Ibadi doctrine".[27] No connection with networks abroad or with international organisations was shown during the trial.

For the first time since the Imamate fell in 1959, Ibadism seemed to have arisen as a rallying reference for political mobilisation. Protest in the name of the Ibadi Imamate could lead to demands for an Islamic government, which would openly contradict the legitimacy of the nation-state built by and around Sultan Qaboos since 1970.

The strong reaction on the part of the regime is therefore not surprising. Nevertheless, several questions remain unanswered. Why did the authorities decide to apprehend these individuals only in 2005, while they claimed to have been watching over them for a long time, during which time they were given complete freedom to spread their ideas, especially within the *sharia* institutes that several of the accused headed? And why did the Sultan decide to pardon all of them only one month after the verdict, if these individuals were as dangerous for the country's stability as the official propaganda asserted? Without necessarily arguing that the whole affair was built up from nothing by the government, one cannot fail to see that the government is the main beneficiary: the Omani regime showed both firmness and magnanimity with opponents or people attracted by opposition. Moreover, at the international level, the United States, in the name of the "war on terror", had put strong pressure on the regimes of the region since September 11. Thus the Sultan aimed at reassuring his Western partners, showing that he was able to maintain the stability of Oman and dismantle every so-called terrorist group before it could do anything.

Just as "Communism" was for long used as a label to discredit any people questioning the current political model, nowadays it is the "fight against Islamism"—an enemy all the more "politically correct" since September 11— that is invoked by the regime in order to blame without distinction every "breach of national security", and then present the use of force as unavoidable. While the actual ideas with which the government charged the accused— most of whom held graduate and postgraduate university qualifications[28]— were not widespread, a large fringe of Ibadi Omani youth felt sympathy towards them. On the eve of the verdict, several hundred demonstrators marched in Muscat demanding their acquittal, with shouts of "our *sheikh*s are innocent".[29] Many more gathered after the verdict to demonstrate against the heavy jail sentences, which led to light clashes with the police. Islamist ideas, even if their holders are not yet politically organised, are constantly spreading in Omani society and channelling economic and social discontent. As a human rights activist noted, the regime proceeded to a "pre-emptive strike"[30] in order to remind everyone where the boundaries not to cross were.

Afterwards 'Abd Allah al-Riyami, who had been active in exposing on the Internet the arrests and detentions of the spring of 2005, publicised by the same means, in June, the arrest and prosecution of a former Seeb representative in the Majlis al-Shura, Tayyiba al-Ma'awali. She, who attended the trial of the thirty-one as an observer, was charged with slandering officials via the telephone and Internet, and criticising Oman's political liberalisation in foreign media. The court sentenced her on 13 July to a year and a half in prison, a penalty reduced to six months by the court of appeal. Her refusal to acknowledge her misdeeds officially, contrary to what the accused in the spring trial did, seems to have prevented her from benefiting from a royal pardon. Moreover, two days before the court issued the verdict against her, 'Abd Allah al-Riyami was asked to present himself to the police for interrogation. During his detention for one week, he was warned that there was an "open file" on him.[31] He was then told he should either stop criticising the authorities or leave the country. Tayyiba al-Ma'awali was freed on 30 January 2006.

In November 2006, the main Internet discussion forum *Omania* was closed down by the Omani authorities and its founder, Sa'id al-Rashdi, arrested. The latter was prosecuted at the end of March 2007, together with three other managers of the website and a dozen individuals who posted messages; they were charged with spreading false information about the economic activities of some members of the government. While all the managers of the website were acquitted, several of the other defendants, who participated in the discussion on-line, were sentenced to 300 to 400 OR fines, and one of them was sent to prison for a month.[32]

Uncertainty about the succession. Before 1996 and the Basic Law, Sultan Qaboos had never said anything about his succession. The principles and the procedures of succession to the throne are formalised—for the first time in Omani history—in Articles 5, 6, and 7. Only Muslim male descendants of Turki bin Sa'id who are legitimate sons of Omani Muslim parents are eligible to become sultan. When the throne is vacant, the "Ruling Family Council" (*Majlis al-'A'ila al-hakima*) is required to meet within three days to designate a successor. Before amendments to the Basic Law announced in 2011, if the members of the Family failed to choose someone, the "Defence Council" (*Majlis al-Difaʿ*) confirmed the person designated beforehand by the sultan in a message addressed to the Ruling Family Council. In 1997, Sultan Qaboos announced that he had "already written down two names, in descending order, and put them in sealed envelopes in two different regions", probably in order to avoid the possibility that a single individual could manipulate the royal will.[33]

To a certain extent the procedure—as it is defined by the lineage of Sayyid Turki—leaves the succession open. No crown prince is designated in Oman, for obvious reasons: not only there was no direct heir in 2017, but Qaboos, who himself overthrew his father, is very careful to avoid being victim of a political practice common in Omani history. Nevertheless, several questions remain. First, the succession provisions have led to discussions among the Omani population, especially among Ibadis. As a government official explained to the author,

"This decision has been difficult to [accept] for many people, particularly among the old ones, because it goes against the Omani tradition and heritage. Ibadi thought relies on consensus and on general agreement to choose the best to lead. The Omanis prefer no choice [to] a bad choice. Now it is out of the question that the next Sultan be of another lineage than Al Turki."[34]

Finally, it is necessary to note the central role played by people outside the Al Saʿid family through the Defence Council, which has formalised their influence in Omani politics since 1970. The Council is created by the Basic Law, and "studies matters concerning the maintenance of the Sultanate's security and defence" (Article 14, Paragraph 2). According to decree no. 105/96, the Council is chaired by the Sultan and is composed of the Director of the Office of the Supreme Commander, the Minister of the Palace Office, the Inspector-General of Police and Customs, the Chief of Staff of the SAF, the respective commanders of the Land Forces, the Air Force, the Royal Guard, and the Navy, and the head of internal security (the ISS).[35] The role of this body external to the royal family raises questions. Up to what point is the royal family ready to be deprived of supreme decision making by a body composed of members who owe their position to Qaboos only? Moreover, in spite of the precautions taken by the ruler, is not there a risk of seeing contradictory messages emerging, a situation which would involve political confusion?

Sultan Qaboos has no direct descendants. This only makes the succession more delicate because it is more open. The highest personalities in official protocol do not seem to be able to claim the throne: Sayyid Fahd bin Mahmud, whose children's mother is of French origin, cannot plan to pass the kingship to one of them after his death while the Minister of Diwan, Sayyid Khalid bin Hilal, does not belong to the lineage of Sayyid Turki. The more probable candidates are thus three sons of Tariq bin Taimur, who are Qaboos' first cousins: Haitham, As'ad and Shihab. Sayyid Haitham is the only one to have held official governmental positions.

Despite all the political uncertainties, politics continues to be largely perceived in Oman as something which divides and which can be a source of problems. Until 2011, the regime had succeeded in anchoring in younger generations' minds that there are better things to do than getting involved in politics. Thus, on the occasion of a discussion relating to a failed coup d'état in Mauritania in June 2003, one person suggested, as a joke, that it would be necessary to plan a revolution in Oman too. A young civil servant of Hirth tribe then exclaimed, referring to the 1950s: "I leave the revolution to you! My family has already tried it, and it did not work! As for me, I will do the revolution this evening, on my PlayStation!"

The rigidity of the system, though seldom openly denounced, is nevertheless felt intensely, as a civil servant who graduated in Kuwait said: "Omani intellectuals are employed by the university, they read books and at 14.30, they go back home and sleep. The government forbids them to carry out interviews and investigations... And in exchange they earn their salaries without any problem! They are afraid because they are told that, if they start working, all that they do can be used by foreigners against Oman."[36]

This co-optation has also affected independent personalities, as a moderate critic explained: "There are intellectuals in Oman, but they do not speak. When you talk seriously, they run away because they are afraid, but also because they are ashamed. They fought for revolution, they had strong ideas but now they totally depend on their position. They know that they are trapped."[37]

Another intellectual regretted that Majlis al-Shura elections in 2003 were not about any real issues at all: "How can we talk about democracy here? There is no press, no journalist, people believe that Majlis al-Shura universal suffrage means democracy but it is not true. No international organisation, no expert will come to observe the elections. Why?"[38] Another interviewee pushed the argument even further: "Anyway, this situation suits everyone because the Americans know well that if we have democracy in Oman, the Islamists will win and the new policy will be hostile to them."[39]

Some among the graduate younger generation do not even hesitate to question the official historiography of the *nahda*: "For us, 1970 is dust now, it is history. What matters for us is what happens now [...] Everyone recalls the *sabla*.[40] But it is a joke! Nothing anymore is discussed inside; only news of marriages, deaths, family rumours are exchanged..."[41]

Until 2011 even if some talked, in private discussions, about the price of the Sultan's new jet or his holidays abroad, criticisms of the ruler were usually made indirectly. They generally took the form of attacks on the incompetence and corruption of ministers or mobilisations about international issues—despite the prohibition of any demonstrations in Oman. For instance, on the occasion of the second Intifada in Palestine, in September 2000, a hundred Omanis organised a sit-in in front of the United States embassy and chanted slogans such as: "Arab leaders, America is the mother of terrorism" or "Arab leaders, are your armies asleep?"[42]

The September 11 attacks and the Taliban regime's overthrow in October 2001 aroused passions all over the country. Two apparently contradictory feelings mingled. The first was amused amazement—not to say jubilation—aroused by the attacks throughout society, and the undeniable popularity of Osama Bin Laden in the following months.[43] This sympathy for an individual seen as a paragon of resistance to the Western world and as the pride of the humiliated Arabs emerges in the words of a young man: "I agree with Bin Laden! Sometimes, he says the truth! These non-believers betray us! All! King Abdullah, King Muhammad VI, Mubarak!"[44] Mentioning both of the Sultan's closest allies is obviously not innocent here...

In the spring of 2003, this identity frustration was gradually transferred to the ground of Iraq. Demonstrations, gathering a hundred Omani people, took place in Muscat and Salalah in the spring 2003. They were closely supervised by the Omani police to stop them overflowing towards major axes of communication or embassies. Slogans made indirect criticisms of the Omani government's international policy rather than the American offensive itself. In Arabic, they referred to the American military aircrafts present on Omani territory: "Shame, shame on Oman!" or "Omanis are free in their country; Americans out!"[45] In private discussions, nevertheless, some Omanis did not hide their support for the American intervention in Iraq. One businessman from Muscat explained that "all the area's regimes are puppets of America. Therefore they can say nothing against America's will to attack Iraq, even if they know that they can be the next on the list [...] I support a change of regime in Iraq from outside; we need change, but we cannot change by ourselves."[46]

For all those who were not hostile to the United States' decision, the same argument is implicit: the Arabs are not able to overthrow their regimes alone;

they need the interference of a foreign actor to accelerate the course of history. To some extent, they join the opponents of the military intervention, who call into question the order established by the region's conservative governments (monarchies or "monarchising" presidential regimes). In both cases, it is the Sultan's political authority, and especially its most centralised part, that is indirectly targeted. In the absence of any possibility of organising politically or expressing proposals for reform, these public demonstrations were used as safety valves, like tiny concessions granted by the regime to an Omani civil society more and more in phase with the wider Arab one.

So, if the Sultanate enjoyed relative political calm until 2011, it was not free from properly political challenges. But in the 2000s the most crucial difficulties were arising in the socio-economic field. The economic slowdown in the 1980s, combined with the emergence of endemic unemployment among the younger generations, led to implementation of policies favouring nationals in employment in Kuwait, Saudi Arabia and Bahrain—with more or less encouraging results.[47] This issue remains more than ever one of the public policy priorities, especially in Oman.

Nationalisation of employment (ta'min)

The authorities' early awareness of the social issues. Although the role of foreign workers in the economy has become one of the most sensitive issues in Omani public debate, it is certainly not something recent. The massive influx of workers from the Indian sub-continent and Middle Eastern countries (Egypt, Sudan, Jordan) in quest of employment started after 1970. Official Omani figures state that foreigners represented 7% of the workforce (both public and private sectors) in 1970—and 65% ten years later! Between 1980 and 1985, the number of foreign workers doubled in the private sector (from 131,000 in 1980 to 275,000 in 1985) as well as in the public sector (27,500 against 15,400).

The first Omanisation steps occurred in the military sector after the end of the Dhofar war. The proportion of national officers in the army increased from 51% in 1980 to 62% in 1985.[48] On the civilian side, the Minister of Labour announced in April 1987 that it was forbidden to hire foreigners in eleven categories of jobs, like public relations officer, security officer, driver, bus or taxi driver, fisherman and shepherd.[49] This decree represented the first major step aimed at slowing down the increase in numbers of foreign workers in the Sultanate.

Sultan Qaboos himself decided to intervene in the debate early on, as in January 1988:

We are giving special attention to the establishment of new rules for regulating the employment of national manpower in the private and government sectors. These rules should secure the gradual replacement of expatriates by Omanis [...] Omanis should [...] play a substantial role in all fields, noone should shun the jobs of his father and forefathers, or hesitate to make use of the job opportunities available in the private sector on the pretext that he holds an academic degree and that he should have a government job.[50]

In April 1990, a British press correspondent noted that "Diversification and Omanisation are Oman's obsessions, the Muscat 'buzz words'".[51] The ruler called on the *sheikh*s and notables to "push youth to get on the job market. This encouragement is their most important duty".[52] In 1995 the Sultan tempered people's concerns by explaining that "Any talk of unemployment in this country is talk of artificial unemployment and not real unemployment. The result of [the 1993] census [...] showed the existence of an estimated half-a-million strong expatriate workforce, while the number of job seekers does not exceed 30,000. Where is the unemployment [...] if the citizen really wanted to work? But if he makes excuses, then it is a different matter."[53]

Underemployment of youth was thus considered to be an individual matter, without any link with the Omani socio-economic structure itself.

In October 1994, the Ministry of Labour and Social Affairs announced quotas to be respected in various branches of the private sector; in 2000, the nationals would have to be 60% of employees in the storage, communications and transport sectors; 45% in finance, insurance and real estate; 35% in industry, and 30% in hotels and catering. The following year, a tax to finance Omanis' vocational training was deducted from companies proportionally to the number of expatriate employees; this had the additional motive of diminishing the salary differentials between nationals and foreigners. Until the mid-1990s, the absorption by the civil and military public sectors of the majority of Omanis entering the labour market had hidden the slowness of Omanisation in companies, which did not take the official injunction seriously.

In parallel to the Fifth Plan (1996–2000) aiming to promote the private sector's share in the economy, a long-term programme entitled "Oman 2020: Vision for Oman's Economy" was established in June 1995. Two series of objectives over a 25-year period were set out. The first was economic diversification: the oil sector's share in Oman's GDP had to fall from 41% in 1996 to 9% by 2020, while that of gas was to increase from less than 1% to 10%, and that of non-oil industries from 7.5% to 29%. The second had to do with human resources and employment. First, it was planned to help raise women's share in the working population from 6% in 1995 to 12% in 2020, so as to reach a total rate of 50% of the working population. At the same time, the rates of nationals in public and private sectors must increase from 68 to 95% and from 7.5 to 75% respectively, while the share of expatriates in the whole population must be reduced from 25% in 1995 to 15% by 2020.

Confronted with young Omanis' reluctance to take private sector jobs, less well paid and categorised as jobs for Asian immigrants, Sultan Qaboos reminded people in November 1998 that "all Omani youth should accept this work unhesitatingly and without false pride."[54] The true turning point in government policy came two years later.

Faster progress since 2000. The Sixth Plan (2001–5) again focused on economic diversification, through tourism and industry, and on the growing role the private sector has to play. On employment, the authorities planned that 134,000 Omanis would enter the labour market during these five years. They estimated the number of jobs available at 110,000, 92% in the private sector.[55] The Plan provided for total Omanisation over five years in 24 low-skilled occupations, including fruit and vegetables truck drivers, food and drink employees and retailers, fuel station employees, telephone services, etc. Other more technical professions, like those of electrician, plumber, goldsmith, tailor, hairdresser and painter, were supposed to follow suit.

In October 2001 Sultan Qaboos convened in Saham and 'Ibri a symposium on the national workforce, in which ministers and private sector representatives took part. The latter were invited to involve in this "national challenge" and comply more strictly with regulations on recruitment of expatriates and attainment of Omanisation quotas. Two months later a Ministry of Manpower was set up, by amalgamating the Ministry of Labour with those of Social Affairs and Vocational Training; Juma'a bin 'Ali was appointed as Minister. In the days preceding the second symposium on Omanisation in February 2003 in Ibra, the authorities uttered an unusual *mea culpa*, by acknowledging the inconsistencies and failures of the former programmes as well as the economic impossibility of doing without expatriates in the near future.[56] A Five-Year Plan for Omanisation (2003–7) was drawn up; it defined for each branch ambitious rates to achieve in 2007. Moreover it focused on the sensitive question of vocational training, the Achilles heel of Omani education. On this occasion, two programmes to help young Omanis to set up their companies were stressed. Called *Intilaqa* ("rise") and *Sanad* ("support"), they allow Omanis to have state-funded training in an institution or a company, after which each can create his own company, while using the franchise of the company in which he has been trained (or receiving state financial assistance, in the *Intilaqa* programme).[57] Moreover the government decided to pay the fees of more than half of the young Omanis trained in private institutions, on condition of assured employment in a company at the end. The state also supplied land free to private higher education institutions, and up to 50% of the capital, and granted them a 10-year exemption from all taxes on companies.[58] In the academic year 2011–12, the Sultanate had 27 private institutions of higher education.

In May 2003, the Ministry of the National Economy announced that Oman's plan was to have in 2020 one million jobs occupied by Omanis, whereas the number of available jobs for nationals and expatriates in 2003 was 750,000.[59] The two following years were devoted to complete Omanisation of other low-skilled positions, like drivers (of buses, heavy vehicles, ambulances, etc.) and food industry employees. In February 2005, on the occasion of the Sultan's annual tour, Qaboos repeated the importance of the young generations' employment issue: "Young people must involve themselves in their job when they get one, and must show an exemplary behaviour. Involvement in the job is a duty, and if the job is available today, it may not be the case tomorrow any more." The Sultan stressed that "The family assumes the responsibility of the children' ideas and behaviour and has to instil in children the spirit of work." Finally he explained, "Unemployment (*batala*) is a terrible word and nobody understands it at all. It is better to use the term 'people in search of employment' (*bahath al-'amal*)."[60]

As for immigration, there was a turning point in official policy in 2000. Although the authorities relied heavily on the people of Omani origin abroad to take part in the country's development in the 1970s, they never welcomed this workforce with excessive enthusiasm. Many of them had to settle in the UAE from the 1980s, as it was already impossible to get residence permits in Oman. At the moment, a *de facto* moratorium on the return of Omanis from Africa seems in force, in order to "avoid 'unfair' competition with locals".[61] The government sets limits to the issuing of Omani documents to Omanis who live in Africa, as they are thought likely to compete with young home Omani job-seekers. One of our informants, who himself is trying to have his Tanzania-passport nephew come to Oman, complains: "To get an Omani visa is like getting a visa for paradise! I hope paradise looks like something else than here..."[62]

Measures to catch illegal immigrants were also tightened, as was shown by strengthened police checks on roads leading to the UAE from 2003, and checks on the coasts also, to intercept clandestine migrants crossing the Gulf of Oman. More than 40,000 illegal Pakistani immigrants are said to have been sent back to Karachi in deplorable conditions every year since 2004. Throughout years 2006 and 2007 flights chartered by the Omani government deported every year more than 15,000 Indians whose passports had been confiscated by the Omani sponsors on their arrival and who were working illegally after their work permits expired.[63]

Balance sheet and prospects. Since 2000, the whole Sultanate has been mobilised to take up the challenge of employment of young Omanis, of whom 50,000 every year leave school and university (with or without degrees) and enter the labour market, while 45% of the population is less than 20 years old. By comparison with similar policies in the neighbouring countries, the Sultanate can be proud of undeniable successes, especially in the civil service sector. In December 2012 that sector showed an average Omanisation rate of 85.8%, constantly rising for the last decade (Table 2). Although the absolute number of expatriates has increased again since 2009, most government departments display very high Omanisation rates,[64] like the Interior (99.9%), and Oil and Gas (99.6%). But the Ministries of Education and Health are far behind (89% and 69.8% respectively), and so are the Diwan and the Royal Court (74.7%). These four departments represent 71% of all civil service employees.

Table 2: Proportion of nationals and expatriates in the Omani civil service sector since 2005 (in December), in thousands

	2005	2006	2007	2008	2009	2010	2011	2012
Number of Nationals	109.4	116.1	124.4	131.2	136.6	140.4	159.3	166.8
Balance of nationals (Compared to the year before)	+5.2	+6.7	+8.3	+6.8	+5.4	+3.8	+18.9	+7.5
Rate of Nationals (in %)	*82.6*	*83.6*	*84.7*	*85.5*	*85.6*	*85.6*	*86.4*	*85.8*
Number of expatriates	23	22.7	22.5	22.3	22.9	23.6	25.2	27.5
Total	132.4	138.8	146.9	153.5	159.5	164.0	184.4	194.3
Total annual growth rate (in %)	*4.2*	*4.8*	*5.8*	*4.5*	*3.9*	*2.8*	*12.4*	*5.4*

Source: calculation based on the figures available on the National Centre for Statistics and Information website (www.ncsi.gov.om).

As for the private sector, the main success has occurred with the *Sanad* programme, which allowed more than 15,000 young Omanis, between 2002 and 2005, to establish their own businesses, sponsored by major companies.[65] Moreover, it is becoming more and more difficult to find expatriates managing groceries or other small shops outside Muscat, and for the first time the number of expatriates employed in the sales sector started to decrease in 2004. Lastly, 92% of employees in the private banking sector were Omani in late 2013.

However, the overall Omanisation rate in the private sector (10.9%) remained low in May 2014 also, because the number of active expatriates has increased tremendously since the beginning of 2006 (Table 3). Among them Indians are predominant, since they represent 39% of expatriates in the private sector; immigrants from the whole Indian subcontinent account for 88.3 % of the foreigners. As for non-Omani Arabs, mostly Egyptians and Sudanese, they represent only 3.1% of foreign workers in the private sector while they are 55 % of those in the public sector. In 2003, a change in the statistical way of counting the workforce in the private sector led to removal from the table of 160,000 immigrants. A prominent businessman of Muscat regretted that "Figures published periodically are contradictory and unintelligible. It is just not possible to get an overview of what happens."[66]

Besides, the public sector has had a wide capacity to absorb newcomers on the job market, by tolerating a high degree of nepotism and easing a rapid turnover of positions with full-rate retirement pensions after a small number of working years. Although the number of civil servants is not in keeping with the effective amount of work to be done, the public sector still grows. This is due partly to the widely shared perception of a paternalist state, depository of the oil rent, which is supposed, more or less explicitly, to have the task of finding jobs for nationals. But young Omanis' preference for public sector jobs, better paid and with adapted work schedules, also contributes very much to it.

Despite the new policy orientation aimed at giving the private sector a major role in youth employment, the private job market is still far from taking over from the government sector as an employment safety valve, because of unresolved structural problems. One of the most sensitive of these relates to nationals' training, more precisely to its adequacy to meet companies' needs. While the progress accomplished for ten years, with the opening of many technical and vocational institutes, cannot be denied, they are able to admit only between eight and ten thousand people every year. Many private sector employers complain that the training given remains far removed from the task the employee will be assigned. Others, used to the extreme flexibility of the

OMAN

Table 3: Proportion of nationals and expatriates in the private sector and on the whole job market since 2005 (in December every year), in thousands (Security and defence forces excluded)

	2005	2006	2007	2008	2009	2010	2011	2012	2013
Number of nationals in the private sector	98.5	114.3	131.8	147.2	158.3	177.7	174.4	172.1	181.9
Rate of nationals (in %)	18.8	18.3	17.1	15.6	15.3	15.7	13.5	11.6	10.6
Number of expatriates in the private sector	424.8	510.7	638.4	794.9	874.2	955.6	1114.6	1316.2	1527.2
Rate of expatriates (in %)	81.2	81.7	82.9	84.4	84.7	84.3	86.5	88.4	89.4
Total private sector employees	523.3	625.0	770.2	942.1	1032.6	1133.3	1289.0	1488.2	1709.1
Total active population (private + public civil sectors)	655.6	763.8	917.1	1095.6	1192.1	1297.3	1473.4	1682.6	–
Overall rate of Omanisation of the job market (in %)	31.7	30.2	27.9	27.5	24.7	24.5	22.6	20.1	–

Source: calculations based on figures available on the National Centre for Statistics and Information website (www.ncsi.gov.om).

expatriate workforce, are critical of Omanis' lack of motivation and work commitment, but also of their poor command of the English language. The Minister of Manpower himself admitted in March 2005 that more than 48,300 Omanis left their jobs in the private sector between 2001 and 2004, either on their own initiative or by decision of the company.[67]

An even more basic problem concerns the asymmetry of status on the job market between Omanis and immigrants, especially those from Asia. The nationals enjoy a set of social measures the expatriates do not have, for instance a minimum wage (OR 325 for a full-time unskilled job[68]) and protection against dismissal except for a serious fault. While these provisions have a legitimate aim of protecting employees, the fact that they lead to a distinction between two categories of employees with unequal rights penalises *de facto* the nationals' access to jobs. A former senior state official who went over to the private sector summarised the situation with explicit words: "Never will a government will be able to force companies to prefer badly-trained Omanis to experienced Indians, with a salary three to five times lower."[69]

The manager of an oil industry supply company said even more explicitly:

It is 50% more expensive to have an Omani employee than an Indian one, the job and conditions being equal, and even if you take into account the legal penalties linked to the issuing of a labour card for an expatriate. You can ask an Indian worker to stay two years night and day at an oil site in the desert for OR 35 per month; with an Omani, it's not possible because he has a family and he will ask to come back from Wednesday night to Saturday morning to Muscat and you have to pay him OR 120! So I prefer to pay an Omani and ask him to stay at home, and keep the Indian guy working.[70]

This practice is not the only one used by businessmen to get round the authorities' orders dealing with Omanisation, as the manager of a training company in the oil sector explained:

Everyone fiddles his Omanisation rates and everyone acts as if there was nothing. There are several techniques for cheating, everyone does it. First, it is possible to include our Omani trainees, who are training in our clients' companies, in our official Omanisation balance sheets. This increases the Omanisation rates artificially. Another system involves paying the Omanis well, so as to make them rise one or several skill levels. Thus a well-paid worker can be registered as a technician, so that the number of Omani technicians or skilled workers of the company increases. The Ministry of Manpower is happy and turns a blind eye to the other Omanisation rates of the company.[71]

Many employers consider frankly that Omanisation is a handicap, some even suggesting that Omanisation could be a "tax on business".[72] This point is obviously disputed by the authorities, which recognise nevertheless that the nationals have some way to go:

> If you take the overall expenditure to hire an expatriate, it is certainly more than what an Omani gets. Besides the salary, an expatriate would require airfare, both for the employee and his/her family; house rent; medical expenses; insurance, etc. If you put all of this together, an Omani is found to be far less expensive [...] The Omanis must be punctual and productive. This is the area where the expatriate workforce is better at.[73]

Moreover, appointment of Omanis to top positions is slow; as a foreign diplomat explained in 2003, "Omani businessmen are assisted only by expatriates. Omanis have often no access to executive positions in top private companies. The reason is obvious: wealthy Omanis do not want their wealth to be known; for that, the Indians are reliable people."[74]

Lastly, PDO's troubles in the mid-2000s have unveiled the truth about its Omanisation achievement (79% in 2011). The company is said to have inflated its Omanisation rates by subcontracting the activities using most expatriate workers (technical assistance, contracting, etc.) through a multitude of small companies. A senior official of the Ministry of Manpower comments: "Most jobs in PDO have become administrative positions. Do you know an executive from the headquarters who takes his car to see in the field how work is going on in the desert? [...] When an employee succeeds in joining PDO, he has achieved his professional goal."[75]

Thus, the Omanisation problem does not boil down to a post-for-post substitution of the expatriate workforce with Omanis; this was explained ten years ago by the officials, referring to the difference between "artificial" and "real" unemployment. While this idea of substitution, which deals mainly with less or unskilled positions, represented for long the greater part of the policies implemented, the authorities seem to have understood since 2005–6 the real dimensions of a process which goes beyond the mere statistical question of the number of expatriates in the private sector and affects definition of the whole social structure in the long term. The policy of jobs indigenisation reveals the existence of structural poverty in many districts of the capital: Wadi 'Aday, Jabru, al-'Amrat and al-Khud. One Swahili-speaking Omani explained the spread of uncertainty even among the middle classes: "Getting OR 250–300 now is regarded as very good."[76]

In 2013, the proportion of Omanis employed in the private sector earning less than OR 300 per month was 65%. Although the Asian expatriates' working conditions were perceived by nationals as unacceptable for themselves only ten years ago, the economic difficulties have led to a scaling down of expectations, as it becomes difficult for more and more Omani families to do without an extra salary, even a low one.

The authorities cannot turn a blind eye any more to the rise of unemployment among the young population. No official rates are available but the rare estimates to hand show a deep-seated phenomenon. The first census in 1993 established that the employment rate among nationals was 11.9%.[77] In May 2003, according to the undersecretary for the National Economy, "up to 60,000 Omanis under the age of 24 are estimated to be unemployed",[78] i.e. 23% of 15–24-year-old non-student people. One year later, unofficial estimates gave an unemployment rate between 12 and 15%, "yet these figures leave unacknowledged what is probably a considerable level of underemployment, particularly in rural areas".[79] In 2005, civil servants of the Ministry of Manpower spoke privately of 300,000 job seekers[80]—an unemployment rate around 25%.

Economic difficulties have direct social consequences. In the mid-2000s, between half and two thirds of 25–29-year-old men were thought to be still single while the proportion of single women among all women of marriageable age rose from 28.9% in 1995 to 41.9 % in 2003.[81] While this increase can be partly explained by longer studies, urbanisation or stronger resistance to family-imposed marriages, the major factor is the weight of the dowry paid by the suitor to the girl's family—the total amount of which oscillated in the mid-2000s between OR 4,000 and 8,000—for many young people from lower classes. To this cost those of purchase of a plot of land and building of a house, which are key elements in the autonomisation of young couples, are added, so that young couples must face heavy debts at the outset. In 2003, the proportion of young couples who had bank loans amounted to 96%.[82] This suggests how popular Sultan Qaboos' gesture of refunding all the private debts of his citizens on the National Day in 1990 must have been.

So it was not very surprising that the inflation at a 20-year high that the Sultanate faced after 2004 became of primary concern. It was estimated at 12.3% for the first half of 2008 by the Ministry of the National Economy. But this average rate does not reflect disparities between consumer goods, as the rate officially reached 35% for metals, 20 to 30% for milk, meat and fish and even 60% for oil and fats. The Sultan granted in November 2005 an extra one month's basic salary to civil service executives and a two-month bonus to civil service employees whose wage was less than OR 300 per month. In 2006, the ruler raised all civil service employees' basic pay by 15% from 1 January 2007, while the minimum monthly wage for Omani nationals working in the private sector was also raised, by ministerial decision, from OR 120 to 140 in February. In February 2008, Qaboos once again issued orders to raise social security family allowances and government employees' basic salaries. This prodigality of the "father of the nation,"[83] aimed at calming down the widespread dissatisfaction, fuelled the rising inflation which is largely due to the Omani rial being pegged at a fixed exchange rate to the depreciated US dollar; this drove up prices of consumer goods, which are mostly imported. Moreover, even though the government imposed in 2007 a 15% cap on rent rises over the two following years, rents and housing prices have experienced a tremendous rise since 2005,[84] partly due to liberalisation of the law on property ownership, which enables GCC nationals to freely own residential and commercial properties anywhere in Oman.

All these factors explain the revival of emigration by young Omanis to other GCC countries. For instance, agents working for Kuwaiti companies come to recruit Omanis directly on the spot. Unable to fill vacancies for drivers or salesmen in Kuwait, they proposed to Omanis in 2003 an OR 200 monthly wage, with free accommodation for six months and a car[85]—working conditions unavailable in Oman for equivalent skills. In March 2003, Oman opened an employment office in Doha, operated by the Ministry of the Civil Service, to direct Omanis in their search. But such migration cannot serve as a long-term employment policy: "Oman does not have any surplus value to offer to its neighbours [...] In the other GCC countries, the Omanis are usually perceived as low-skilled workers. It will be possible to export Omani workers when Oman itself is managed by Omanis..."[86]

A further structural obstacle to Omanisation lies in the political-economic "conflict of interest" at the top levels in the country. Several cabinet members are still involved directly or indirectly in business. These decision-making people must avoid questions being asked about the nation's general interests they are supposed to promote (like the Omanisation policy) and the particular interests they defend as businessmen. From this point of view, the official "national challenge" of Omanisation goes far beyond the employment issue and calls into question the whole economic structure on which Oman has relied for thirty years. Numerous critics attack a supposed "economic resistance to change" and denounce an existing order that, they suggest, nobody among the elites has a real motivation to reform; in private, a top official said frankly in 2003:

> The Ministers are only interested in their own resources, it is not any more the general interest, but the personal one [...] Each government department pursues

its own policy without any cooperation with the others [...] Ministers are all multimillionaires [...] Furthermore, many of them do not even have secondary school certificates, they belong to the generation that came to power in 1972. They do not want any modernisation or opening up policy. They slow down the development of the country.[87]

Resolving this economic dilemma is a major condition for success for a transition process in two directions: towards the substitution of expatriate workforce with national workers, and of an oil-rent-based state economy with a diversification of national resources. These challenges are linked to each other—a reality whose implications the authorities grasped at a late stage, as a member of the Consultative Council noted in 2005:

> Three or four years ago, the government pushed the private sector to hire Omanis. It looked like forcing. With time, the government analysed that what was done was wrong [...] Omanisation is not a replacement process. It is necessary to ask instead how to appoint more Omanis! We will always need expatriates [...] The managers will take the Omanis at the end, even with OR 50 more to pay, because their own sons will find soon the same problem. It is a question of national responsibility.[88]

More alarmist, an executive officer in the Ministry of Manpower said privately:

> Unfortunately Omanisation is still perceived as a process of substitution in the minds of the authorities. It has not yet become a question of skills, of comparative quality, but only of nationality. The government is not pushing the Omanis because they are competent but because they are Omanis [...] The Omanisation policy cannot succeed in that case. It is a long-term policy we should have decided in 1970 [...] It has not been thought out and we will have to face the consequences now [...] I think the government understands now that Omanisation means the creation of new jobs, new activities. But all this cannot be applied within five years.[89]

What substitutes for oil?

Forced to accelerate drastically the scope of economic diversification, the Sultanate decided—in the Fifth Five-Year Plan, but even more in the Sixth (2001–5) and the Seventh—to work simultaneously on three main issues: the development of the gas sector, tourism and non-oil industries.

High hopes for natural gas. In November 2002, a mini-scandal emerged when it was proven that Shell, through PDO, had overestimated by approximately 40% the oil reserves it owned in Oman.[90] The Minister of Oil and Gas, Muhammad al-Romhi, announced the dismissal of the PDO chairman, who had at the same time been undersecretary in the Ministry for thirty years, and took the company's chair himself from May 2003. This decision coincided with a fall in production from 900,000 to 650,000 barrels per day over two years, for reasons the Minister himself explained: "We are producing close to 4 million b/d of water. The big problem we have is disposing of this water, which is very costly [...] In the future we will have to drill very deep wells with huge pumps in order to get rid of our excess water."[91]

Ironically the techniques of extraction in the northern wells require the injection of water, which could be transferred by pipeline from the south. The high cost delayed the decision to undertake this work, but the total national daily production grew again from 2007 and reached 941,000 barrels a day in 2013.[92]

In December 2004, to restore investor confidence, the PDO concession, covering most of the territory initially until 2012, was extended until 2044. At the same time, the government decided to invest more than $1.5 billion to set up EOR (Enhanced Oil Recovery) projects aiming at increasing in the long run the production rates of the wells in the south.[93] Nevertheless, in June 2005 the development and exploitation of the promising Mukhayzna field, whose production reached 123,000 b/d in 2013, were entrusted to a foreign consortium dominated by the American company Occidental, while in August the government announced for the first time in ten years that some PDO blocks would be opened to bidding for exploitation by foreign companies. This was a huge affront for an institution which had until then been the economic and social window of the country, in particular for Omanisation of jobs.

In this context, natural gas has been for long a focus of the authorities' hopes for diversification of public revenue. In 1992, plans were established for the creation of the first liquified natural gas (LNG) complex in Qalhat, close to Sur, managed by a new company, Oman LNG, a consortium in which the state holds 51% and Royal Dutch/Shell 30%. Gas exploration and extraction are operated by PDO, while the government owns 100% of the gas produced. Production of LNG started in February 2000 and exports to South Korea and Japan in April 2000. The 25-year contracts with those two countries were followed in May 2002 by a 20-year agreement with the Spanish group Union Fenosa. In January 2003 the construction began of a third liquefaction train, operational in 2006, whose ownership and management were contracted to Qalhat LNG, in which the state owns 46.84% of the shares. At the moment Oman's total reserves of gas are estimated at nearly 30 trillion cubic feet (0.5 % of the world reserves),[94] while production amounts to 1.07 trillion cubic feet for the year 2013 and is constantly increasing.

To promote use of gas resources, the Sultanate launched several large-scale industrial projects. The most important is the Sohar industrial port, under development since 1998. On the site, various activities are planned for a total investment of $15 billion.[95] A second national refinery started operations in October 2006, and the site also incorporates a polypropylene plant, fed by the refinery's output and producing since December 2006 (Oman Oil owns 25% of the capital); a methanol plant, whose products were first shipped in September 2007, managed by the new company Oman Methanol Company, the capital of which is shared between OMZEST (30%) and foreign partners (70%); an aluminium smelter, owned by Oman Oil (40%) and the Abu Dhabi National Energy Company PJSC—TAQA and Rio Tinto-Alcan (together 60%), started production in June 2008; a urea and ammonia plant, set up by the Suhail Bahwan group, which started production in 2009; and petrochemical infrastructure (ethane cracking, polyethylene plants, etc.) managed by Oman Oil Refineries and Petroleum Industries Company (ORPIC). Moreover, the Sohar industrial area has a sea water desalination plant, two power plants, and Oman's first steel plant, in operation in 2008. The whole Sohar industrial site was originally scheduled to generate more than 8,000 stable jobs and 30,000 other jobs indirectly in the Batina region. In addition, a fertiliser plant (Oman-India Fertiliser Company, OMIFCO), in partnership between Oman (Oman Oil holds 50% of shares) and India (two Indian companies own 50%), was inaugurated in January 2006 in Qalhat. Finally, in Salalah, a methanol plant, wholly owned by Oman Oil commenced operations during the first half of 2010 and has the ability to produce 3,000 tonnes a day of methanol.

Thus the future use of natural gas in Oman seems to be the subject of a considered and ambitious plan. Multiple outlets for natural gas, in the shape of raw materials for export, raw materials for local industry (fertilisers, polypropylene, methanol) and a source of energy (aluminium factory and power plant), make it possible to consider the future with serenity. However, there are some uncertainties involved, particularly in terms of regional competition and outlets. Indeed, Oman must face the presence, in the area, of Qatar and of Iran, where costs of extraction are far lower than in the Sultanate. The same problem arises for aluminium, as Bahrain is already the fifth world producer and plans to expand its smelter to achieve the second position, while Dubai is also very active.

Moreover, natural gas will never replace oil for public revenue, as is recognised by the authorities when they assess the hoped-for share of gas in GDP in 2020 at 10%. Public revenue linked to natural gas for 2012 reached OR 1,583 million—only 16% of the revenue from oil. Moreover, the contracts on the gas market are determined before production, in the long term, and thus do not allow adjustment of production according to the economic and political context. Besides, activities in relation to natural gas are characterised by a high technical level and financial and material capital intensity, and require a very small workforce, mostly highly qualified. So, while the prospects for gas give grounds for optimism, there remain many unknown variables. The Sultanate has therefore turned to other economic sectors, in particular heavy industry and tourism.

Heavy industry and tourism. The Sixth Five-Year Plan defined tourism development as one of the sectors with strong potential for employment of nationals. Oman benefits from obvious human assets (the hospitality of the inhabitants) and political and environmental ones (a large variety of landscapes easy of access, the historical heritage), but opening the country to tourism has been done with care, as is shown by the authorities' determination to emphasise "selective quality tourism"—meaning tourism reserved to wealthy and easily controllable elites of the West. Since July 2003, a single-entry tourist visa for Western visitors has allowed people to stay for one month, with a possible one-month extension. It can be obtained directly on arrival in Oman. As for charter flights, they exist only in the monsoon period (July and August) and go only to Salalah, as the authorities fear the social and environmental effects of uncontrolled mass tourism.

The government's initiatives became concrete in June 2004, with the creation of a Ministry of Tourism, the first in any GCC state. Since November 2004, a decree of the Ministry of Housing has authorised a non-Omani to own a land or a home in areas devoted to tourism and established by law.

Several large-scale projects have recently been set up: the Barr Jissah complex first of all, at the south-eastern exit from Muscat, initiated by the Zubair group (holding 60% of shares). On the sea shore, these four luxury hotels and extensions cost nearly $200 million and opened in December 2005. Moreover, the state, in partnership with the Dubai-based Al Futtaim group, launched in May 2005 the first phase of another complex, The Wave, worth $4.5 billion, along 7 km of sea shore behind Seeb Airport. Even more ambitious, on Sawadi beach, between Sohar and Muscat, the government approved plans for the Blue City project, worth $20 billion. Covering 35 km^2, this project was supposed to accommodate 200,000 residents in 2020, but heavily suffered from the 2008 real estate crisis (see chapter 8). Lastly, there are other projects like the $1 billion refurbishment of Yitti village, in 2009, and the construction of several hotels in Dhofar, Musandam and Ra's al-Hadd.[96]

While Oman accommodated 1.8 million visitors in 2012—less than 10% coming from other GCC countries—the tourism sector's contribution to GDP is estimated at less than 3%. And many questions arise about the authorities' strategy. While the huge investment authorised in the above mentioned projects seems profitable, the opportunities for tourists to spend money (craft industry, recreation, etc.) are few. The country had in 2012 a hotel capacity of 18,500 beds (67% in Muscat and Salalah),[97] but limited tourist information allows the visitor to orient himself.

Basically, while wanting to reconcile tourism development with a legitimate will for social and environmental conservation, the government has not yet found the right balance which would allow the country to benefit from its potential. The Omani authorities do not want the country to become another Dubai and emphasise that projects implemented should in no way call into question what makes the essence of the Sultanate. But there is slippage as the government grants the investors a much greater latitude of action than before and only retains a role of facilitator.[98] This pre-eminent influence of private interests in the development projects' management became obvious when local businessmen involved in The Wave and Blue City succeeded in obtaining a green light from the ruler, in spite of the concerns, shared by the ruler himself, of departments in charge of safeguarding the environment.[99]

In addition to gas and tourism, the non-oil industrial sector is the object of particular care. Since 1985 the government has created the Rusail industrial area, west of Muscat, which benefits from exemptions from customs duty. Seven other zones (Raysut, Sohar, Nizwa, Sur, Buraimi, al-Mazyuna, on the Yemeni border, and Sama'il) have been set up. Two cement major companies—Oman Cement and Raysut Cement—and the Oman Mining Co., with mainly public capital, which started to produce copper ore in south of Sohar and to refine it since 1983, are significant. Flour mills should also be mentioned, with the creation in 1975 of the Oman Flour Mills company, in which the state owns 51% of the capital; this sector was liberalised in 1995, when Salalah Mills Company, chaired by Sheikh Sa'id al-Shanfari, was created.

Port activities play a central role in this strategy of diversification. By making Salalah port the leading element in the South's economic development when a free zone was opened in early 2006, the government wishes to compete with Dubai for container shipping. As in Muttrah, Sohar and Khasab, lengthy work will increase port capacities, while Duqm's dry dock, built at a cost of OR 700 million on the Indian ocean coast, has been operating since 2012. Duqm airport will be completed in 2018.

Agriculture and fisheries are the last axis of economic diversification. In 2003, the census reported that 58,000 people (7.8% of the working population) drew their main income from agricultural activities—including 9,200 in fisheries—with a very low rate of Omanisation (24.5%). The main Omani vegetable products remain dates—palm trees are estimated to occupy 60% of the cultivable surface—coconuts, bananas and tomatoes, while livestock are mainly camels, goats and sheep. In February 2005, the ruler reaffirmed the need to be aware "of the importance of the priority to grant to national products. We cannot prevent the other products to enter the country [...] but if somebody finds an Omani product slightly expensive, it is necessary to give it priority, rather than to spend such a difference of price in things without utility."[100]

In May 2004 a royal decree created a Development Fund for Agriculture and Fisheries under the supervision of the Ministry. In 2000 Oman was estimated to have reached 64% self-sufficiency for vegetables, 53% for milk and 44% for eggs.[101] However, while agriculture and fishing products are the first earner among Oman's exports other than oil and gas, the sector generates only 1.2 % of GDP and 2.2% of activity independent of oil and gas. In addition, agriculture absorbs nearly 90% of the country's water consumption. For two decades, uncontrolled water use in the Batina has caused the drying up of ground water supplies and consequently invasion by sea water. The socio-economic stakes that agriculture represents were not enough for the authorities to take the necessary decisions in order to deal with the salination of the most fertile lands of the country, in spite of the lasting consequences that it is likely to have on the ecosystem. Lastly, like plots of land for building, cultivable plots are the objects of wild speculation, which leads to concentration of the best lands (Batina, Salalah plain) in the hands of a minority.[102]

In addition, in order to widen the state's financial resources, the government announced in 1993 that all companies, whether Omani or foreign, would pay taxes on profits from the following year.[103] Since September 2003, all the companies registered in Oman are subject to the same rules: below OR 5,000 profit no tax is collected; beyond this threshold, profits are taxed at 12%. In the case of non-GCC foreign companies' branches established in Oman, profits beyond OR 5,000 can attract taxes at between 5 and 30%.[104] Moreover various indirect taxes on citizens, like municipal taxes on restaurants, on leasing or on real estate transactions, are in force. Since 2000 several direct taxes have been set up, like a tax on crossing the United Arab Emirates border. But a more symbolic development has been the end of the total exemption from health care payment for nationals, with the introduction of an annual family medical card (OR 1) together with a 200 baisas fee for medical consultation. Lastly, more and more drugs, which are no longer provided by hospitals, must be bought at pharmacies with no refunds. Total tax revenue collected by the state rose in 2012 to nearly OR 746 million, including 353 million in taxes on company profits.

The call to the national and foreign private sectors. The diversification policy was supported by a strong desire to promote the private sector, aiming both to attract foreign capital and to support the role of local companies in economic diversification. Since 1996, besides fiscal alignment with the Omani companies law, foreign investors in Oman have also had exemptions from taxes (for the first five years) and from customs duties (for imports for processing in Oman), and finally the possibility of repatriation of profits. A 1994 royal decree, copied from those of 1972 and 1974 on investment and trade, limited to 49% the shares foreigners can hold in an Omani company or in a company established in the territory. An additional law of November 1994 made it possible for foreigners to hold up to 100% of shares if the project "contributes to the development of the national economy", a formula which allows the Ministry of Commerce and Industry to give authorisation at its own discretion.

The liberalisation took a new step after 2000 as the foreign shareholding allowed in an Omani company was extended in 2001 to 70% in all sectors, and even 100% in finance (banking, insurance) since 2003 and in the telecommunications since 2005. Last but not least, the Sultanate became the 139th member of the World Trade Organisation in November 2000, and signed on 19 January 2006 a bilateral free trade agreement with the United States; many services are excluded from it, in order to preserve the local network of small and medium-sized enterprises, while the Omanisation requirements are still valid, even in the sectors concerned by the agreement.[105]

Oman thus chose to focus on the private sector as "the main contributor of growth"[106] and on the disinvestment of the state from various sectors; a royal decree of 1 May 1996 established the practical modalities for implementing privatisation, through an inter-ministerial committee in charge of determining the sectors and the projects to be dealt with. The government has focused on the water, electricity, transport and telecommunications sectors, with unequal success.

One of the most advanced sectors on the privatisation track is electric power; the Manah plant, opened in 1996, was the first power establishment in the GCC states to be privately owned. It was financed by a consortium of Omani partners (Tawoos, WJ Towell, National Trading Company and Zubair). Two other plants (al-Kamil and Barka') opened in 2004 with the same legal status (IPP-Independent Power Project). The first is owned by a subsidiary of the French GDF Suez, while the second is held 58% by the Saudi ACWA Power and 7% by Suhail Bahwan. The Salalah plant, inaugurated in May 2003, is operated by Dhofar Power Company, in which the government-owned Electricity Holding Co. has a majority holding. Sohar IPP, in operation since 2006, is operated by Sohar Power, owned by GDF-Suez (35%) and the Dubai-based MENA Infrastructure Fund (20%). Both Rusail IPP (in operation since 2006) and Barka 2 IPP (since 2009) are owned by a consortium composed of GDF Suez, Mubadala of Abu Dhabi and National Trading. Lastly, both Sohar 2 and Barka 3 IPPs, in operation since 2013, are owned by a consortium comprised of GDF Suez (46%) and Suhail Bahwan (22%).

In the water sector, the government encouraged in 2002 the reopening of the Muscat wastewater treatment project, after it was closed in 1998. A government-owned company, Oman Wastewater Services (renamed Haya Water), was set up in order to implement this $1 billion project, aimed at connecting water to 80% of Muscat's population before 2018. Al Ansab sewage treatment plant (STP) was launched in 2009 by the Omani company Galfar while the construction of a new STP in Darsayt was contracted in 2011 to a consortium of Cadagua (Spain) and Galfar.

In July 2004 two privatisation laws were promulgated, one dealing especially with water and electricity, identifying means and procedures for reforming the public services to be privatised. The revenue from these sales is to be paid into the State Reserve Fund. The law planned that the responsibilities of the Ministry of Electricity and Water would be divided among several entities, before its dissolution. The former publicly-owned power plants were to be transferred to independent publicly-owned companies and then privatised. Other companies are in charge of, respectively, buying electricity from the production companies, transporting and distributing it. Last but not least, a holding company is responsible for the state interests in the companies, while a regulation authority is responsible for supervision of all the actors.

In the air transport sector, the Omani state decided in 1998 on privatisation of both international airports, Muscat and Salalah. In October 2001, a joint venture of Bahwan Trading (35%) and two British companies (British

Airports Authority and ABB Equity Ventures) acquired 70% of a new company, Oman Airports Management Company. But in November 2004 the state announced that it was taking back control of both airports after financial disagreements. The state restarted the procedure from scratch and in January 2005 made a Danish consultants' firm responsible for studying the extension of both airports. While so many years have been lost, the contract (worth OR 700 million) for the construction of a new terminal at Muscat airport was awarded in 2010 to a consortium comprising Bechtel (USA) and Bahwan Engineering. The same year, a joint venture of Galfar and India's Larsen & Toubro was awarded the main contract (valued at OR 294 million) for the expansion of Salalah airport.

The last important axis of the Oman privatisation process is the telecommunications sector. In 2002, the Telecommunications Regulation Authority (TRA) in charge of competition regulation in the sector, privatisation of the sole operator Omantel and granting of new licenses was established by royal decree. In December 2003, the TRA announced the complete liberalisation of the sector. Two months later, Omantel was granted the two first licenses by royal decree, one for fixed lines, the other for mobiles. A new commercial entity, Oman Mobile Telecommunications, was created in May 2004 to deal with mobile phone services. In June the Qatari company Qtel, in partnership with the Danish group TDC, was awarded the contract for the second mobile phone license and set up the Nawras company. After several delays, 30% of Omantel's capital was put on the market in June 2005. In 2008 the TRA awarded a second fixed-line licence to Nawras. In 2013 Connect Arabia, owned by a consortium led by Virgin, was awarded a 15-year licence to provide telecoms services in Oman, providing that it sold 40% of its shares through an IPO within five years.

The Minister of the National Economy inaugurated in September 2003, near Sultan Qaboos University, the first Omani technology park, Knowledge Oasis Muscat (KOM). Devoted to gathering on a single site various activities connected with information technology, it houses call centres of local and international companies (Omantel, Gulf Air, etc.), headquarters of companies and research centres and technical colleges for computer and applied sciences.

While the privatisation programme has speeded up considerably since 2003, there were serious hiccups in its implementation which led to frequent delays, not to mention a resounding volte-face (in the air transport sector) and scandals. In what was known as the "electricity fraud case" 31 individuals, including a former Omani Ambassador to the UK, a State

Council member and the son of a minister were convicted of misappropriation, bribery, abuse of position and forgery, and sentenced to various jail terms. Among them the Electricity Undersecretary was found guilty of accepting bribes and misusing his position; he was finally sentenced to 14 years' imprisonment.[107] All the accused were pardoned by the Sultan in July 2006. Some months earlier, an inspection team of the Capital Market Authority unearthed smuggling operations for sale of subsidised gas in National Gas. Several top officials of the company were accused of siphoning away gas to neighbouring countries since 2001.[108]

In addition, the economic liberalisation has suffered from the caution investors have shown—in particular foreign ones—towards the Omani market, as the Sultanate remains in a back position compared with neighbouring countries regarding the share of foreign direct investment in GDP. The Omani authorities have focused on this issue in recent years, by giving prominence to a stronger role for foreign capital, even if it means the emergence of lasting inflation and acceptance of a pause in the Omanisation policy in employment. The new tax system, which came into force in 2010, is an illustration of this strategic U-turn. Even if this measure could lead to a strengthening of their foreign competitors, Anwar al-Sultan, a director of W.J. Towell Group and brother of the then Minister of Commerce, explained his satisfaction with it: "The new corporate tax law [...] is meant to spur foreign investment into the country. The more foreign investment that comes to the Sultanate, the more advantages it will bring for Omanis in terms of jobs and to the country as a whole".[109]

The major weakness in the long run relates to the extreme dependence of the economy on a restricted number of actors, who were the main recipients of the three last decades' development and of the oil rent, and who are the only ones to invest enough funds to give impulse to a true entrepreneurial economy—no more a rentier one. In 2001, Omani holdings abroad were estimated at $15 billions, the equivalent of the country's entire GDP.[110] This indicates the scepticism with which the Omani business elites have been considering the local market, and the fumblings of privatisation in Oman tend to prove that massive repatriation of holdings abroad is not for now. Opening up the private sector did not produce a redistribution of economic dividends to new business classes. In almost all cases the contracts have been won by the same top business groups (in partnership with foreign investors) that are already ingrained in the heart of the political-economic decision process. From this point of view, rather than encouraging an economic mobility that would put into question the established authoritarian order and contribute to a renewal, or at least a revitalisation, of the Omani socio-economic fabric, the Omani privatisation process has done nothing but confirm the hierarchy of established social and economic positions.

8

NATIONAL IDENTITY CHALLENGED?

Social and demographic changes in Oman for the last decade have not led the regime to give the impression of being ready to concede even a piece of political power. Moreover, when it decided to bring in elements perceived as outsiders (as in the State Council), they were only people that the regime selected itself, at the moment when it was ready to do so.

Nevertheless, Oman has experienced a significant revival of communal prejudices, first between nationals and expatriates, but more interestingly within the Omani society itself. The Omani state, both as a geographical territory and as a scene of ambitions and encounters, has contributed to making an individual aware of his origin, his social class, and his language—in a word, his "identity". And the first economic difficulties produced growing frustrations and demands based on identities or elements of difference that are all the more easy to apprehend for being based on the need to find one's position on the nation's symbolic scene in order to exist socially. The encapsulation of infra-national legitimacies into the state, the monopolisation of tribal or ethnic registers to the state's benefit (chapter 6), in a word the voluntary—but not politicised—perpetuation of local particularisms by Sultan Qaboos' regime, have contributed to the resurgence of "visible differences" and prejudices, just when the first changes for the worse in the social and economic situation came.

Consequently, a re-polarisation of the Omani society is currently occurring, through solidarity groups which are defined on a "traditional" (tribe, clan, etc.) basis or else a completely new one (language community, geographical or regional origin), but always within the state. While this polarisation occurred in the economic field for a long time through clientelism or "*wasta*", primarily because of the stakes provided by the oil rent, those are not its mode of expression any more. It appears also through genealogical and historiographical re-writing in order to calm suspicions about these groups' loyalty to the nation and even to overbid in reassurances of belonging to the nation. The question then is, what is the political consequence of these new infra-national identities, and to what extent they are a threat to the Omani national identity built up by Qaboos.

Deepening cleavages

The Sultanate has experienced a revival of communal prejudices between nationals and immigrants, especially those originating from the Indian subcontinent. This phenomenon, which is not new, has increased because the worsening of economic conditions and the indigenisation of jobs have led to direct competition between these two communities.

Omanis and expatriates: worsening daily relations. Soon after Sultan Qaboos came to the throne, when the authorities openly called upon a foreign workforce to fill many skilled or unskilled positions, social tensions appeared; in September 1971, a thousand Omanis demonstrated in Muttrah against the inflation linked to the arrival of immigrant workers and the return of Omanis from abroad. PDO sites were attacked, while shops owned by Indians and Somalis were looted. A curfew was imposed in the urban area for several days.[1] Cities like 'Ibri, Rustaq and Nizwa experienced strikes, as well as the Fahud oil site.[2]

As in the other rentier Gulf States, relations between nationals and expatriates were marked by the *kafala* principle, the sponsorship by a national of authorisation for foreigners to stay in Oman to work. The *kafil*, who is legally responsible for the expatriates' actions, usually confiscates an immigrant's passport and can cancel the authorisation at any time if he feels that he does not need the worker's services. This sponsorship system spread the conviction that the immigrant workers, in particular those from Asia, have come to serve the nationals. Some Omanis have specialised in a trade in visas (worth OR 300 to 400) by offering letters of accreditation to foreigners without providing them employment on their arrival. As major companies generally refuse to hire immigrants without passports, they have to take low-skilled and ill-paid employment, as fisherman, farmer or housemaid for example. Rare are the

Indian or Pakistani workers who are not, or have not been for a large part of their stay, in such an irregular situation.

A feeling of superiority has been anchored into minds in the years during which the Omani who had been considered as "poor"—compared to his neighbours of the Gulf—acquired a status of "rich" by comparison with Egyptians and Indians living in his country. A contemptuous and haughty indifference towards immigrants has gone with tight separation between social spheres. This gap is reinforced by stereotypes, illustrated by jokes and anecdotes about a venal, covetous Egyptian ready for any sort of deal or an awkward Indian, driving badly or cheating. But the more constricted economic situation has greatly upset this order. On the social level, the policy of replacing expatriate workers has contributed to sharp tension in daily relations. Immigrants from the Indian subcontinent often perceive the arrival of Omanis in their working environment with contempt. They do not fail to remind them that they, the immigrants, have played a core role in the country's development, and condemn the low motivation of Omanis at work as well. These tensions arise from the expatriates' concern about their future, as the arrival of an Omani colleague in a nearby position is usually perceived as the first step towards their own ousting. Occasional demonstrations have been organised by poor immigrant workers whose salary had not been paid for months, their employers expecting that their precarious situation would not allow them to rise up.[3]

The recrudescence of micro-social tensions has led the Minister of the National Economy to try to reassure immigrants regularly, by stressing all that Oman got from them:

The omanisation measures have made a small section of the public believe that all expatriates will lose their jobs or they will be driven out. This is not so [...] The Sultanate is greatly indebted to those expatriates who have been part of the nation-building process [...] We still need the expatriates' experience, knowledge and expertise in various sectors [...] Any version to the contrary is false.[4]

Omani and expatriate workers find themselves side by side on the job market, in competition for the same position or required to cooperate—not just to coexist any more. It is difficult for the Omani employees to agree to be put on professional equal footing with, or to obey, immigrants they were used to considering as working to serve Oman. Moreover, economic difficulties for Omanis have led to a general feeling that the country is run by the "Indians" and that an excessive part of the national wealth is diverted to India and Pakistan:

If an Omani is appointed as a boss in the place of an Indian, the Indians will create huge problems for him. He will experience a nightmare. And the big boss only looks at the output: business is business! In this country, it is not Omanisation, it is Indianisation![5]

Condescending contempt on the part of Omanis towards underpaid immigrant workers has given way over the years to rancour coupled with fear of immigrants from whom they are not symbolically separated any more. However, it is within Omani society above all that exacerbation of prejudices is most revealing.

Grievances based on religion. Until the early 1990s, "for most of the Omanis [...] it was the practice which defined the belonging to Islam, purely and simply".[6] If some were aware of differences of interpretations or practices, they were not criteria for hostile polarisation.

Despite the official teaching of religion which aims at promoting a "generic" Islam, the general spread of access to school and basic knowledge, and migrations within the national territory, have led to a growing awareness of mutual religious differences. Through the Sultanate's involvement in the Middle East's political and strategic debates, mutual perceptions have been modified. The most revealing example related to the 1986 controversy between the Mufti of Oman and the Saudi scholar 'Abd al-'Aziz bin Baz about Ibadism.[7] While initially this event was seen in Oman as a national issue, in which the Mufti took part because he was Omani, it later contributed to the emergence of debates within the Ibadi community itself.[8] The 1990s saw the emergence of more structured language in Inner Oman, aimed at giving Ibadi followers the possibility of debating with other Muslims, in Oman or abroad. At the moment, the religious factor is displayed to make arguments against other social changes considered as negative. One Sunni housewife, a 30-year-old native of Muscat, complained about the changes in her town:

> Since 10 or 15 years ago, Muscat has changed. I think that it is because of these people who come from the interior to work here; they are not educated, they have no money, and they are very religious. Their way of life changed a lot but their mentality did not evolve at all; they want to implement the same rules in their village and here.[9]

In the same way, Muscat is experiencing increased religious polarisation about places of worship according to confession (Sunni or Ibadi); this was unknown in Oman before, as for long everybody used to pray together. The strongest religious polarisation is directed against the Shi'a of the coast, who are seen as a homogeneous group, usually identified with the Lawatiyya. With reference to their cohesion and their economic successes, they are frequently accused of having pushed for a Lawati lobby in the state's top positions. Influenced by collective memories of the pre-1970 period—when Muttrah traders, who were mostly Lawatiyya, had the monopoly of sugar and rice imports—many Omanis from the interior are still convinced that the Lawatiyya are able to press their interests through threatening trade stoppages.

This mistrust only increased after the 1979 Iranian revolution; frequently the loyalty of the Shi'a to the Omani nation is questioned by others, while some even accuse them of sympathy towards Iran. In 1997 rumours proliferated because of the regime's silence about the arrests of Shi'a accused of transmitting documents to Iran (see chapter 7); the Lawatiyya were depicted by others as a "fifth column" working for Teheran, as they did before 1970 (it was suggested) for the British. On their side, the Lawatiyya often complain about their isolation and their frustration at not being considered; these stereotypes mutually strengthen each other, through a "performative effect" which acquires reality. The opinion expressed by an Ibadi senior official summarises the feeling of many Omanis:

> Have you read the [2002] US State Department report on Oman? They talk about discrimination against Shi'a here. It is not true! They are hardly 5,000 (*sic*) and they control all the economy. This so-called discrimination is a political weapon to put pressure on Oman.[10]

If dividing lines based on religion are deepening, they do not hide those related to language, skin colour or even geographical origin.

Ethno-linguistic stereotypes and prejudices. In Oman, the groups that are objects of the most common stereotypes are Bedouin (*badu*) and Blacks; sarcastic stories scoff at the Bedouin's avarice, opportunism and lack of education, or their difficulty in adapting to technical modernity. Social stigmatisation of descendants of client or slave groups is still very present, in spite of multiple mixing of population over time, especially through matrimonial strategies.

Men's marriage with the "nearest woman through men" (the father's brother's daughter) represents officially 35% of unions in Oman. If unions where bride and groom are genealogically related are taken into account, consanguine marriages represent more than 55% of all Omani unions.[11] In the case of a marriage between two individuals from different families, codes are strict. A woman cannot marry a man of lower class (the principle of "masculine hypogamy"), even in her own tribe, as transmission of socio-tribal rank is patrilineal. Thus, theoretically, if the father is perceived to be "Arab", then his children will be perceived as such, independently of their mother's origin. In marriages between two members of different tribes, scrupulous care is usually taken to ensure that bride and groom are from the same social status (what is called "status parity" or *kafa'a*).[12]

It is thus inconceivable—and this is perfectly admitted by everybody—that a *khadim* or *zuti* boy could ask the hand of an "Arab" girl, as it would undermine the honour of the latter's family members. As Mandana Limbert notes, the Mufti of Oman himself regularly repeats that it is forbidden for a woman to marry a man of lower status, even if he comes from a rich family.[13] The example of a *wali* of *zuti* origin whose son wanted to marry a not *zuti* girl is significant: the father himself refused this marriage for fear to having to face a refusal from the girl's family. Relaxation of this double rule—masculine hypogamy and status parity—is obviously possible but it remains rare, even in Muscat. A *qabili* Omani said harshly, "I think that the one who wants to marry *a zutiyya* has a mental problem".[14]

The argument usually used by *qabili* in refusing to let a daughter marry a non-Arab man lies in the absence of Arab-established genealogy. Indeed, one of the characteristics of the so-called "Arab-native" families is the theoretical possibility of going back several generations and proving a noble and "pure" ascent. Among clients and slaves groups, this genealogy is not established up to two or three generations. This is expressed by the over-repeated formula, "We do not know where they come from"—i.e. what is the rate of Arab blood non-*qabili* populations have inherited. The least "portion" of black blood took someone past an informal "line of colour" determining who is not "white". Thus social categorisation of the individual, theoretically established on a skin colour basis (black/white), has in fact little to do with skin colour itself. Such an uncompromising attitude explains why people of mixed Arab and slave birth, as well as their descendants, are often socially assimilated to slaves, despite their Arab paternal descent. This is especially the case for the child born to a *sheikh* and a young female slave; the mixed-race children of a *sheikh* are still automatically excluded from succession to the title of *sheikh*.[15]

Maybe the testimony of a *qabili* Omani, married to an Omani of Egyptian origin, gives the best illustration of the hierarchy of social conventions in matrimonial strategies:

> When I said to my father that I wanted to marry and that I had somebody in mind, he asked me several questions successively. The first was: 'Does she speak Arabic?', then he asked whether Arabic was her mother tongue. When I answered yes, I saw

a sigh of relief because it meant that she was not of Baluchi origin or Swahili-speaking. Then he asked me her tribe's name. When I said that she had none, he changed his mind because it meant that she could be *khadima* or *zutiyya*. For my father, the worst is to marry a Black or a *zutiyya* or a Baluchi rather than with a Muslim foreigner. If I had suggested to him that I might marry a Swahili girl, I believe he would have finally agreed because she is of Omani origin, her family's roots and culture are Omani.[16]

More complex is denigration of three groups—Dhofaris, Swahili-speaking Omanis and Baluchi-origin Omanis—which has been going on for several years. These groups, which do not have any genealogical, linguistic or geographical homogeneity, have a point in common which makes them more vulnerable to stigmatisation: they are external to the Ibadi and Arabic-language heart of Oman. These groups lack at least one of these features of "Omanity" as it has been imposed since 1970, so that they are permanently needing to justify their belonging to the nation.

In his memoirs, a British officer quotes a saying of northern Omanis who were in Salalah in the early 1970s: "If your path is blocked by a snake and a Dhofari, kill the Dhofari first". And the author adds that the Dhofaris who went to Muscat "were treated with the contemptuous respect reserved for someone culturally inferior but physically dangerous".[17] Despite the ending of the Dhofar war more than twenty-five years ago, the particularism of "the Southern province" remains strong in discussions and relations with northern Omanis. One Sultan Qaboos University (SQU) teacher, a native of the north, recognised that "It is very difficult, for me as for the students, to have Dhofari friends. They consider me as 'Omani'. SQU students who are natives of Dhofar do not mix with others."[18]

Sociability networks of Dhofaris who live in Muscat are indeed founded on the common regional origin. In Salalah, the word "Omani" refers in all cases to an Omani who is a native of the north (whether Arab or Baluchi). Many people in Salalah still refuse to define themselves as "Omani", preferring to call themselves "Dhofari". In 2004, when somebody involved in a car accident was injured, the news that the individual in question was "Omani" spread among passers-by—it was a way to reassure everyone, because nobody there could know him or be linked to him by kinship. Such an attitude is not specifically a political expression. It is in fact an expression of particularism which is considered a matter for pride. It rests on the memory of the pre-1975 period, when the few northern Omanis settled in Dhofar, especially from Hawasina and Ma'amari, were military personnel in charge of guarding the palace and the town. Even now, the word "Husni" is used in Salalah to talk in a disrespectful way about Omanis—

that is, Omanis from the North—and designate a depraved and dishonest peo-ple.[19] Thus the traumas of the Dhofar war are far from being cured and could be one of the major challenges to the successor to Qaboos, who benefits, in the eyes of the south's population, from his mother's ancestry.

This atmosphere also affects young Omanis of Baluchi origin, and particu-larly those who live in outlying districts of Muscat (Jabru, al-Khud, al-'Amarat); they are the subject of many fantastic ideas, because of the difficulty a great number of them have in speaking Arabic, the language of administra-tion and hence of integration. For many Omanis, "Baluchis" of Muscat are identified with some illicit behaviour, like drug trafficking or clandestine immigration from the north of the Gulf of Oman. Moreover, the Baluchi-native Omanis' religious observance is easily questioned, in particular in an ironic way through funny stories. Marriages of male or female Omani Arabs with Baluchi-native Omanis are still extremely rare, even in Muscat—with the exception of the "Arab Baluch" who has acquired the status of an "Arab tribe" (*qabila 'arabiyya*) just like other noble Omani tribes (see below)—as a *kha-dim*-native Omani noted: "Once, a girl said to me that I had no chance with her because her father forbade her to fall in love with *a khadim* or a Baluchi."[20]

This is often associated with the rancour towards a population considered to have been too loyal to the Sultan and his British allies in the past:

> As for the time they settled in Oman, there is no difference between Baluchis from Inner Oman, who are well integrated, and the others. The difference is between those who helped the English and those who did not want to [...] Such behaviour remains in the minds, one cannot make them disappear! In my ministry, we often make jokes about Baluchis, by telling them: 'It is normal that you take such or such decision, you are the friends of the English and always helped them!' Of course, it is a joke, all that is over. Baluchis of the interior, they are Omanis, a tribe like any other. They like Oman as everyone.[21]

This perception is confirmed by a SQU professor. After he had explained that talk of identity problems was a manipulation from abroad to destabilise the country, he declared:

> So the Baluchis took part in the Omani nation-building? Are you joking? [...] [The English] did everything to divide us so that Arabs were weak! That is why Baluchis came to Oman: to fill the army positions and to help the English. Not a single Arab was ready to do that, none accepted that![22]

In this climate of frustration, the following episode in August 2004 is not surprising. While I was waiting for a taxi, a car stopped and made a sign for me to get in. Many Omanis working in the public sector increase their incomes by becoming taxi drivers in the evening with their own vehicles. But this occasional taxi driver was a fifty-year-old soldier, who used his brigade's pick-up. During the conversation, his "broken Arabic" speech[23] led me to ask him his town and family name. His answer—"No tribe, I am Baluchi"—was the beginning of a diatribe about changes occurred in Muscat, where he lived all his life:

> Before, these tribes did not exist. I am the son of my father, and himself the son of his father, and that is all. In Muscat, everyone lived together, one did not know his neighbour's tribal name. The Omanis, the Arabs, are those who made distinctions when arriving in Muscat. As they make distinctions between themselves, then they wanted to create some between us to create divisions. They completely destroyed Muscat. Arabs all are devils! (*kul 'arab, kul shaytan*)

If contemporary Oman is experiencing a resurgence of prejudices and internal frustrations, this particularly involves groups that we can describe as "peripheral" in the demographic and historical structure, as they do not belong to the Arab and Ibadi heart of the territory. The paradox—or the explanation—is that these *'asabiyyat* have a central position in the socio-political architecture erected by Sultan Qaboos. By their political and economic role (Shi'a of Muscat, Swahili-speaking Omanis) or their military role (Baluchis), they imposed themselves as allies the new authority could not do without.

In quest of more state

In 1963, Clifford Geertz established that "primordial sentiments" like tribes or ethnic groups on the one hand, and allegiance towards the state on the other, could not be regarded as directly opposed. Solidarity groups reorganised in contact with, and within the framework of, the modern state are not a non-soluble residue of a supposed traditionalism, but a consequence of political modernity.[24] The state is both the framework in which the political game takes place and the stake of that game, since what counts is being recognised by other actors as legitimately entitled to occupy political and economic positions. In contemporary Oman, no group—if we except Dhofar, on which we will focus later—wants the disappearance of the central state. On the contrary, what is sought by communities is to find positions in its heart.

Clientelist practices and recognition claims. Until recently, a state of abundance—of material resources, public sector jobs, etc.—combined with the subtle action of the authorities to integrate and co-opt actors into the modern state, contributed to moderating the '*asabiyya* game, without destroying it. However the prospect of a reduction of the "cake", added to the authorities' intransigence about sharing any part of the political decision making process, has for more than a decade led to increased frustration and thus an increase in particularistic claims. The increasing scarcity of resources the state can redistribute has led each person to reassert his belonging to this or that so-called "primordial" group, in order to keep social visibility in a state which is still the horizon they all look to. But while a politicisation of these groups remains improbable under Qaboos' rule, there is current debate relating to loyalty to the Omani nation.

The authorities have for long tolerated clientelism in public sector recruitment, as a way for sub-national groups to appropriate the modern state's institutions in concrete fashion. But social intermediation (*wasta*) is also common in the attribution of contracts, in judicial decisions or in relations with public services (hospitals, schools, immigration offices, etc.). It is not rare to hear an Omani complaining that he "does not know" anybody in a hospital or in a government office, which implies that his application will never be taken into account. An expatriate civil servant, specialising in Omani economic issues, notes:

> As for major economic projects involving foreign companies, clientelism is difficult to put into operation because struggles take place at a top political level. At a lower level—for current contracts, which involve local companies—clientelism is of primary importance. The authorities try to keep the balance between all groups or tribes; the major part of a manager's time is spent in public relations, to increase his influence.[25]

These practices illustrate both the adaptation of individual strategies to the evolution of the socio-economic model and a growing "request for more state". Sultan Qaboos understood this as early as the 1980s, by tolerating a symbolic sharing out of public administration among tribal and community fiefdoms. Through particularistic behaviour observed in Oman, every group shows a determination to find its place within the state and, by consequence, a desire for recognition as fully belonging to the Omani nation embodied by the state.

Banyans and Lawatiyya in quest of 'Omanity'. Among the Banyans, there is a dichotomy between a dozen or so families, well integrated into the politico-economic sphere and holding Omani nationality—like the Khimji family, one of whose members (Kanak) was promoted *sheikh* of the Banyans in 1979 by the regime—and the rest of the community, which only has Indian passports and lives in nostalgia for former prosperity, the memory of which is transmitted from father to son. Thus a small Muttrah trader proudly showed a 1930 letter from the Sheikh of Dubai to his grandfather, confirming contracts for arms; he did not fail to explain that at that time his grandfather could "make Khimji wait for one hour on the doorstep", considering that the latter's current wealth is due to "contacts with Sultan Sa'id in the 1940s and 1950s and the assistance he brought to the British at that time."[26] He showed embarrassment when the Omani identity cards issue is mentioned but proclaims proudly that he is still of Indian nationality. While denying that he has tried at all costs to obtain Omani nationality, he acknowledged that the routine procedure did not succeed. He is proud not to have tried by *wasta*, as if he wanted to stress that, while he refused to lower himself to begging a favour, the government was ready to grant it to him on that condition only. As for land issues, the 1973 law established an exception for non-Omani Banyans, who were granted property deeds for what they owned at that date (in particular, houses in Muttrah and Muscat). The trader added: "I have deeds I inherited from my father and my grandfather on many lands in Inner Oman. Even if they are perfectly valid, they are not needed now... If I see people and tell them: 'Your grandfather signed this or that,' they will throw me into the sea! And they are protected by the government..."

Then he showed with pride a letter from the former Minister of National Heritage, Sayyid Faisal, attesting that his family was well deserving of the nation. Banyans often have a feeling of abandonment, even of injustice, feeling that they are pushed aside from society, and the official emphasis on the Arab and Muslim features of the post-1970 Sultanate allows no solution for the problem of their future integration. A forty-year-old Banyan businessman who has tried to get Omani nationality—until now unsuccessfully—explains:

> Sometimes an old Omani says to me: 'You do not know what is Oman, you should not speak!' But I answer: 'Do not forget that you came here thirty years ago; my family has been there for 70 years.' But in general, with the old generation who knows the value of Banyans, our relations are good. With young people, it is different because they perceive all Indians in the same way.[27]

If the Lawatiyya's room for manoeuvre seems broader than the Banyans', because they belong to the Muslim *umma*, their visibility in society is much stronger, because of their incomparable political and economic weight, while their religious beliefs (Shi'i Islam) lead inevitably to them being suspected of sympathy towards Iran. Thus the Lawatiyya are necessarily more liable to find

OMAN

themselves at the heart of the others' frustrations. As Olivier Roy notes, "One of the perverse effects of the *asabiyya* game is the presupposition of belonging which is charged to any actor [...] even if he affirms its will to be above *asabiyya* and communities [...] Individual strategies of promotion can happen through the support of the group only, since there is no recognised general and impartial framework of social promotion."[28]

The Lawatiyya's success in finance and the intellectual skilled professions shows that they have developed what Max Weber called an "ethics of excellence". Lawatiyya and Baharina have known how to capitalise on the double advantage of having always been external to pre-1970 political debates and having technical and linguistic skills much higher than those of Omanis of the interior who remained in Oman. While some Shi'a complain about what they consider as discrimination against them in appointments to "visible" political positions, one thirty-year-old Lawati's joke illustrates the state of mind within the community:

> It never was or will be our goal to take political power in Oman. Anyway, we have it already... It is often said that money makes power. In Oman, we have the money; therefore we are the ones who hold the power....[29]

However, in order to overcome political suspicions, they overbid in declarations of loyalty to the Sultan. As a Lawati *imam* explains, "The Shi'a have traditionally defended the Sultan's interests against attacks from other tribes [...] In many towns, Shi'i districts are close to the forts, which means that they have their roots here."[30]

But in the current context, ostentatious shows of loyalty are not enough any more. They are even perceived as counter-productive, by reviving jealousy and frustration. Lawatiyya face the challenge of a collective identity, which needs to work on its own history and memory.[31] It is not uncommon to hear the term "Indian Shi'a" to describe the Lawatiyya, as opposed to "Arab Shi'a"—the Baharinas—as a Bahrani businessman notes: "There are two groups of Shi'a in Oman: Shi'a of Muscat and Shi'a of Muttrah. Shi'a of Muscat are Arab Shi'a, they are called 'Baharina'. Shi'a of Muttrah are of Indian origin; you can see their faces, they do not seem to be Arabs."[32]

Thus, if they do not want the Other to impose the criteria of their identity, the Lawatiyya have been forced to build a genealogy which connects them to the Arabian Peninsula and establishes their Arab origin. Constant mutual outbidding in claims of "Omanity" in the country constrains them—maybe more than the other groups, because of society's perception of them as a close-knit and influential community—to demonstrate their belonging to the post-

1970 nation and their fidelity to the values defined by the regime. According to the words of an Omani historian, "the Lawatiyya want to be recognised as an old Arab tribe like the others."[33] The purpose here is not to bring an answer to the debate on the Lawatiyya's ethnic origin, which remains unresolved. What matters is rather the means employed to justify their belonging to the Omani nation and to try to calm down suspicions towards them. The re-reading[34] of their own history by Lawatiyya scholars highlights this strategy.

Currently, several historical interpretations exist in Oman regarding the origin of the Lawatiyya. One of them asserts that they descend from al-Hakam Al-Lat, who took part in the first Arab campaigns in the Indian subcontinent and thereafter became governor of Sind province.[35] But the most widespread story considers that the Lawatiyya are related to the Bani Sama bin Lu'i, an Arab tribe from the Hijaz. According to the Lawati author Jawad al-Khaburi,[36] the Ahl Lawatiyya settled in Oman during the pre-Islamic migrations; later they participated, among people from Oman, in conquests by Muslim armies in the Indian subcontinent around the year 15 after the Hijra, and then settled in Sind and Punjab provinces, where first they adopted a local language, close to Gujarati and Sindi, and secondly a part of the group converted to Isma'ili Shi'ism. This contributed to their marginalisation at the political level; they were then forced to concentrate on economic and commercial activities.[37] An alternative interpretation among Lawatiyya even connects the Bani Sama with Kharijites who fled to Oman and were expelled to India later.[38] In all these accounts, the return to the Arabian Peninsula is said to have happened in the seventeenth or eighteenth century.

All these historical interpretations attach great importance to the Arab-Muslim origins of the Lawatiyya. By a historiographic shift of the major argument which underlies their stigmatisation in contemporary Oman, their ancient presence in the Indian subcontinent finds its justification in their pure Arab genealogy and their early devotion to the expansion of Islam. And the Lawatiyya do not fail to point out their Arab origins to distinguish them from the Khodjas whom they consider as Hindus converted to Islam.[39] These recent conceptual reinterpretations of their own history are intended to tally with the requirements of the contemporary Omani state's historiography. The need for "Omanity" imposed by the Other is so strong that it goes as far as advancing the idea of an original rooting of the group in Omani territory, even in Ibadism.

The Omanis of Baluchi origin. Because Baluchi immigration to the southern coast of the Gulf of Oman started centuries ago, and given the conditions under which these migrations took place (military recruitment, tight control by the Sultan and the British, etc.), the current Omani population of Baluchi origin displays very strong social and geographical heterogeneity. Thus they never represented a solidarity group as such. But the role played by some families allied to the Sultan needs to be emphasised—apart from the merchant families we referred to above, like Zubair and Al Nasib, who early distinguished themselves from the rest of the community—as intermediaries between government and newcomers throughout the twentieth century. Sheikh Sa'id bin Rashid was certainly the best known personality, as one of his relatives declared: "All Baluchis of the Gulf belonged (sic) to Sheikh Sa'id. They all knew that Sheikh Sa'id was their *sheikh*. He was a friend of the leaders of Emirates, Kuwait, Bahrain... And he was the one who 'made the passports' for Baluchis in all these countries."[40]

The prestige of these notables, charged with assisting local rulers in the social and political control of Baluchi immigration, only reinforced the distinction they themselves emphasised between the Muscat-settled Baluchis—who are those who migrated most recently—and those of the interior, settled mainly in 'Ibri and Quriyat. The latter are currently known in Oman as "Arab Baluch". In contrast to those in Muscat, they are proud of not speaking the Baluchi language any more and of being considered, in particular in marriage strategies, as an Arab original (*asli*) tribe. Some of these families have even converted to Ibadism. Sultan Qaboos always took care to show them goodwill; thus Sheikh Sa'id bin Rashid's son Sheikh 'Abd Allah, a former Ambassador to Turkey, has been a State Council member since 2003. Moreover, he is frequently consulted by the Ministry of the Interior on the appointment of *sheikh*s *rashid* in *wilaya*s where Baluchis are numerous (Muscat governorate, Batina, 'Ibri, Quriyat, etc.).[41]

The current recrudescence of community polarisation has not allowed better integration of the most recent Baluchi newcomers. Like Lawatiyya, Omanis of Baluchi origin have been called on constantly to reassert their attachment to the national community. Stating that "Oman is a large family, our family", the dignitary of Baluchi origin quoted above explained that the Baluchis of Oman are "an element of Oman" and that there has been no new Baluchi immigration to Oman for thirty years. To stress the loyalty of Baluchi-native Omanis, he added that they do not have any more land or houses in Baluchistan and that the links with that region only amount to visiting relatives there. Later, he explained his pride that they have "become like Omanis", understood as real Omanis from the interior, and showed documents of

Yemeni authorities and Ibadi Omani scholars attesting the "Arabness" of Baluchis, a "tribe descending from Qahtan" sent (it is suggested) to what is now Baluchistan to propagate Islam. He considered that he could therefore legitimately reclaim the terms traditionally used by interior Omanis, describing his group as a "tribe, the largest tribe in Oman".[42] Thus Baluchis of Oman are not only Baluchis who live in Oman, but Omanis of Baluchi origin: their political strategies use the Omani categories of identity and socio-political positioning, and are consciously within the framework of the contemporary Sultanate of Oman.

Another identity strategy has led some Baluchi Omanis to dispute the claim of Arab ancestry of Baluchis and reassert their pride in a specific Baluchi identity within the Sultanate:

> We must stop forcing ourselves to talk Arabic. Arab Baluchis do not exist! You can be Arab or Baluchi but cannot be both. No problem if one says 'Omani Baluchi'. When we have a language, it should not be lost, nor repudiated [...] We would like to promote local languages and support the teaching of Baluchi, Swahili or Jabbali at school [...] At a demographic level, Baluchis are maybe 20 or 30% of Northern Oman's population; then there should be 20 or 30% Baluchis in the Majlis al-Shura![43]

The Baluchi identity feeling this intellectual called upon is embodied within the scope of the Omani state and not in a separatist or transnational perspective: "Of course, all Baluchis of Oman have family contacts with Baluchistan. But social structures and ways of life became very different; for instance, names of Baluchi tribes in Oman do not exist in Baluchistan."[44]

Both different strategies illustrate the rooting of a Baluchi identity feeling in Oman, which has emerged within the framework of the central state— through unofficial permission by the regime for administration departments being "reserved" to Baluchis, appointment of Baluchi *sheikh*s, etc. This Omani Baluchi feeling lies within the general context of polarisation of society since the mid-1990s, which has seen also the emergence of new *'asabiyyat*.

Modern *'asabiyyat*

Tribes do not represent any more the point of impact of clientelist strategies within the framework of the national state. But the dwindling of the resources offered by the state and deepening lines of cleavage in society have led to the repositioning of some primordial *'asabiyyat* "whose existence and mode of operation precede the setting up of a State society [but] use it to their own advantage"[45]—the Lawatiyya are an illustration of this—and the constitution of new 'asabiyyat that have their raison d'être in the state. The outward appearance of these modern 'asabiyyat is broadly shaped by traditional symbolic categories, but they emerge in the framework of a state only, and can be explained only by the action of the state on them (and vice versa). The "Swahili" example is particularly enlightening.

The Swahili-speaking Omanis. Very few Omanis who settled in Africa were able to make the journey to Oman and back to have a more realistic perception of the "native country" than the one passed on by imagination and dreams. Therefore the trauma they experienced upon finding a poor desert territory was nothing compared with the gap they felt between the welcome they expected to receive and the distrust they faced, as much from the authorities—which sometimes saw their education and cosmopolitanism as a threat to social stability—as from their own tribes. Mutual frustrations soon developed. The native Omanis complained about the sudden inflation, imputed to the arrival of a richer population, thought to have ideas above their status. On the contrary, the returnees accused their fellow countrymen of ingratitude and of failing to acknowledge the role they played in the social and economic "take-off", as one woman who came to Oman from inland Tanzania in 1972 highlighted:

"People from Ibra were not happy when we came back. They did not help us, they said that we had gone away… But they forgot that, if we had not sent them money, they would have all died!… When we came back, we went to see the *sheikh* to know where the family's properties were. But the cousins said that now all belonged to them, that they themselves had stayed to take care of the family's assets and cultivate the lands. They held that they had the right to keep it. We got nothing when we came back."[46]

As the years passed, the mutual prejudices intensified. The back-from-Africa Omanis were criticised for their allegedly less formal behaviour, especially regarding relations between male and female, compared with families which had not migrated. Whatever social positions they had held in East Africa, prejudices and social tensions affecting Swahili-speaking Omanis focused especially on Arabness and Islamic observance. For three decades now, mastery of the Arabic language as a basic marker of contemporary "Omanity" has gone hand-in-hand with the state's focus on the Arab identity of Oman. A young Omani whose family moved back from Rwanda in 1994 explained his linguistic difficulties thus:

When I arrived, they made me come down four school levels. I know people who have been unemployed for seven or eight years and who stopped going to school early as Arabic was too difficult and they did not understand anything. The only solution for me to get the secondary school certificate is that the *marabouts* cast a spell on me![47]

Even if the Arabisation of the young generations improved, through education in Oman's Arabic-language state schools, Swahili remains the vernacular language for the Omanis who lived in Africa, even among the members of the royal family who lived in Zanzibar. This produces complex situations within families:

I am able to think in French only. My daughter, who came from Rwanda to Oman when she was three, is the only member of the family to be really good at Arabic, because she has been educated in the Arabic system. I speak Swahili with her, or sometimes English. With my wife, it is half French, half Swahili.[48]

The Omanis who came back from East Africa constitute a highly heterogeneous group, with many marks of division, according, for example, to the date a person came back to Oman, their native tribe (to which every member has remained closely linked, as shown by the role tribal *sheikh*s played to validate genealogies for back-from-Africa branches), and even the place of residence in Africa. Perceptions of old divisions inherited from the "African" period remain acute, both in collective consciousness and in actual social practices. For instance, an old woman who came back from Burundi in the early 1990s gave her perception of the dividing line between "Anglophone Swahili-speaking Omanis" and Francophone ones:

The main difference is connected to education: in Burundi, we were brought up like Belgians, while the Zanzibaris have been like English. When the Zanzibaris came to Oman, they behaved like upstarts. Moreover, we don't speak the same Swahili as the Zanzibaris, theirs is more refined. Thus they laugh at us because of our accent. While their Swahili is like English, indolent, like when they eat coconuts![49]

In contrast, a Zanzibari Omani working as a senior civil servant stated:

People who are native of the islands are more educated, and we are certainly more traditional and conservative regarding our way of life: we have always been aware that we have the duty to preserve the heritage and the values of the sultanate [of Zanzibar]. The people who were born in Rwanda and the Congo are more plain-spoken. They work hard, they are brave and tough, sometimes a bit too much....[50]

Then, before arriving in Oman, the returnees had no real *esprit de corps*. Thus the gathering together of these different Omani populations, who only shared the fact of having lived in East Africa and bringing "Swahili" cultural referents back with them, was certainly not voluntary or spontaneous, but a consequence of the post-1970 Omani context. This led to the creation of a new *esprit de corps*, the criteria for which were established by the others, the home Omanis. The old woman quoted above bewailed the way they were all lumped together: "We were all called 'Zanzibari' (with a contemptuous motion of the hand) and could not do anything about it. It is difficult to accept but the Omanis say that we are all Black people, so... What can we do?"[51]

It is thus as a consequence of their—peaceful—confrontation with the other Omani people that a particular group feeling emerged among those who were collectively called, in the common discourse, "Zanzibaris" or "Swahilis". Since 1970, this new group identity has adopted survival strategies which are comparable to those used by other Omani *'asabiyyat*. From a social point of view, the Swahili-speaking Omanis consolidated their positions through nepotism. Through their client networks, people in charge of an administrative department have been inclined to favour the recruitment of relations from their group. In 2006, a majority of PDO's young employees and trainees spoke Swahili, wherever their family had previously lived in Africa.

Marriages between Swahili-speaking Omanis of low or middle social class and other Omanis remain uncommon. Many young Swahili-speaking Omanis, whose "creolised" way of life was a consequence of the time their families spent abroad, have experienced difficulty in complying with the strict rules governing relations between the sexes observed in Oman. On the other hand, Omanis who did not live in Africa will rarely agree to allow a son to marry a young woman who is perceived to be "independent" in her lifestyle and less "well-behaved" from a religious point of view. "Swahili" weddings are occasions for the assertion of a "Swahili cultural particularism" regarding music and festivities. The ceremonies, mixing families from various social classes, are entertained by musical groups invited from Tanzania or the Congo especially for the occasion. Another important element in males' life is that many back-from-Africa Omanis enjoy gathering on Thursday nights in places like "Swahili bars", which remind them of the "good old days" and are devoted to "African" food, music and dancing.

The Swahili-speaking Omani community illustrates, then, the formation of an *'asabiyya* independent of genealogy, relying instead on a single criterion, which is easily mobilised at a national level: the practice of a vernacular language.[52] But this new *'asabiyya* is not the only one.

New polarisation criteria: native region and social class. The administrative division of the country into new geographical entities in 1990 led to the appearance of new regional solidarities, because of the restructuring of the country's territory around regional capitals that are destined to develop (such as Nizwa, Sur, and Sohar) and become links between their regions and the national capital. These towns, which were only tribal strongholds until 1970, went through a huge process of development. This was a consequence of the location there of local branches of the administration or of new educational structures (universities, training centres for teachers and nurses, etc.). Rural-urban drift, unknown until this time, brought about a dilution of former local identities in a wider regional community. This new trend is particularly strong when it comes into contact with the outside (i.e. with other regional solidarities). In the eyes of the new generations, the tribe or the village is now less important in identifying who is a member of another group than the regional centre in which the latter studied or trained. New regional identities have emerged all over the country (such as *dakhli*, from the interior; *sharqi*, from the east, etc.) and have given rise to a new trend in nepotism, which is no longer based solely on family relations, but also on professional and educational networks.

Moreover, political and economic elites, now without ethnic or tribal distinctions, are integrated in a new upper class, disconnected by geography and way of life from the rest of the population. Members of this aristocracy share much more values among each other than with members of the groups they genealogically belong to. Class solidarity has grown up in an ethos of substitution for ethnic, tribal or communal factionalism. An *'asabiyya* is emerging, based on money and on a common interest in safeguarding control of the economic levers.

These changes in Omani society lead to resentment on the part of a broad fringe of the younger generations, who experience daily difficulties. The origins of those "happy few" are constantly pointed out, as well as their reluctance to obey the 1980 law on the duty to bear a patronym:

> They change their family name, as did Muhammad bin Musa bin Yusef al-Lawati. He created a new tribe, the Al Yusef, and he writes on his business card: 'Muhammad bin Musa Al Yusef'! Same thing for Muhammad Zubair. He never gives 'al-Hutti' or 'al-Balushi' and calls himself Muhammad bin Zubair. Why?[53]

Great wealth or a pre-eminent position of power can quickly arouse suspicions and be alleged to derive from condemnable acts. Someone who has acquired a status which socially marks him apart—especially when his rise has been fast—has to make others benefit from it, by redistributing earnings, if he does not want to attract rumours and suspicions and the idea that only shame about ill-gotten wealth is likely to explain his discretion. Apart from the royal family, there is only prominent family which is not the subject of popular sarcasm: the Bahwan. They are known in Muscat for their generosity and piety, which they demonstrate on Muslim feast days, through gifts and collective meals for the needy or through the Sa'ud Bahwan Foundation. No doubt this ostentatious charity explains the place the Bahwan family has in civil society's opinion.

Socio-spatial differentiation in Muscat appeared in the late 1970s and has only increased throughout Sultan Qaboos' rule: "The address has become a social indicator."[54] Wealthy social classes thus move in a closed world, geographically isolated—in outlying areas of Muscat like al-Khuwair south, some places south-east of Muscat and the Qurum heights. These zones, protected from the rest of the town, are polar opposites of the poor districts, which are also located away from the main axes of communication, hidden from tourists. In the latter districts (Wadi 'Aday, Madina al-Nahda, Jabru, al-Khud, etc.) where almost only Omanis live, mainly of Baluchi and Swahili origin or of *khadam* descent, unemployment and Arabic-illiteracy rates are very high. It was not uncommon in the late 1990s for police to be unable to enter Jabru, after riots against them by young inhabitants, while the Madina al-Nahda district has been called "Chicago" by its young inhabitants.

Is the regime or the nation threatened? The Sultanate is crossed by multiple identity and social dividing lines, made sharper by the economic difficulties which have restricted room for manoeuvre for the regime and for the oil rent's redistribution. These tensions generally take the form of questioning of the "Omanity" of the others and their loyalty to the Omani nation. One intellectual explained his fear thus:

"The feeling of belonging to a great nation exists indeed, but in the interior of the country. For the others, it does not mean anything. [...] For the moment, religion does not have any relevance in the national identity debate. But I fear that it can be used later on with political ends, as one sees in other countries of the region."[55]

Others are well aware of the political choices imposed by the official historiography:

The problem is this—what is Oman? If I put the Sultan aside, what remains as national 'cement'? The country looks like an archipelago. And I wonder how a dialogue can be established between all these groups. Asking how the country will fare after Sultan Qaboos and how we will do without him is forbidden. But the people want to know, I think![56]

These words reveal a growing feeling of anxiety affecting all sectors of society. People have become aware of the symbolic centrality of the person of Qaboos, who has been a reassuring paternal figure for thirty years. At the same time, they are aware that he is not eternal, and that sooner or later, the Sultanate will have to find its own way without its protector.

In this perspective, Oman's relation with the UAE is particularly interesting. Many Omanis consider the former Trucial Coast as a natural prolongation of their own nation, calling it "*sahl 'Uman*" (Oman coast). It is a job market attracting many low-skilled Omanis, a geographical sales outlet for the Omani exporting companies, a source of supply for petty illicit dealing and private trade, but more particularly a place where many Northern coast Omani individuals and families, of all social conditions, go at weekends, to have fun or on the occasion of commercial deals. Dubai attracts both fascination and repulsion. Fascination for this city and its inhabitants, not so long ago dependent on the power balance in Oman but now, within a generation, a paroxystic emblem of economic opulence; repulsion aroused by the impact, from the Omani point of view, of this material wealth on the ways of thinking of Dubai inhabitants.

Dubai's symbolic, cultural, economic influence, and by extension that of the UAE, on the Sultanate of Oman have only strengthened during the last twenty years, especially on the economic and human geography of Oman. For technical reasons (it is impossible to gain admission to Sultan Qaboos University with lower secondary school certificate marks than those required), financial reasons (inability to pay for education in private Omani institutions), or personal ones (the possibility of returning regularly to Oman), 8,400 Omani students (81% girls) were registered in UAE universities in 2011 (a substantial number in weak ones, like 'Ajman), that is 56% of all Omani students abroad.[57]

The Omani authorities have moreover to face the issue of the strong extraversion of Northwestern Omani *wilaya*s towards UAE development poles. This historical obsession of Muscat rulers about the very populated areas of Dhahira and West Batina escaping their allegiance, to the profit of Saudi Arabia half a century ago and the UAE nowadays, is still present under Qaboos' rule. John Peterson noted the prevalence in post-1970 cabinets of personalities from Dhahira; originating from tribes who had established ties with Riyadh in the 1950s, they were said to receive preferential treatment aimed at diverting them from the enticements of the late Sheikh Zayed.[58] It is not without significance that Sultan Qaboos' annual tours in 2005, a few months after the death of the UAE president, and in 2010 were concentrated on the north-west, where a majority of the active population works in the UAE, and whose *sheikh*s are linked to Sharjah and Dubai families by marriage, family agreements or business.

Regarding Oman's north-western provinces and the UAE, the political situation became steadily more tense through 2006, as Oman was wary about the renewed interest Saudi Arabia seemed to have in oil reserves in the al-'Ain-Buraimi oasis; there were also the recurrent official UAE criticisms of Muscat's lax policy on migration control. Indeed, many Pakistanis and Afghans were said to be passing illegally through the Gulf of Oman and then the Sultanate to find jobs in the UAE. These issues led the Sultan to set up the Buraimi area as a governorate in December 2006. Moreover, this area has been given special attention in the seventh Five-Year Plan (2006–10), with ambitious public investment plans (transport infrastructure, schools, etc.) as well as tax concessions to the private sector to encourage industrial or tourism projects. The consequences of the tremendous economic and social transformations in Dubai and Abu Dhabi are thus felt directly in the identity of northern Oman.

Nevertheless, the Omani nation, such it was built after 1970, certainly exists in 2017. The register of infra-national identities and their current recrudescence is not opposed to that of the nation, but complementary to it. Neither the Omanis of Baluchi origin, nor the Swahili-speaking Omanis, not even those of the interior express the will to dissociate themselves from Oman or to reject the validity of this framework of references—on the contrary. Each group asserts a greater acknowledgment of its belonging to the "Oman" entity and hopes that will reinforce its own positions in the heart of the state. Accordingly there is competitive bidding of declarations of loyalty to the nation, each group making objections to the Other relating to its history, its past or some social attitude, to denigrate or downgrade that Other's "Omanity", while claiming itself to be more "Omani" than the others. From this point of view, Oman's modern national unity is not weakened by infra-national belonging feelings. Going further, one could even consider that belonging to the nation benefits from the existence of local identities, which work to root the nation's legitimacy in the eyes of the individuals. If the expression of these particular identities on the public scene represents a threat, it is a threat to the political system itself, to the rules imposed by the regime—

a monarchy in the hands of a single man, without counterbalance and without any possibility of alternative expression—and not to the firmly-established framework in which it is held: the nation.

The major exception concerns Dhofar. Dhofari particularism is based on the shared perception of a central state-led "internal colonialism" process— the regime being accused of siphoning off wealth extracted from under the soil of the South. The issue of Dhofar integration into the Omani nation brings in the centre/periphery dialectic, which is not posed in the same terms for groups in the North of the country. The latter can claim to be included in the core of the central state: this is the case for Omanis of Baluchi origin (in the army), Lawatiyya (in the economy and trade) or Ibadis of the interior (as depository of the nation's religious values and historical heritage). While the same is also true for some Dhofari tribes (Shanfari, Rawas), and while many Dhofaris are proud "to be represented" at the top level—through the Sultan's maternal ascent—these elements have never been able to mask the peripheral character of this region. Much more than for the rest of the country, for Dhofar the succession to Qaboos will represent a major test of people's adhesion to the country's post-oil development and the role they wish to play in it.

9

THE OMANI SPRING

TESTING THE QABOOS STATE

That was a great time. We were one hand, we were one voice, we trusted each other; we were not scared of internal security. We knew that we would be arrested, but we did not care.

Omani human rights activist, about the Omani Spring, Personal interview, Beirut, December 2013

In 2011 and 2012, the Sultanate of Oman experienced its widest popular protests since the end of the Dhofar war in the 1970s. The depth of the social malaise in the country was illustrated by two month-long peaceful sit-ins between February and mid-May 2011 as well as by sustained protests calling for political reforms in summer 2012 and renewed mobilisations in summer 2013. In particular, the death of two protesters shot by security forces in the northern town of Sohar in February and April 2011 caught many observers by surprise. Although the protests have not led to any formal political change, as of 2017, the impact of the events in the mid- to long-run has proved as massive as they were unexpected by the regime. The Omani Spring represents the most blatant symptom of the unprecedented challenges to the old authoritarian rentier model of development confronted by the Qaboos State. It has been revealing of an anxiety concerning the perceived lack of a long-term economic and political vision, which has not stopped growing but remained unheeded for years and has finally intruded into the streets and online since 2011.

Unheeded pleas for help

As well as the obvious impact of regional dynamics on the events that have been shaking the Sultanate since 2011, one has to keep in mind the series of challenges calling into question the socio-political order established in Oman in the 1970s. 32% of Omanis aged between fifteen and seventeen in 2007 were not enrolled in school, and half of those who finish high school do not have the opportunity to continue into higher education.[1] The arrival on the labour market of a huge contingent of young people coincides with an economy which remains extremely dependent on oil-derived revenue. In 2015, the oil and natural gas sectors accounted for 42% of Oman's GDP and 79% of government revenues (after the transfer to reserve funds).[2] The limited results of the Omanisation policies favouring nationals in employment and the slowness of the process of diversifying sources of revenue have been illustrated by dramatic social inequalities, endemic unemployment, and poverty resulting from deregulation and privatisation policies. When the protests started in January 2011, estimates at the national level showed a persistent 20% unemployment level among nationals—and certainly above 25% among eighteen-to-twenty-four-year-olds. These figures leave unacknowledged what is probably a considerable rate of underemployment, particularly in rural areas. 38.1% of Oman's unemployed are young people, and of those, 84.7% of them have never previously been employed.[3] In February 2011, the proportion of Omanis employed in the private sector and earning less than OR 200 per month was 70%.[4]

Political grievances have developed in a fertile ground too, with a significant recent history of political action. In 2005, several waves of arrests involving personnel of the Education and Islamic Studies colleges of Sultan Qaboos University as well as senior military and civil officials led to the sentencing of more than seventy people (see chapter 7). Concomitantly, embryos of civil society, composed of young Omanis with high educational and intellectual capital which legitimised their involvement in the decision-making process, started developing. New Internet forums opened, where most of the participants chose to appear in the discussions with their real name, even when tackling sensitive issues, with the declared aim of promoting new social and political debates in Omani society. Despite systematic harassment and arrests of online activists, online accounts of fraudulent practices by key figures of the regime (the ruler excepted) became common. In April 2009 'Ali al-Zuwaidi, the moderator of a popular Internet forum, received a one-month prison sentence for publishing a government directive that banned live radio phone-in programmes because they "encouraged public criticism". In summer 2010, intellectuals and human rights activists took the opportunity of the fortieth anniversary of Qaboos's accession to the throne to submit an online petition to the ruler, calling for wide-scale reforms—such as the promulgation of a "new constitution" leading to a parliamentary monarchy, or measures against corruption among top political incumbents.

Breaking the fear barrier

In this context, these warning signs of the approaching storm should have been interpreted by the authorities as such and taken seriously. However, the first protests in Muscat in January 2011 and the general climate of frustration that sparked the fire in Sohar in February caught the regime by surprise, against all expectations.

On 17 January 2011, 200 people assembled in Muscat to protest against government corruption and economic hardship. This was followed in February by a series of nation-wide protests, each attended by several hundred people demonstrating against low salaries, the high unemployment rate among Omanis and the lack of legislative powers of the Majlis al-Shura, elected by universal suffrage. In late February, fresh protests were held in Sohar. Thirty-to-forty young unskilled people native to neighbouring cities, convened for the ump-teenth time by the administration to be told that no job offers were available for them, decided to start a sit-in inside the local branch of the Ministry of Manpower on 26 February. Promptly evacuated by the police, they decided to gather at Sohar's main Globe roundabout, on the Muscat-Dubai road, but were arrested in the middle of the night and taken to the central prison. When the news became known in the morning, skirmishes developed around Sohar police station, where the crowd believed that the individuals were detained, and one protester was shot dead and many others injured the day after when the police fired at the crowd. From that moment on, Sohar's Globe roundabout, renamed "Reform square" (*maidan al-islah*), became the gathering place of the protest-ers—who were mostly young, unskilled or low-skilled and native to the Batina region—while a sit-in, lasting for two months, was organised simultaneously in front of the governor's office in Salalah and another one in front of the *wali*'s office in the eastern town of Sur.

For the first time since the end of the Dhofar war, expression of alternative ideas and informed criticism of ongoing policies entered the streets. The now famous "The people want the fall of the regime" sung in squares in Tunis and

Cairo was re-appropriated in Oman and adapted into "The people want the reform (*islah*) of the regime" or "The people want the fall of corruption" (*isqat al-fasad*). Other slogans ("Yes to a new Oman", "We need freedom" or "You may restrict our hands but you cannot restrict our dreams of a better life") openly asked for structural reforms. Far from calling into question the authority of the ruler, the strikes and demonstrations that mushroomed all over the country—from 'Ibri in the West to Ja'alan Bani Bu 'Ali—between February and May 2011 expressed cries for help addressed to the Sultan by a population worried about the future and increasingly unable to meet the requirements of daily life, as illustrated by the list of demands displayed on the Sohar roundabout during the first days of the protests and addressed to Sultan Qaboos in person. They revolved around better wages and pensions, job opportunities and proactive measures to curb rising prices and inequalities,[5] but also called for the Sultan to personally intervene to end the reign of *wasta* and corruption in the public sector and to dismiss and put on trial long-serving ministers and top officials widely perceived as embodying corruption (including the ministers of the Royal Office, National Economy, Commerce and Industry, Information, and Justice, as well as the Public Prosecutor).[6] In Muscat, the sit-in led by intellectuals and human rights activists in front of the Majlis al-Shura—a symbolic refusal to endorse an elected body without real power—called concomitantly for the creation of another government university, free and open media, the promulgation of a constitution replacing the Basic Law promulgated by the Sultan in 1996 and guaranteeing the separation of the three powers and, above all, the appointment by the ruler of a prime minister. At the same time, accounts of harassment by security forces, violations of basic human rights, and denunciations of the existence of a security and police state (*dawla al-amn wa-l-bulis*), suggested in particular by the much-repeated expression "Sultanate of fear", mushroomed on the Internet and Twitter. As one intellectual who participated in the Muscat sit-in explained in 2012,

> Omanis were not silent by choice before 2011, rather they were silenced by the regime. The Omani population was very quiet because of repression and fear: "Don't talk about politics: you will be taken behind the sun!" In 2011, they have managed to break free from the Sultanate of fear ... The regime saw the image of the 1970s and the Dhofar war coming back, while it had been working hard since then to avoid it! ... Omanis feel they are powerful, they have the possibility to change things. Let's hope that we will break free forever from that fear.[7]

Protesters from five sit-ins (Muscat, Sohar, Salalah, Sur and Ja'alan) and belonging to all kinds of ideological background created a national coordination society named *al-Islah* (the Reform). A central committee and a head were elected who tried to register this society—the first of its kind in Oman—with the Ministry of Social Development. Their application was rejected. Besides the fact that political societies are banned in Oman, another reason for this rejection had to do with the meaning of the word *islah*. Beyond its obvious religious connotation, referring to the various reform movements in Islamic intellectual history and the twentieth-century use of this term by political Islam movements, the authorities considered it a taboo word, "since *islah* implies that there is something wrong and that it needs to be fixed." Media were instructed to use the terms *tatweer* (evolution) or *taghyeer* (change),[8] both more neutral terms referring to the improvement of a system which is already supposed to be working well.

The Sohar paradox

The fact that the most important demonstrations took place in the town of Sohar is highly symbolic. Like all other regions of Oman, the Batina region has benefited since the 1970s from the regime's strategy to realise the unification of the territory under the single authority of Sultan Qaboos, financing his state-building endeavours with the oil rent. However, well until the early 2000s, Sohar remained a semi-rural provincial town, neglected by the post-1970 centralised modernisation process, like other regional centres. The lack of employment opportunities in the Batina (besides in local branches of government and public sector administration) explains why the United Arab Emirates (UAE) has remained a job market that attracts many low-skilled Omanis (see chapter 8). In particular, Omani nationals, many of them from the Batina, were highly represented in the UAE Armed Forces until the beginning of the twenty-first century.[9]

In this context, Sohar people viewed the establishment of the industrial site and freezone, conceived by the regime as an international showcase of the economic diversification of the country, as a godsend. Yet the transition of Sohar within a few years from a small, sleepy provincial town into the industrial capital of the country led to a disintegration of the social fabric. The establishment of the port resulted in tremendous demographic changes. Between 2003 and 2010, the total population in the *wilayas* of Sohar and Liwa increased by 33% and 31% respectively.[10] This demographic boom is due to the fact that the number of expatriates more than doubled in Sohar (from 20,400 in 2003 to 47,400 in 2010) and even tripled in Liwa (from 2,800 in 2003 to 8,500 in 2010) in a seven-year period.[11]

At the same time, the majority of the Batina population had no access to the benefits of the local economic boom, and experienced stagnation or diminution of their living standards. Inequalities exploded, between pockets of wealth (including luxury gated townships reserved to expatriate executives of industrial groups present on the port) and the rest of the region, which has been hard hit by increases in all prices (rents, materials, consumption goods). This economic boom disproportionately benefited a handful of local notables and foreign GCC nationals, as well as the top Omani business groups already embedded in the heart of Muscat's political-economic decision process, which took advantage of the dramatic rise in land prices. An illustration of this phenomenon has been the involvement in Sohar's business opportunities of royal family members, the most prominent of them being the ruler's first cousin and potential successor, Sayyid Haitham bin Tariq. He is the main shareholder of the National Trading Company, which had remained discreet until recently.[12] The group, which has acquired a disproportionate visibility in the 2000s as a holding company for investment and project development, has been involved in the construction of two major power plants (Manah and Sohar) and is the agent in Oman for several multinational companies including Alstom and Thyssenkrupp. Sayyid Haitham is also involved in a number of other prominent projects, in particular the Blue City project, in which he shared a 30% stake with another Omani investor. However mismanagement, a legal battle between the project's owners, and personal greed, with the 2008 regional real estate crisis on top of it all, resulted in Oman's most resounding bankruptcy ever and the infamous necessity for the state's sovereign Oman Investment Fund to buy a substantial amount of Blue City bonds in 2011 and 2012.[13]

Nuisances created by industries in Sohar port helped trigger local popular frustrations as well. Since as early as 2004, inhabitants from villages close to the Sohar industrial port have been trying to alert the authorities to the impact of emissions by polluting industries located in the port area, which were claimed to have caused a steep increase in cases of cancer and respiratory diseases, and even the forced displacement of residents from their villages. The issue became more prominent after 2009, when local residents managed to get their voice heard at the national level, by multiplying public interventions on radios and TVs, despite all efforts by the government and business interests to obstruct any investigation and to cover up the problem.

More generally, though the protests around the country have primarily been motivated by social and economic issues, two noticeable dimensions should be highlighted. First, while it is clear that mobilisations were not organised on a sectarian (ethno-linguistic, regional or religious) basis or around sectarian-oriented demands (claiming rights for a particular community or group), it cannot be denied that the visibility of Islamists quickly grew among the protesters and that the latter played a crucial role in channeling discontent—probably not so much because of the attractiveness of their ideologies *per se*, but rather because they offered one of the few easily identifiable counter-discourses and forms of collective organisation. The influence of underground Muslim Brotherhood cells and networks kept expanding in the Sur, Salalah, and Sohar protests, while the Salafis were very much present in all Batina protests, Sohar and Shinas in particular. Interestingly, Ibadis and all components of Sunni Islamists, along with a significant number of young secular intellectuals, temporarily managed to suspend their disagreements and made a united stand in these movements, especially in Muscat (with an effective entente between Ibadi Islamists and Muslim Brothers) and in Sohar (where the Muslim Brotherhood and Salafis coordinated very efficiently).

Moreover, interestingly, the province of Dakhliyya, where absolute poverty is probably as common as it is in Batina and Dhofar, remained untouched by the Omani Spring. More than Ibadi particularism, this immunity can probably be explained by a combination of different factors. One has to do with the twentieth-century history of Oman. As explained by an Internet activist native to the Interior province:

> The memory of the Jabal Akhdar war in the 1950s, when the Sultan's Armed Forces and the British destroyed the Imamate, is still alive. People in Inner Oman remember how bad the al-Busa'idi were and know they are all alike. In Dhofar, they have this same memory of the war against the Sultan, but it is different because this memory is a good one: they won the war and pushed out Qaboos's father.[14]

Due to this historical legacy, Qaboos has always been very careful not to alienate the stronghold of the Ibadi Imamate in the interior of the country. In particular, tribal and religious leaders of this region have been granted prominent positions in the new state with continuing effective access to central authority. Therefore, the feeling of abandonment by the central state experienced in the Batina and among other communities since 1970 has been less pronounced in Dakhliyya. This, combined with the memory of the 2005 wave of arrests among Ibadi activists, probably contributes to explaining the absence of protests in Dakhliyya.

Last but not least, unlike to Batina and Dhofar, where social structures have not resisted the tremendous changes instigated by a badly digested modernisation, the "traditional" social organisation in inner Oman remains very solid and has served to palliate growing inequalities and frustrations. Both the Mufti of Oman and the Ibadi religious establishment in Nizwa retain a high degree of prestige, and their statements since 1970, unfailingly in favour of the preservation of the socio-political order, are still greatly respected. Thus despite the failures in Batina and Dhofar of the encapsulation policy implemented by the Sultan for several decades to keep all prominent actors under his control, the Dakhliyya served in 2011 as a successful counter-example.

Resorting to the coercive methods of the past

In an attempt to appease the protesters and to pull the rug from under their feet, the regime used, as previously, the oil rent as an emergency job and subsidy faucet to save time. The private sector minimum wage for nationals was increased by 43% to OR 200. After a first minor re-organisation of the Council of Ministers that had been announced in mid-February 2011, Sultan Qaboos made further concessions on 27 February, including the introduction of a monthly allowance (OR 150) for job seekers registered at the Ministry for Manpower, the creation of 50,000 new jobs for Omanis in the public sector (predominantly in the defence and security sectors), the doubling of the monthly allowance for families benefiting from the social security law and the increase of student allowances.

Clashes with riot police intensified in Sohar while traffic at the roundabout remained closed and blockades of the main access to Sohar's port and industrial area were frequently organised between late February and early April 2011. Symbols of the state's authority and the properties of those who represent it were targeted. In Ja'alan Bani Bu 'Ali, protesters attacked a number of public offices, including the local branch of the Ministry of Housing and the *wali*'s office. Sohar protesters forced a number of government buildings to close while a police station and the *wali*'s office were put on fire. Epitomising the conflict of interests between business and politics and excessive profits accumulated by a few regime insiders during the town's economic boom, Sohar's main supermarket (Lulu), the building and the land of which belonged to the Minister of Royal Office 'Ali al-Ma'amari, was burned down and ransacked. On 5 and 7 March, in the largest cabinet re-organisation in forty years, Sultan Qaboos dismissed one-third of his cabinet, including long-serving officials—such as 'Ali al-Ma'amari; Ahmad Makki, the Minister of National Economy; and Maqbul al-Sultan, the Minister of Commerce and Industry. He also announced a few days later the establishment of a ministerial committee to examine the possibility of granting legislative powers to the Majlis al-Shura. These decisions were intended to publicly reaffirm the Sultan's centrality when it comes to embodying both national unity and the struggle against corruption. Even if positively received, the firing of these dignitaries as scapegoats made responsible for the system's failings—like the gestures towards Islamists, such as the Sultan's approval of the establishment of Islamic banks in May 2011—did little to dull the protesters' resoluteness.

From this perspective, a number of the other old recipes used in the past to prevent social claims or the emergence of alternative discourses have lost their efficiency. The repeated labeling of the protesters as "scum" (*ra'a*) and "vandals" (*mukharibin*) by senior officials and national media was evidence of the regime's incapacity to accept the legitimacy of the expression of alternative opinions without accusing them of breaching the public order. Through a well-proven technique, the government also described the protesters as being under foreign influence, in order to discredit them and their demands. Rumours spread by security-circulated text messages and tweets flourished about supposed Emirati involvement in the organisation of the Sohar protests, on the aftermath of the announcement of the disclosure of an Emirati-backed spy network targeting the Omani leadership.[15] Similarly, protesters in Ja'alan and Dhofar were said to be supported by the Saudis, because of the local population's Sunni affiliation. However, these unfounded allegations did not attract much attention. Attempts were made to buy off individuals perceived as leaders of the protests, by offering them money and positions as directors in government departments—usually without success.[16] CEOs and human resources departments of private companies based in Batina were contacted directly by police and Ministry of Manpower officials and instructed to create jobs overnight for "Sohar roundabout's young people", whose names they were given.[17] Moreover, the manipulation of local identities and tribal issues to channel claims and demands, as a divide-and-rule technique to prevent the emergence of political mobilisations, proved inefficient too. The Ministry of Interior tried to involve tribal *sheikh*s and *wali*s to appease the protesters on several occasions and to promise them jobs in the security forces. These mediations were explicitly turned down by the protesters, especially in Sohar, with insults and obscene gestures, as a clear illustration of the actual level of prestige and authority enjoyed by tribal leaders after decades of Qaboos's co-optation policy. Also it seems that the authorities lacked an accurate perception of the protests. Despite all the evidence that overthrowing the regime had never been on the protesters' agenda in 2011, police and security investigations soon used the term "opponent" (*mu'arid*), and various factors tend to show that they were looking for a structured underground organisation (the conception of which was far from the actual chaotic coordination between the different sit-ins and the clumsiness of some of the means of action). A number of protesters arrested were asked about the names of the "leader" of the movement, but also their supposed connections to the Muslim Brotherhood and to other foreign political movements such as the Free Syrian Army.[18]

After the Sultan's royal decree announcing his intention to grant the Council of Oman greater legislative and regulatory powers, which coincided with the GCC's plans to set up an aid package worth $10 billion to help Oman cope with protests and, a few days later, Saudi and UAE forces' entry in Bahrain on 14 March 2011, it became clear that the ruler, like his GCC counterparts, did not intend to go beyond what he fundamentally considers the red line: that is, the centre of political power (combining the executive and the legislative power) remaining his personal prerogative, closed off from contestation.[19] When it appeared that the limited concessions the Sultan was ready to grant to the protesters did not produce the desired effect, the months of April and May 2011 showed that a security-obsessed answer was privileged and that repression remained an active strategy to choke off dissonant voices: another protester died in clashes with the police in Sohar in April. Peaceful gatherings at Sohar, Sur and Salalah roundabouts were cleared by riot police using tear gas and backed by helicopters, tanks and armed cars. Several hundred protesters, beaten and dragged from their cars in the street or from bed in the middle of the night by masked members of the Sultan's Special Force, were arrested all over the country. Immediately after their arrest, many were blindfolded, ankle-shackled with hands tied behind their back, put in a bag with two holes for breathing and sent by military plane to Sama'il central prison. Internet discussion forums were closed, repeated intimidations and arrests of journalists and human rights activists occurred while a number of them were victims of libel and blackmail campaigns by the intelligence service and the official media. Activists, bloggers, and also students travelling back from abroad have been regularly summoned for interrogation and forced to sign promises that they will stop all political activity and sever contact with international human rights organisations, while relatives have received explicit threats. The systematic practice of physical and psychological mistreatment, which in many cases amounted to torture (politically motivated disappearances and incommunicado detention in a secret location for weeks; death threats; virginity tests for female protesters; forced confessions; solitary confinement in 4-square-meter cells without windows and with loud music and bright light for twenty-four hours; sleep depravation; extreme temperatures; restricted access to toilets, etc.), were reported.[20] A creeping militarisation of the territory took place, as shown by the transformation of Sohar into a forti-fied city in April and May 2011, and the drastic increase of police controls and check-points on roads to the UAE until 2014. In May 2011, Sultan Qaboos also expanded by royal decree (no. 59/2011) the powers of the police. Amended article 50 of the Penal Procedure Law allows them to detain indi-viduals (without an arrest warrant from the public prosecution) for longer (up to fifteen days) before bringing them to court—and even for up to thirty days without charge "for crimes related to national security or mentioned in the anti-terrorism law."

Significant investments in the security sector (police, intelligence), which aim to strengthen political control and pre-empt future unrest, have also been a priority since 2011. Defence and national security forces consumed 36.5% and 33.1% of the state's expenditure in 2012 and 2013 respectively, and 13.9% of the country's GDP in 2014—one of the world's highest rates.[21] According to the Stockholm Institute for Peace Research Institute, Oman registered a 51% rise in defence spending in 2012—the sharpest worldwide.[22] This went with a tightening of legal provisions criminalising the expression of non-conformist or critical opinions. The new cybercrime law issued by Royal Decree no. 12/2011 in February 2011 marks a serious restriction on freedom of expression, imposing jail sentences of up to three years for using the Internet to "produce or publish or distribute or purchase or possess whatsoever that might violate the public ethics" (article 17) or "prejudice the public order or religious values" (article 19). A few weeks later, the prerogatives of the Public Prosecutor were expanded by royal decree, with all powers of the Inspector General of Police and Customs mentioned in the Public Prosecution Law to be assigned to the Public Prosecutor. As explained by a leading Omani finan-cial journalist, "the Public Prosecutor answers directly to the Sultan [now] and can investigate anybody."[23]

In June and July 2011, more than 100 individuals from Sohar, Salalah, Sur and Ja'alan were sentenced to jail on such charges as "blocking traffic" and "illegal gatherings." In particular twenty-seven Sohar activists were sentenced to jail terms on various charges related to "illegal gatherings," "incitement to cause riot" and "public disorder." Seven of them, tried under the terrorism law, received a thirty-month jail term on the accusation of "possessing material with the intention of making explosives to spread terror" while seven others were given five-year jail terms for "sabotaging and destroying public and private properties" and "forcefully stopping work at government offices, blocking roads and disrupting traffic at Sohar port."[24]

Finally, in October 2011 several articles of the Penal Law were amended by royal decree, including article 135 imposing jail sentences for "the publication of false news, statements or rumors liable to incite the public or undermine the prestige of the state or weaken trust in its financial state," and article 137 which states that "anyone participating in a gathering of at least 10 persons, with an intent to affect the public system, can be punished with a gaol term of one month to one year." These amendments criminalised the specific character of these protests, even down to methods (for example, road blocks) and the protesters' appearance (for example, wearing masks or veils in a public place or any other concealment preventing identification). The same month, the administrative re-organisation of the territory dismantled Batina and Sharqiyya regions, dividing them into two, and transformed all regions into governorates, with all governors (except those of Muscat and Dhofar, who keep ministerial rank) exercising their prerogatives under the strict supervision of the Minister of Interior.

Limited political concessions

Even as the regime moved to crack down on dissent, the Sultan made several concessions designed to emphasize his attentiveness to the public's aspirations for greater participation in decision-making.

In October 2011, 1,133 candidates, including seventy-seven women, stood in the elections to the Majlis al-Shura. 60% of Omanis eligible to register to vote did so (522,000) and 76% of registered citizens actually cast their vote. Thus 46% of eligible people voted. The higher turn-out than in 2007 was likely a reflection of Omanis' expectations that the council would promote greater reform. Except for the fact that candidates were allowed to hold public meetings in halls or electoral tents for the first time in 2011, campaign rules were as restrictive as in the 2003 and 2007 elections. Three individuals who took part in the protests earlier in the year were elected.[25] Unsurprisingly, clientelism, tribal or ethnic affiliations, and money offered by candidates were also the key determinants of voters' choices in 2011. The campaign coincided with the trial of the editor-in-chief and a reporter of the independent newspaper *al-Zaman* for publishing an article giving evidence of corruption in the Ministry of Justice. In September 2011, the primary court sentenced both journalists to five months in prison for "insulting the Minister of Justice and his undersecretary" and ordered the closure of the newspaper for one month.[26]

Five days after the elections, the Sultan made substantial amendments to the Basic Law, expanding the prerogatives of the Council of Oman. These new amendments give the Council of Oman the possibility to propose laws on its own initiative, which must be referred to the Council of Ministers for consideration (article 58, bis 36). Also, draft laws prepared by the Council of Ministers should be referred to the Council of Oman for approval or amendment before being submitted to the ruler for promulgation (article 58, bis 35). However serious restrictions to the Council of Oman's legislative prerogatives apply. Laws "which the public interest requires" should be submitted directly to the ruler by the Council of Ministers. Moreover article 58, bis 40 states that the Council of Oman can provide recommendations only (that the Council of Ministers is free not to consider) in relation to development projects and the state annual budget, which is prepared by the Financial Affairs and Energy Resources Council, chaired by the Sultan and composed of cabinet members, the deputy chairman of the Central Bank and advisers to the Sultan (Royal Decree no. 60/2011).[27] The new amendments also give the Majlis al-Shura the ability to elect its own chairman (article 58, bis 12)[28] and to interpellate and question service ministers, who have to send them an annual report on their activities. However, the Majlis al-Shura still cannot question ministers linked to national sovereignty (Foreign Affairs, Defence, Finance, Interior) and the opinions and the decisions of the two councils are not binding on the Sultan. At the opening session of the Council of Oman on 31 October 2011, the Sultan made his first long-awaited public address since the protests. However, this speech fell far short of the population's expectations and appeared very disappointing to many since no major announcement was made, except promises to combat unemployment and corruption.

Following the Sultan granting the Council of Oman greater powers to propose and amend laws, a number of Majlis al-Shura representatives took full advantage of what seemed to many a change of the chamber's status. Criticism of government policies within the chamber and grilling of ministers, making the most of Omanis' general distrust towards cabinet members, intensified. Live coverage of these sessions of parliamentary questions on the national channel (and their extensive re-distribution, via small videos, on social networks) only increased the national visibility of these representatives, whose perception of their responsibilities and positions in the general balance of powers illustrated a qualitative evolution compared to their predecessors. A vivid example of this determination by some Majlis al-Shura members to use what they consider their popular legitimacy derived from the ballot box and to profit from the necessity for the Sultan to open up greater opportunities for the Council to express its voice (at least, formally) was the test of strength between the Council and the cabinet that took place in 2012. While it is outside the Majlis al-Shura's prerogatives as set by law, and the initiative was rejected by the Council of Ministers in June 2012, the Chamber officially approved in November 2012 the formation of a Defence, Security and Foreign Affairs permanent committee. Tellingly, this decision, which was not formally opposed by the ruler, was seen as a small safety valve in the post-Arab Spring context during which cabinet members embodied the widespread perception of an elite busy safeguarding its political and economic privileges.

Another October 2011 amendment to the Basic Law dealt with the succession process (see chapter 7). Chairmen of both the Consultative Council and State Council, along with three Supreme Court members and Defence Council members, are henceforth to confirm the appointment to the throne of the person designated beforehand by the former ruler in a letter to the Ruling Family Council.

The same month, a Sultan's decree announced the set up of municipal councils in all eleven governorates, composed of members representing *wilayas* and elected by universal suffrage (all Omanis over twenty-one registered on the voting lists) for a four-year renewable term, in addition to ex-officio members representing ministries.[29] *Wilayas* with up to 30,000 inhabitants are represented in the municipal council by two members, while those having more than 30,000 but less than 60,000 have four representatives, and larger *wilayas* have six representatives. All municipal councils are chaired by the head of the governorate, appointed by the Sultan. According to the municipal council law promulgated on 26 October 2011, municipal councils enjoy advisory powers only. They provide opinions and recommendations on the development of systems and municipal services in the governorate (infrastructure, health, environment, local taxes, etc.). On 22 December 2012, the country held its first ever municipal elections. Of 1,475 candidates (including forty-six women), 192 were elected, including four females. Turnout was low. Only 50.3% of the total 447,500 voters installed on the electronic identity card system cast their vote. At least fifty applications for candidacies submitted by individuals who took part in the 2011 protests were rejected by the election committee both in 2011 and 2012 for "security reasons."[30]

Another reform implemented (by Royal Decree in February 2012) was the restructuration of the Supreme Judicial Council, which oversees the judiciary, draws up general judicial policy, looks into nominations referred by the respective authorities to fill positions in the judiciary, the Administrative Court and the Public Prosecution, and proposes and reviews draft laws on judicial matters. While the reform increases the Supreme Judicial Council's independence from the Minister of Justice, by removing the latter from the Judicial Council and by drastically restructuring the management of judicial affairs away from the Ministry's influence (Royal Decree no. 10/2012), it reasserts the Sultan's primacy and control over all competent authorities, since the Supreme Judicial Council is chaired by him and decisions taken by the council in his absence have to be ratified by the monarch. Probably never before in Oman has the judicial system been so dependent on one man's goodwill.

In yet another attempt by the regime to show its determination to fight endemic corruption within state institutions, the government body formerly known as the State Audit Institution was renamed as the State Financial and Administrative Audit Institution (SFAAI) and its prerogatives expanded (by Royal Decree no. 27/2011). Its missions now include the provision of a framework for efficient management of public funds, the obligation to detect financial and administrative irregularities and to ensure transparency in financial and administrative transactions, and to make recommendations for the avoidance of conflicts of interest. The end of 2013 and the spring of 2014 were punctuated by a litany of reports announcing prosecutions and convictions of government officials and businessmen on various charges related to abuse of office and corruption. Among the most prominent people to be prosecuted have been the former long-serving (1996–2011) Secretary General of the Ministry of National Economy Muhammad al-Khusaibi, who briefly held the position of Minister of Commerce and Industry in early March 2011 and who was very close to the Zawawi family; Indian businessman P. Muhammad 'Ali, co-founder and managing director of the Galfar group, Oman's largest construction company; and long-serving (since 2004) CEO of government-owned commercial company Oman Oil, Ahmad al-Wahaibi. Companies involved in contracts and projects related to Sohar port were affected. In particular, former executives of state-owned Oman Refinery Company and Aromatics Oman Company received heavy jail sentences for abuse of office, money laundering and accepting bribes to facilitate the award of public contracts.[31] But despite all the hopes put in the SFAAI's ambitious mission, the people involved in these cases were only scapegoats, as none of them was among the big economic and political players who had attracted the protesters' wrath and who have been embodying the conflicts of interest between politics and business since the 1970s.

On the social and economic side, as a journalist explains, the regime "has been striving by all proper means to prevent a new social conflagration."[32] While the number of scholarships to study abroad has exploded since 2011, the Council of Ministers announced in February 2013 a new rise in the minimum gross salary for nationals working in the private sector by 62% with effect from July 2013. It consists of OR 225 as a basic salary plus OR 100 as transport and housing allowance. Moreover, royal orders were issued in November 2013 to standardise all grades and salaries for employees in the public sector, and to standardise pension benefits and liabilities of beneficiaries towards the pension funds, as per the pension system for employees at the Diwan of Royal Court—all with effect from 1 January 2014. That follows a 70% increase in government spending between 2011 and 2014.[33]

Since 2014, falling oil prices have become a new source of pressure. The price of oil which Oman needs to balance its budget doubled to "over $100" per barrel in 2015 from $54 on average in 2006–2010, the undersecretary of the Ministry of Oil and Gas said in February 2015.[34] In these conditions, the government posted huge budget deficit of $13.8 billion in 2016 (or about 20% of the country's GDP), compared to the originally projected deficit of $8.6 billion. In 2017, Oman's government plans to cut its budget deficit to $7.8 billion, partly through limitation of opening of new jobs in the public sector, raising electricity tariffs rates for large corporate and government consumers, new taxation on tobacco and alcohol, and changes to fees charged for hiring foreign workers. The government also announced that it would partly cover the deficit this year with $5.5 billion of international borrowing.[35] Furthermore, in December 2013, Sultan Qaboos issued royal orders to set up the main committee, chaired by Sayyid Haitham bin Tariq, responsible for developing and drafting a new long-term national strategy entitled "Oman Vision 2040." This is to replace the old Oman Vision 2020 (drafted in 1995), the objectives of which proved already unreachable in the mid-2000s and which became definitely obsolete with the Omani Spring.

Lastly, the Oman Chamber of Commerce and Industry law too was amended by Royal Decree no. 59/2013. The chairman and seven members of the board of directors (out of a total of twenty-two members, fifteen being elected) had been appointed by royal decree, but now the chairman and the full fifteen-member board of directors are selected through election every four years.

From high expectations to disillusionment

However, this combination of measures alternating limited concessions, arbitrary gestures of benevolence and relentless crackdowns on any discordant voice, which was supposed to re-assert the grip of the state on Oman's turbulent peripheries, did not stop the contestation. Popular frustration with the slow pace of reform became evident again all over the country in May 2012. Around 1,000 oil workers went on strike in Muscat, Fahud and other oil fields, demanding better pay and working conditions. At the same time, protests developed in Batina in support of the Liwa member of the Consultative Council, Talib al-Ma'amari, a Salafi forty-year-old professor of Arabic literature at Sohar University, who faced calls from the Public Prosecution for his parliamentary immunity to be lifted, following posts on his Facebook page criticising senior officials of the Ministry of Housing. This political activism, and especially his role as champion of the cause of the victims of Sohar's industrial pollution, was crucial in his election to the Majlis al-Shura in 2011. These 2012 mobilisations resulted in further clashes with police and arrests but the Majlis al-Shura rejected the request to lift Talib al-Ma'amari's immunity. In early June 2012, the government adopted a hard line: the Public Prosecutor, on the basis of the amended article 135 of the Penal Law, announced that anyone who publically criticised the government would be charged with sedition. He threatened he would take "all appropriate legal actions" against writers, bloggers and sit-in participants who are said to act "against values and morals of the Omani society" and to "prejudice the national security and public interests."[36] The summer of 2012 illustrated this move, with a new crackdown on civil society all around the country, leading to the arrest and sentence to jail terms (from six to eighteen months) of more than forty writers, human rights activists, lawyers and bloggers (a number of whom were subjected to practices of mistreatment amounting to torture) on various charges related to "illegal gathering," "violation of information crimes law" and "defamation of the Sultan". Repeated protests in Liwa and Sohar, coupled with blockages of Sohar industrial area, were staged on a weekly basis in the second half of 2012. Clashes between riot police and local youths in villages of the province were commonplace in 2012 and 2013, to the point that North Batina police and security forces were placed on orange alert state on several occasions and a curfew had to be imposed and armoured vehicles deployed in villages north of Sohar in October 2013. As a Sohari businessman explained in November 2012, "nowadays young people aged 13 to 18 are confronting security forces on a weekly basis in some villages. It becomes like a game for them, a pastime, a prerequisite to become 'a real man' in the eyes of peers..."[37] In January 2013, another journalist from *al-Zaman* neswspaper was sentenced to a one-year prison term for lèse-majesté.

In March and July 2013, Sultan Qaboos pardoned and ordered the release of all individuals sentenced and imprisoned for political reasons, including the fourteen activists from Sohar who were serving since June 2011 terms of between thirty months and five years. The Sultan also ordered those dismissed from private and public jobs after the 2011–12 protests to be reinstated. This decision was intended to close the delicate chapter of social and political contestation opened two years before, which the authorities have liked to consider only a parenthesis in a cautious and harmonious development process conducted since the 1970s. Yet the intimidation and arbitrary detention of activists have continued and, according to Human Rights Watch, basic rights have been "routinely trampled" since then.[38] In August 2013, renewed demonstrations and blockages of Sohar industrial area to protest against pollution caused by industry led to a new crackdown by riot police and arrests, including Talib al-Ma'amari. Despite his parliamentary immunity, he was sentenced in October 2014, after more than a year of detention, to three years in jail on charges of illegal gathering and undermining the status and prestige of the state, on the basis of articles 135 and 137 of the Penal Law.[39] This harsh sentence on one of the most popular Majlis al-Shura representatives, considered a "real political leader"[40] in North Batina, appears to be an unequivocal message addressed by the regime to the Majlis al-Shura members that the semi-freedom of expression tolerated after 2011 is no longer desirable, and that the existence of a proper parliament in Oman, with actual legislative powers, is definitely not on the agenda. Not surprisingly, the virulence with which ministers are grilled has dramatically decreased since 2013, while one of the most obvious illustrations of the Majlis al-Shura's timid emancipation process since 2011—the Defence, Security and Foreign Affairs permanent committee—has been virtually dormant since 2013.

Writer 'Ali al-Rawahi was summoned and detained incommunicado for five days in December 2014 after tweeting that Oman had become "a family company managed by thieves and of which the people are the clients ignoring their rights and how to claim them."[41] In March 2015, poet Sa'id al-Darudi was sentenced in absentia to 18 months in prison, following a Facebook post claiming 'I am not Omani, I am Dhofari' on charges of disturbing public order and creating discord and hatred. The same month, prominent human rights defender from Dhofar Sa'id Jaddad, who had been arrested in July 2013, following his calls for political and social reforms, was convicted of "undermining the prestige of the state," and "using information networks to disseminate news that would prejudice public order." He was sentenced to three years' imprisonment, based on his online activities, including a public letter he wrote to United States President Obama asking for human rights improvements in Oman. On 14 January 2016, the independent magazine *Muwatin* (Citizen), whose editor had sought political asylum in the UK in 2015, announced that it would stop publishing until further notice because of what it described as "circumstances beyond its control, the most important being the safety of writers and journalists of Muwatin."[42] The following month, former diplomat and online activist Hassan al-Balushi was convicted by Sohar Primary Court of "insulting the Sultan," "public blasphemy of God's holiness" and "using information networks in prejudice against religious values" and sentenced to jail for three years. In August the Ministry of Information ordered the permanent closure of the independent *al-Zaman* newspaper after reports on alleged corruption of top officials in the judiciary. While the Appeal Court overturned in December 2016 the decision to shut down the newspaper, its editor-in-chief Ibrahim al-Ma'amari and its deputy editor Yusuf al-Haj were sentenced to six months and one year of jail respectively.[43] In the meantime, another independent newspaper, *al-Balad*, announced its decision to close in October 2016, due to the harassment of the internal security.

Moreover, in October 2013, teachers from government-run schools throughout the country held a four-week strike, the most powerful one on record. At the height of the strike, 35,000 teachers, demanding in particular a proper salary structure according to seniority and the possibility to form an elected union,[44] were participating and 740 out of 1,047 public schools were shut down. A few days later, in reaction to strikes that have affected key economic sectors of the country since 2012, the Minister of Manpower issued a new resolution prohibiting workers from striking or instigating strikes at establishments that provide "essential public services"—oil facilities and oil refineries, ports and airports.[45] However other strikes in prominent private companies, including in the petrochemicals and retail sectors, took place in spring 2014.[46]

A new Nationality Law, promulgated by sultan's decree in August 2014, gave the state the power to strip Omani nationals of their citizenship if they "engage in a group, a party or an organization that adopts principles or doctrines that can harm the interests of Oman" or "worked for a foreign country in any way whatsoever ... and failed to fulfil the Omani government's order to abandon such a work."[47] These provisions can obviously be used to threaten or quell peaceful dissent. Pursuant to this legislation, the Ministry of Interior stripped nationality of ten Omanis with dual passport in February 2016.

The need to open a new chapter

The regime's repressive response to the popular demands plunged many Omanis into deep bewilderment. Hitherto, before 2011, Omanis had not been used to seeing public criticism of ongoing policies erupt onto the street. Instead, a climate of national unanimity predominated in the media and in officials' public speeches, while Omanis had been told for forty years to rely on the reassuring paternal figure of the Sultan (*Baba Qaboos*) to arbitrate and resolve all public matters. The regime had been allowed to give credence to the idea that "the cost of resisting injustice outweigh[s] that of resignation to it."[48] This made the political system predictable, even if it remained deeply arbitrary: the regime would strike neither blindly nor without distinction but surgically against the one who crossed the red line. This came as a confirmation to the majority that politics is a dangerous game and that it is possible to enjoy a very satisfying life if one does not meddle in it.

Even among cabinet members, the fear of speaking up and displeasing the ruler, but also the culture of political insecurity, has been cultivated in order to make sure that everybody has internalised the fact that no position can be taken for granted—as explained by a retired senior civil servant:

> When you speak to ministers or to high officials, they know the problems better than you. But they don't want to hear because they are afraid: they don't know who you are, who you are sent by. They have not seen the Sultan for one, two, three years, and they feel totally isolated. They don't trust anybody and they don't want to take the risk of making you believe that they are weak or vulnerable ... They all want to get on a boat which is sinking. They all want positions while a change must take place.[49]

For instance, local observers explain the dismissal of a number of ministers in March 2011 by their incapacity to report the actual situation on the ground—for fear of facing reprimand and losing face and position.[50]

This legitimation strategy has also taken the form of an implicit blackmail, on the premise that a strong regime is preferable to the alternative of chaos. Civil wars in Yemen and Iraq, but also political instability in Kuwait and Bahrain, have frequently been used to put the extreme personalisation of power in Muscat into perspective, by explaining that Omani political stability, despite the system's imperfections, is still preferable to state of entropy in neighbouring countries. As a consequence, the system could remain extremely stable despite the repression that was taking place within it. The main achievement of such a legitimation strategy happened in 2010, when the United Nations Development Programme awarded the Sultanate the title of top mover in terms of Human Development Index progress between 1970 and 2010.[51] Ironically, less than two months later the Omani regime had to face its toughest challenge since the end of the 1970s.

From this perspective, the Omani Spring has revealed how the extreme personalisation of Oman's political system since 1970, which proved to be the best antidote against the emergence of alternative discourses to Qaboos, has reached its limits. The ruler, having fired high-profile ministers in 2011 who served for a long time as political fodder, has nobody anymore who can be sacked in order to calm down discontent, as one Internet activist from the Interior explained in 2012:

> People's faith in Sultan Qaboos is still high, however, there is no one else anymore to blame for the failure of the reforms. That's why I think that if he will appoint a prime minister he will be "Sponge Bob", just someone who will suck all the dissatisfaction which may be directed towards the Sultan otherwise.[52]

Direct criticism of the Sultan became common during the course of the protests. In Salalah in 2011, demonstrators openly questioned the ruler's responsibility for economic mismanagement ("If you didn't know [the malpractices], it is a disaster; but if you did know, it is an even bigger disaster")[53] or threatened him in veiled terms, by referring to the Dhofar war ("The one who forgets the 1970s should think of the grand-children of the free men").[54] His reluctance to break taboos on key issues—for example the appointment of a prime minister and the laying down of foundations for governance of a post-Qaboos Oman—has done nothing but fuel this widespread anxiety. Also incomprehensible for many was Sultan Qaboos's absence of media intervention or personal meeting with representatives of the protesters. His decision to entrench himself in his palace in Manah (Dakhliyya) until October 2011 further illustrated his unwillingness to either challenge his image as an arbiter above mundane problems or take the risk of denting his prestige by having to face overt popular criticism.

Activists who were convinced of the ruler's belief in reform before February 2011 later expressed their huge disillusionment with the regime's response to society's call for help. As a Muscat activist acknowledges,

I was convinced there was a clash between two wings within the authorities. And I discovered that the reformist wing is so weak that it is not even worth relying on it, not even worth expecting something from it … It's very sad that [the Sultan] doesn't understand that he may not leave the power peacefully. That's such a pity, I am really sorry to say that he doesn't understand people have no patience any more. I myself am no more patient. Maybe he's the most disillusioned of all of us … I'm sure he's bored with his people: "I gave them all for 42 years and they thank me like this. They don't deserve me!"[55]

The young Omani civil society is composed of educated males and females who no longer agree to abdicate their right to take part in the political and economic decisions the country is facing, as their parents did in the name of social welfare (which is out of date) or for the requirement of national unity behind the ruler. The official narrative stressing the Omanis' duty of loyalty towards the "father of the nation" in the name of the *nahda* ideology seems like a broken record that has proved inaudible in a country where 84% of the population was born after 1970 and 70% after 1980. It is openly challenged by activists and bloggers who now make a clear distinction between the current regime and the Omani nation. One of the leaders of the 2011 Muscat sit-in puts it bluntly:

In 2011, we wanted to understand what the causes of our country's disease are. We wanted to remove the corrupted elite [around the Sultan] from the political system and see if this could sort out the problem. We managed to make these elites go … but we have quickly understood that the body was still deeply infected.[56]

Online writers and protesters who openly criticised the ruler's proximity to British and US interests and compared his management of the oil rent and the country to that of a private firm were quickly arrested and condemned to jail for lèse-majesté. In November 2012, on the occasion of 'Aid al-Adha, Sultan Qaboos visited Musandam and Sohar—his first visit to the town since the beginning of the protests—with the obvious intention of suggesting that the general situation was "back to normal". This visit was heavily choreographed, with huge deployment of security forces placing the town under siege and pre-emptive detentions by the security forces of young people accused of making fun of the visit appeared on social networks. Even more, graffiti calling for the overthrow of the Sultan appeared on Sohar walls.

The retired senior civil servant mentioned above, who takes care, by way of introduction, to clarify that he "loves His Majesty" and "will be loyal and indebted [to him] all [his] life", explains:

I am not afraid of activists but rather of young poor population who has nothing to lose and whose anger can be destructive […] Ordinary people don't believe [the

Sultan] can change anything to the situation. He is perceived as far and disconnected from real issues. The old man is alone, terribly alone, he has very few friends
or people he trusts.[57]

The protests have obviously not developed with the same intensity and to the
same scale as have uprisings elsewhere in the Arab world. But the Omani Spring
has produced a result of no less critical significance for the future of Omani politics: that is, the de-sacralisation of Sultan Qaboos. It goes without saying that
Qaboos remains the only candidate for power. However, many Omanis are now
aware that the Sultan will be held accountable for decisions that will impact the
post-Qaboos Oman for generations, since the absence of a prime minister and
of senior cabinet members leaves him in the firing line, as jokes about him that
have thrived on Internet can testify to. One teacher explains:

> Qaboos is an old man, he is a man who is alone and who does not understand his
> country anymore. He does not trust anybody, only a close circle of individuals who
> are the only ones to report to him on the situation in the country ... I am afraid [the
> Sultan] may squander all he has built and the popular recognition he has accumu-
> lated for forty years. I am supporting the nomination of a Prime Minister or a
> Crown Prince as soon as possible, in order for Qaboos to keep his image of "Son of
> God on Earth" that he has built for himself.[58]

In July 2014, the Sultan traveled to Germany to receive medical care. A
short television address in early November followed by his return to Oman in
March 2015 provided a feeling of temporary relief to many, who are well
aware of the considerable turmoil his sudden demise may provoke. However
it failed to silence rumors of cancer, especially since Qaboos undertook
another two month-long medical trip to Germany between February and
April 2016.

In October 2015, 590 candidates contested the elections for the 85 seats of
the Consultative Council. In June, the Ministry of Interior had banned 174
candidates from taking part in the elections, including three incumbent
Council members, for political reasons. The voter turnout stood at 57%, reg-
istering a 20% drop compared to 2011, illustrating the disillusionment of
many young Omanis after four years of political standstill. Of the 20 female
candidates, only one won a seat.

After the Omani Spring, the regime has desperately attempted to perpetuate what the United Nations special rapporteur called in September 2014 a
"pervasive culture of silence and fear affecting anyone who wants to speak and
work for reforms in Oman".[59] This only confirms the authorities' disarray in
the face of a development they can no longer stop: the flourishing criticism of

the elite's political management of this critical juncture in Oman's history. These grievances are made explicitly in the name of Oman and out of concern for the future of the country. As one of the Sohar activists summarises, "Qaboos has become somebody like anybody else, he can make mistakes like anybody else".[60] This dramatic change in the relationship between society and its leadership confronts the Qaboos State with unprecedented questions whose answers can no longer be delayed.

NOTES

INTRODUCTION

1. The Economist, 18 November 2000.
2. W. Thesiger, Arabian Sands, New York, Longmans, 1959.
3. For more details about this region, see the works of Dawn Chatty, like Mobile Pastoralists: Development Planning and Social Change in Oman, New York, Columbia University Press, 1996.
4. M. Weber, Economy and Society, New York, Bedminster Press, 1968, vol. 1, pp. 212 ff.
5. A. Przeworski, "Some Problems in the Study of the Transition to Democracy", in G. O'Donnell, P. Schmitter and L. Whitehead (eds), Transitions from Authoritarian Rule. Comparative Perspectives, Baltimore, Johns Hopkins University Press, 1986, pp. 52.
6. L. Anderson, "Absolutism and the Resilience of Monarchy in the Middle East", Political Science Quarterly 106, 1 (1991), p. 3.

1. FOUNDATIONS OF THE MODERN STATE

1. See Tuhfat al-a'yan bi-sirat ahl 'uman [the work of the notables in the history of the people of Oman], book 1, Seeb (Oman), Maktabiyya Nur al-Din al-Salimi, 2000, p. 29.
2. For a detailed study of the socio-economic history of Oman, focusing on the role of the *falaj* in the geographical organisation of settlement, see J. Wilkinson, Water and Tribal Settlement in South-East Africa, Oxford, Clarendon Press, 1977.
3. Literally "those going out". The term gained the pejorative overtone of "secessionist".
4. See T. Lewicki, "al-Ibadiyya", in Encyclopaedia of Islam, new ed., Leiden, E.J. Brill, vol. III, p. 649. John Wilkinson (in The Imamate Tradition of Oman, Cambridge University Press, 1987, p. 153 and p. 340) is doubtful about the historical reality

of the content of this doctrine, which may have been reconstructed and formalised much later.

5. Apart from the periods of territorial expansion, in Africa or the Indian subcontinent, the Imamate revenues were always very weak, restricted to Islamic alms and taxes on agricultural production and trade with the coast of Oman.

6. The Imamate Tradition of Oman, op. cit., p. 187.

7. One of the "bearers", 'Abd Allah bin Rustam, conquered the town of Tahert (now Tiaret in Algeria) and made it the capital of the Rustemid Imamate (776–909), which represented the apex of Ibadism in North Africa. Nowadays the Ibadi remnants in the Maghreb, heirs of this golden age, are in Algeria (Mzab), in Tunisia (Djerba) and in Libya (Jabal Nafusa).

8. J. Wilkinson, The Imamate Tradition of Oman, op. cit., p. 72.

9. See for instance the use of the term "the true Oman" to designate the mostly Ibadi interior region, in C. Le Cour Grandmaison, "Présentation du sultanat d'Oman", in P. Bonnenfant (ed.), La péninsule Arabique aujourd'hui, Paris, Editions du CNRS, 1982, vol. 2. We prefer here the more neutral term "interior Oman", which refers to the expression used in Oman by a majority of the population. It covers a mostly Ibadi population, which invokes an Arab tribal ascendancy and is native to present-day Dakhliyya, Dhahira, North Sharqiyya and South Batina governorates.

10. For an extensive study of the quarrel, see J. Wilkinson, The Imamate Tradition of Oman, op. cit., pp. 166 ff.

11. Ibn Battuta, Travels in Asia and Africa. 1325–1354 (selected by H. Gibb), London, Routledge, 1929, p. 303.

12. The notion of sheikh in Oman encompasses three things which usually go together but can be dissociated: religious knowledge, age and a hereditary familiar social distinction. Here, sheikh designates especially the last-named feature.

13. R. Bocco, "'Asabiyat tribales et Etats au Moyen-Orient; confrontations et connivences", Monde Arabe Maghreb Machrek 147 (1995), p. 5.

14. In Oman, 'arab does not necessarily denote Bedouin descent.

15. Interview, 8 February 2003.

16. E.E. Evans-Pritchard, The Nuer. A Description of the Modes of Livelihood and Political Institutions of a Nilotic People, Oxford, Clarendon Press, 1960 (original 1940), p. 149.

17. D. Eickelman, The Middle East and Central Asia. An Anthropological Approach, Upper Saddle River, NJ, Prentice Hall, 2002, 4th ed., pp. 131–2.

18. I paraphrase Jean-François Bayart, according to whom "ethnicity is a process of culture and identity, rather than a given structure": The State in Africa: The Politics of the Belly, London, Longman, 1993, p. 56.

19. J. Wilkinson, The Imamate Tradition of Oman, op. cit., pp. 123 and 139.

20. See Ibn Khaldun, The Muqaddimah: An Introduction to History, Princeton University Press, 1980, chapter 2.

21. J. Wilkinson, The Imamate Tradition of Oman, op. cit., p. 124.
22. Interview, 2 December 2002.
23. See for instance H. Ghubash, Oman. The Islamic Democratic Tradition, New York, Routledge, 2006.
24. For a detailed study of Sa'id's move to Zanzibar, see M. Bhacker, Trade and Empire in Muscat and Zanzibar: Roots of British Domination, London, Routledge, 1992.
25. Many works have contributed to knowledge of Omani connections with East Africa. See for instance Abdul Sheriff and Ed Ferguson (eds), Zanzibar under Colonial Rule, London, James Currey, 1991.
26. C. Le Cour Grandmaison, "Rich Cousins, Poor Cousins: Hidden Stratification among the Omani Arabs in Eastern Africa", Africa 59, 2 (1989), p. 178.
27. In this book, as in the usage of actors themselves in three languages (Arabic, English and French), the term "return" is used of the resettlement in Oman, from the 1960s until now, of individuals and families who claim Omani ancestry and who previously lived in East Africa. Talk of "return to the native country" only partially covers the facts, as most of them had personally never set foot in Oman before their "return". But we retain this explicit vocabulary which attests both to their will to appear distinct from the African societies (especially their former slaves) among which they lived for decades and to the complexity of their symbolic ties with Oman since their re-settlement in that country.
28. John Peterson, "Oman's Diverse Society: Northern Oman", Middle East Journal 58, 1 (2004), p. 46.
29. This figure is an estimate based on fieldwork in Oman, since the official documents never mention figures for religion and tribal or ethnic groups.
30. S. al-Mughayri, Juhaynat al-Akhbar fi Tarikh Zinjibar [Established facts about the history of Zanzibar], Muscat, Ministry of National Heritage and Culture, 1995.
31. M. E. Limbert, In the Time of Oil: Piety, Memory, and Social Life in an Omani Town, Stanford, Stanford University Press, 2010, p. 145.
32. S. Miles, The Countries and Tribes of the Persian Gulf, Reading, Garnet, 1994, p. 526 (1st ed. 1919).
33. C. Niebuhr, Description de l'Arabie, Copenhagen, Nicolas Möller, 1773, p. 264.
34. C. Allen, "Sayyids, Shets and Sultans: Politics and Trade in Masqat under the Al Bu Sa'id. 1785–1914", University of Washington, unpublished PhD dissertation, 1978, pp. 118 ff.
35. F. Barth, Sohar: Culture and Society in an Omani Town, Baltimore, Johns Hopkins University Press, 1983, p. 212.
36. During the 1991 Gulf war and after the American invasion of Iraq in 2003, these families accommodated Basra and Kuwaiti relatives who fled the war zones.
37. A. al-Salimi, op. cit., book 2, pp. 259 and 265.
38. L. Layne, Home and Homeland; the Dialogics of Tribal and National Identities of Jordan, Princeton University Press, 1994, p. 7.

39. John Lorimer assembled all this information in Calcutta: Gazetteer of the Persian Gulf, 'Oman, and Central Arabia, Gerrards Cross, Archives Editions, 1986 (1st ed. 1915), 9 vols.

40. For instance, A. al-Salimi, op. cit. and Ibn Ruzayq, Al-fath al-mubin fi-sirat al-sada al-Busa'idiyyin (The brilliant conquest in al-Busa'idi's history), Muscat, Ministry of National Heritage and Culture, 2001 (5th ed.; orig. 1858).

41. See S. a-Kharusi, Malamah min al-tarikh al-'umani (Features of the Omani history), Seeb, Maktab al-damri li-nashr wal-tawzi', 2002 (3rd ed.; orig. n.d.); or S. al-Siyabi, 'Uman abr al-tarikh (Oman through history). Muscat, Ministry of National Heritage and Culture, 2001 (4th ed.; orig. 1982), 4 vols.

42. R. Zahlan, The Making of the Modern Gulf States: Kuwait, Bahrain, Qatar, the United Arab Emirates and Oman, London, Unwin Hyman, 1989, pp. 13–14.

43. J. Peterson, Oman in the Twentieth Century. Political Foundations of an Emerging State, London, Croom Helm, 1978, p. 60.

44. Ibid., p. 48.

45. Ibid., p. 170.

46. For an in-depth account by the British representative of the circumstances prior to the signing, and of the agreement itself, see R/15/6/264 (reprinted in R. Bailey (ed.), Records of Oman, vol. 3, Farnham Common, Archives Editions, 1988, pp. 198–211).

47. Personal translation.

48. In R. Bailey (ed.), op. cit., p. 205.

49. Quoted by J. Wilkinson, The Imamate Tradition of Oman, op. cit., p. 251.

50. See J. Kelly, "A Prevalence of Furies: Tribes, Politics, and Religion in Oman and Trucial Oman", in D. Hopwood (ed.), The Arabian Peninsula. Society and Politics, London, George Allen and Unwin, 1972, p. 122. For a contradictory interpretation, see St. John Philby's despatches in Middle East Journal, 13, 1 (1959), pp. 126–7 and 13, 4 (1959), p. 487.

51. B. Berman, "Ethnicity, Patronage and the African State: The Politics of Uncivil Nationalism", African Affairs 97, 388 (1998), p. 315.

52. J. Wilkinson, The Imamate Tradition of Oman, op. cit., p. 8.

53. F. Bailey, Stratagems and Spoils. A Social Anthropology of Politics, Oxford, Blackwell, 1969, chapter 8.

2. TWO LEGITIMACIES AND NO STATE

1. Quoted by J. Peterson, Oman in the Twentieth Century, op. cit., p. 104.

2. Ibid., p. 52.

3. Ibid., pp. 89–90.

4. D. Eickelman, "From Theocracy to Monarchy: Authority and Legitimacy in Inner Oman, 1935–1957", International Journal of Middle East Studies 17 (1985), p. 11.

5. J. Wilkinson, The Imamate Tradition of Oman, op. cit., p. 259.

6. J. Townsend, Oman. The Making of a Modern State. London, Croom Helm, 1977, p. 46.

7. In R. Bailey (ed.), Records of Oman, op. cit, vol. 1, 1988, annex 1, p. 130.

8. D. Eickelman, From Theocracy to Monarchy, op. cit., p. 11.

9. J. Peterson, Oman in the Twentieth Century, op. cit., pp. 96 ff.

10. In Oil and Politics in the Gulf; Rulers and Merchants in Kuwait and Qatar, Cambridge University Press, 1995, 2nd ed., p. 110.

11. C. Allen, "Sayyids, Shets and Sultans...," op. cit., 1978, p. 187.

12. Interview, 11 March 2003.

13. R/15/6/25, in R. Bailey (ed.), op. cit., vol. 6, p. 432.

14. R. Landen, Oman since 1856: Disruptive Modernization in a Traditional Arab Society, Princeton University Press, 1967, pp. 139–40.

15. Interview, 19 March 2003.

16. M. Field, The Merchants; The Big Business Families of Saudi Arabia and the Gulf States, Woodstock (NY), The Overlook Press, 1985, p. 158.

17. J. Peterson, op. cit, p. 73.

18. Ibid., note 7, p. 104.

19. C. Allen and L. Rigsbee. Oman under Qaboos: From Coup to Constitution, 1970–1996, London, Frank Cass, 2000, p. 22.

20. J. Wilkinson, op. cit., p. 4.

21. Muhammad bin 'Abd Allah al-Salimi, Nahdat al-a'yan bi-hurriyat 'uman (The notables' renaissance in the liberation of Oman), Cairo, Matabi' Dar al-Kitab al-'Arabi bi-Misr, 1961.

22. J. Wilkinson, op. cit, p. 5.

23. W. Thesiger, Arabian Sands, op. cit., p. 305.

24. See R/15/8/62/51, quoted by D. Eickelman, From Theocracy to Monarchy, op. cit., note 42, p. 24.

25. R. Landen, op. cit., p. 303.

26. In 1951, the Dhofar area of the concession was relinquished and the company became Petroleum Development Oman, a name kept until now.

27. They were to become the Trucial Oman Scouts the following year.

3. THE FOUNDING CONFLICTS OF THE MODERN NATIONAL IDENTITY

1. For more in-depth discussions of the 1954 election, see J. Peterson, Oman in the Twentieth Century, op. cit., pp. 181–2 and J. Wilkinson, op. cit., pp. 308–9.

2. Journalist James Morris gave an enthusiastic account of it in Sultan in Oman, London, Faber and Faber, 1957.

3. J. Peterson, Oman in the Twentieth Century, op. cit., p. 29.

4. J. Beasant, Oman. The True-Life Drama and Intrigue of an Arab State, Edinburgh, Mainstream Publishing, 2002, p. 77.

5. In March 1957, the MOFF took the name of the Oman Regiment, while the Batina Force became the Northern Frontier Regiment. Both troops were placed under the general supervision of Col. Waterfield (see J. Peterson, "Britain and 'the Oman War': an Arabian entanglement", Asian Affairs, 63, 3 (1976), note 12, p. 296).

6. R. Bailey (ed.), Records of Oman, op. cit., vol. 9, pp. 314–15.

7. Quoted by J. Wilkinson, op. cit., p. 291.

8. New York Herald Tribune, 24 July 1957.

9. Debates in the House of Commons on 22 July 1957, in R. Bailey (ed.), op. cit., vol. 9, p. 264.

10. P. Allfree, Warlords of Oman, London, Robert Hale, 1967, p. 171.

11. A. Shepherd, Arabian Adventure, London, Collins, 1961, p. 102; D. Smiley, Arabian Assignment, London, Leo Cooper, 1975, p. 58.

12. D. Eickelman, From Theocracy to Monarchy, op. cit., pp. 19–20.

13. J. Peterson, "Britain and 'the Oman war'", op. cit., pp. 292–3.

14. P. Allfree, op. cit., p. 140.

15. H. Ghubash, Oman, op. cit, p. 183.

16. Le Monde, 21 January 1961.

17. J. Peterson, "Britain and 'the Oman war'", op. cit., p. 294.

18. The Guardian, 4 September 1971.

19. See the first bulletin emitted by the Imamate office in Baghdad in May 1962, reproduced in A. Burdett (ed.), Records of Oman; 1962, Farnham Common, Archives Editions, 1997, p. 604.

20. Letters written by the Political Resident (Bahrain) to the British Consul in Muscat, dated 16 February 1963, and by the British Ambassador in Damascus to the Foreign Office, dated 18 June 1963, in A. Burdett (ed.), Records of Oman; 1963, Farnham Common, Archives Editions, 1997, pp. 612 and 618.

21. Statistical Yearbook 2016, Muscat, National Centre for Statistics and Information, August 2016.

22. Foreign Office telegram to the Political Agent on 29 July 1960, quoted by F. Owtram, A Modern History of Oman. Formation of the State since 1920, London, I.B. Tauris, 2004, p. 109.

23. The most important texts of the different Fronts between 1965 and 1974 are reproduced in Documents of the National Struggle in Oman and the Arabian Gulf, London, The Gulf Committee, 1974.

24. F. Trabulsi, "The Liberation of Dhufar", MERIP Reports 6 (1972), p. 8.

25. For an in-depth study of the ideological evolution of the movement, see F. Halliday, Arabia without Sultans, London, Penguin Books, 1974, chapter 11.

26. F. Trabulsi, op. cit., p. 9.

27. From 1972, when Iran established closer ties with Iraq and China, the USSR and

Libya were to be, with South Yemen, the most reliable supporters of the rebellion.

28. Le Monde, 19 June 1970; The Economist, 18 July 1970.

29. J. Peterson, "Guerilla Warfare and Ideological Confrontation in the Arabian Peninsula: the Rebellion of Dhufar", World Affairs, 139, 4 (1977), p. 282.

30. D. Arkless, The Secret War; Dhofar, 1971–1972, London, William Kimber, 1988, pp. 82–3. Several times napalm spreading has been mentioned (see for instance The Economist, 18 October 1969), and this was confirmed to us by local people (Interview, 3 September 2003).

31. In December 1971, PFLOAG (Dhofar) and NDFLOAG (North) merged into the Popular Front for the Liberation of Oman and the Arabian Gulf (PFLOAG).

32. Documents of the National Struggle, op. cit., pp. 64–8.

33. Financial Times, 15 November 1972.

34. Le Monde, 16 March 1976 and International Herald Tribune, 18 July 1979.

35. Interview, 6 March 2003.

36. J. Peterson, "Guerilla Warfare...", op. cit., p. 285, and F. Halliday, op. cit., p. 345.

37. J. Peterson, "Guerilla Warfare...", op. cit., p. 286.

38. F. Trabulsi, op. cit., p. 9.

39. D. Smiley, op. cit., p. 17.

40. J. Peterson, Oman in the Twentieth Century, op. cit., pp. 85–6.

41. Letter of the Political Resident in Bahrain to the Foreign Office, 29 May 1959, in R. Bailey (ed.), op. cit., vol. 9, pp. 681–2.

42. J. Peterson, Oman in the Twentieth Century, op.cit., p. 85, and J. Beasant, op.cit., pp. 88–9.

43. J. Wilkinson, op. cit., pp. 302 and 317.

44. "The Sultan's Personality", in R. Bailey (ed.), op. cit., vol. 10, p. 337.

45. F. Halliday, op. cit., p. 313.

46. D. Smiley, op. cit., p. 41.

47. B. Pridham, "Oman: Change or Continuity?", in I. Netton (ed.), Arabia and the Gulf: From Traditional Society to Modern States, Totowa, Barnes and Noble, 1986, p. 135.

48. D. Smiley, op. cit., pp. 40–1.

49. B. Pridham, op. cit., p. 140.

50. Interview with one of the missionaries who came to Oman in 1955, 1 March 2003.

51. J. Peterson, Oman in the Twentieth Century, op. cit., p. 207. See also O. Winckler, "The Challenge of Foreign Workers in the Persian/Arabian Gulf: the Case of Oman", Immigrants and Minorities, 19, 2 (2000), pp. 35–7.

52. R. Landen, op. cit., p. 156.

53. N. Vatin and G. Veinstein, Le sérail ébranlé. Essai sur les morts, dépositions et avènements des sultans ottomans. XIVe-XIXe siècle, Paris, Fayard, 2003, p. 72.

54. For a detailed account of the events, see J. Beasant, op. cit., p. 115 and A. Takriti, "The 1970 Coup in Oman Reconsidered", Journal of Arabian Studies 3 (2013).
55. Sa'id bin Taimur is buried in the Muslim cemetery of Woking, in Surrey (J. Beasant, op. cit., p. 64).

4. LEGITIMISATION BY THE WELFARE STATE

1. In State in Society: Studying How States and Societies Transform and Constitute One Another, Cambridge University Press, 2001, pp. 257–8.
2. Statistical Yearbook 2016, op. cit.
3. D. Greig, International Law (2nd ed.), London, Butterworths, 1976, p. 93.
4. Speech on the occasion of the first National Day on 23 July 1971, reproduced in The Royal Speeches of H. M. Sultan Qaboos bin Said. 1970–2000, Muscat, Ministry of Information, 2001, p. 17.
5. Interview, March 2003.
6. The Times of Oman, 13 April 2005.
7. J. Kelly, "A Prevalence of Furies: Tribes, Politics ad Religion in Oman and Trucial Oman", in D. Hopwood (ed.), The Arabian Peninsula..., op. cit., p. 141.
8. C. Allen and L. Rigsbee, Oman under Qaboos, op. cit., p. 195.
9. Interview, 31 May 2003.
10. Quoted by F. al-Sayegh, "The UAE and Oman: Opportunities and Challenges in the Twentieth-First Century", Middle East Policy 19, 3 (2002), p. 134.
11. Agence France-Presse, 22 June 2002.
12. Jeremy Jones and Nicholas Ridout, Oman, Culture and Diplomacy, Edinburgh University Press, 2012; for Oman-Great Britain and Oman-United States relations since 1970, see F. Owtram, A Modern History of Oman..., op. cit., chapter 6.
13. C. Allen and L. Rigsbee, op. cit., pp. 180–1.
14. F. Mermier, "De l'invention du patrimoine omanais", in M. Lavergne and B. Dumortier (eds), L'Oman contemporain; Etat, territoire, identité, Paris, Karthala, 2003, p. 245.
15. Sultan Qaboos also encouraged diplomatic rapprochement between Pakistan and India, as in 1985 when he hosted both countries' presidents on the occasion of Oman's National Day.
16. R. Zahlan, The Making of the Modern Gulf States..., op. cit., p. 137.
17. J. Townsend, "Le sultanat d'Oman; vers la fin d'un particularisme séculaire?", Maghreb-Machrek 94 (1981), p. 41.
18. C. Allen and L. Rigsbee, op. cit., p. 191.
19. O. Da Lage, "L'URSS amorce une percée diplomatique dans le Golfe", Le Monde Diplomatique (November 1985), p. 6.
20. Interview, 30 September 2003.
21. The Times, 18 November 1974.
22. F. Owtram, op. cit., p. 175. In both cases, it is planned that no foreign troops can

be stationed permanently on Omani territory, so as to make these agreements as invisible as possible.

23. C. Allen and L. Rigsbee, op. cit., p. 200.
24. J. Kechichian, Oman and the World, Santa Monica, Rand, 1995, p. 246.
25. Statistical Yearbook 2016, op. cit.
26. F. Scholz, "Social Segregation and Comparative Poverty in the Expanding Capital of an Oil State", in M. Bonine (ed.), Population, Poverty and Politics in Middle East Cities, Miami, University Press of Florida, 1997, p. 147.
27. C. Allen and L. Rigsbee, op. cit., p. 162.
28. Le Monde, 14 May 1976.
29. F. Halliday, Arabia without Sultans, op. cit., p. 291.
30. Interview, 15 January 2003.
31. Statistical Yearbook 2016, op. cit.
32. Ibid.
33. Ibid.
34. M. Lavergne, "Le territoire omanais", in M. Lavergne and B. Dumortier (eds), op. cit., p. 179. In October 2006 a fourth governorate was established: Buraimi.
35. There are 61 wilayas in 2017.
36. E. Gellner, Nations and Nationalism, Oxford, Blackwell, 1983, p. 37.
37. B. Pridham, "Oman: Change or Continuity?", op. cit., p. 138.
38. Ibid., p. 139.
39. Financial Times, 13 March 1984, p. III.
40. On the other hand, young Omanis can attend international schools (British and Egyptian ones, for instance) only with special permission.
41. Statistical Yearbook 2016, op. cit.; C. Allen and L. Rigsbee, op. cit., pp. 168–9.
42. For 1993 figures, Status of Woman in the Sultanate of Oman, Muscat, Ministry of Social Affairs, Work and Vocational Training/UNICEF, 2001, p. 24; for 2003, Statistical Yearbook 2003, Muscat, Ministry of Information, 2003, 14th edition; for 2010, Oman Observer, 9 April 2013.
43. This allowance is worth 120 Omani rials (OR) if the student is not accommodated in a university room (1 OR= 1000 baisas= 2.6 US dollars).
44. B. Pridham, op. cit., p. 141.
45. Statistical Yearbook 2016, op. cit.
46. Ibid.
47. Interview, 15 March 2003.
48. Statistical Yearbook 2016, op. cit.
49. F. Halliday, op. cit., p. 292.
50. Socio-Economic Atlas, Muscat, Ministry of Development, 1996, p. 6.
51. Except societies with a majority of public capital, and army and security forces.
52. Statistical Yearbook 2016, op. cit.
53. N. Ayubi, Over-Stating the Arab State: Politics and Society in the Middle East, London, I.B. Tauris, 1995, p. 323.

54. H. Mahdavy, "The Patterns and Problems of Economic Development in Rentier States: the Case of Iran", in M. Cook (ed.), Studies in the Economic History of the Middle East, London, Oxford University Press, 1970.

55. M. Chatelus, "De la rente pétrolière au développement économique: perspectives et contradictions de l'évolution économique dans la péninsule", in P. Bonnenfant (ed.), op. cit., vol. 1, p. 83.

56. H. Beblawi, "The Rentier State in the Arab World", in H. Beblawi and G. Luciani (eds), The Rentier State, London, Croom Helm, 1987, pp. 51–2.

57. G.Luciani, "Allocation vs. Production States: A Theoretical Framework", in ibid., p. 69.

58. H. Beblawi, op. cit., p. 52.

59. J. Davis, Libyan Politics: Tribe and Revolution, London, I.B. Tauris, 1987.

60. J. Crystal, op. cit.

61. G. Luciani, "The Oil Rent, the Fiscal Crisis of the State and Democratization", in G. Salamé (ed.), Democracy without Democrats? The Renewal of Politics in the Muslim World, London, I.B. Tauris, 1994, p. 132.

62. J. Crystal, op. cit., pp. 7–8.

63. Ibid., pp. 8–9 and 75.

64. J. Peterson, Oman in the Twentieth Century, op. cit., pp. 203–4.

65. At the beginning of 1970, Sultan Sa'id and sheikh Ahmad al-Harthi had agreed to the engagement of Qaboos to Ahmad's daughter. But the Sultan was deposed and this engagement was forgotten (J. Townsend, Oman. The Making of a Modern State, op. cit., p. 72).

66. C. Allen and L. Rigsbee, op. cit., p. 35.

67. Le Monde, 30 May 1971.

68. Ibid.

69. Besides the experts mentioned above, several businessmen revolved round the Sultan, among them Robert Anderson, a former US Secretary of Treasury (see J. Townsend, Oman, op. cit., pp. 88 ff.; J. Peterson, Oman in the Twentieth Century, op. cit., p. 216).

70. Le Monde, 29 May 1971.

71. J. Townsend, Oman, op. cit., pp. 127 ff.

72. One of the most influential members was 'Abd al-Hafidh al-'Ujayli, a Dhofari of African origin who had an engineering diploma from Kiev and had married a Russian wife. He was appointed Minister of the Economy in late 1971. After holding the portfolios of Communications and Public Services, then of Agriculture and Fisheries during the 1970s and 1980s, he is currently chairman of Bank Dhofar.

73. J. Townsend, Oman, op. cit., p. 139.

74. Ibid., pp. 93 and 119.

75. M. Herb, All in the Family. Absolutism, Revolution and Democracy in the Middle Eastern Monarchies, Albany, University of New York Press, 1999, pp. 8 and 145.

76. J. Peterson, Oman in the Twentieth Century, op. cit., p. 208.

77. J. Townsend, Le sultanat d'Oman, op. cit., p. 47.

78. See chapter 9.

79. J. Crystal, "Coalitions in Oil Monarchies: Kuwait and Qatar", Comparative Politics 21, 4 (1989), p. 435.

80. J. Peterson, Oman in the Twentieth Century, op. cit., p. 99.

81. C. Allen and L. Rigsbee, op. cit., pp. 45 and 195.

82. J. Peterson, op. cit., p. 195.

83. H. Beblawi, op. cit., p. 56.

84. K. al-Naqeeb, Society and State in the Gulf and Arab Peninsula; a Different Perspective, London, Centre for Arab Unity Studies, 1990, p. 115.

85. Interviews, January 2003.

86. Four companies share most of wholesale trade and food distribution in Oman: Khimji Ramdas, Khalijana (owned by Suhail Bahwan group), Muttrah Cold Stores (WJ Towell group) and Bhacker Suleiman Jaffer.

87. Interview, 4 March 2003.

88. Interview, 21 January 2003.

89. J. Townsend, Oman, op. cit., p. 138.

90. C. Allen and L. Rigsbee, op. cit., p. 118. Restrictions were to be tightened in Article 53 of the Basic Law, in 1996 (see chapter 7).

91. International Herald Tribune, 9 February 1976.

92. Interviews, 21 January 2003 and 13 February 2006.

93. The Finance Council created in November 1974 had the right to examine the expenditure of every ministry, especially when dealing with public contracts with private companies.

94. J. Crystal, Oil and Politics in the Gulf, op. cit., p. 187.

95. G. Luciani, Allocation vs. Production States, op. cit., p. 75.

96. L. Anderson, op. cit., p. 14.

5. NATIONAL IDENTITY BUILDING

1. B. Anderson, Imagined Communities: Reflections on the Origin and Spread of Nationalism, London, Verso, 2006 (1st ed: 1983).

2. E. Hobsbawm, Nations and Nationalism since 1780: Programme, Myth, Reality, Cambridge University Press, 1990, p. 78.

3. A. Dieckhoff, La nation dans tous ses Etats; les identités nationales en mouvement, Paris, Champs-Flammarion, 2002, p. 76.

4. Statistical Yearbook 2016, op. cit.

5. Interview, 14 August 2004.

6. A.-M. Thiesse, La création des identités nationales; Europe XVIIIe-XXe siècle, Paris, Seuil, 2001, p. 240.

7. The impact that socialisation by school system has had on Ibadi self-perception is studied by Dale Eickelman, "Ibadism and the Sectarian Perspective", in B. Pridham (ed.), Oman: Economic, Social and Strategic Developments, London, Croom Helm, 1987, pp. 38 ff.

8. Le Monde, 6–7 April 2003.

9. L. Roussel in Le Monde, 6–7 April 2003.

10. Interview, 10 May 2003.

11. For instance: "Census counts because you count" (8 September 2003); "Census is the means to inventory of the most precious nation's wealth... People" (27 August 2003).

12. The Times, 18 November 1974.

13. See al-Khalij, 12 October 2005 and Gulf News, 12 September 2006. The first two private radio channels (one in Arabic, one in English), both owned by OHI group, were launched in 2007; Sabco launched a new Arabic one in March 2008.

14. The Oman Observer, 29 October 2005.

15. D. Eickelman, "Mass Higher Education and the Religious Imagination in Contemporary Arab Societies," American Ethnologist, 19, 4 (1992), pp. 648–9.

16. C. Allen and L. Rigsbee, op. cit., p. 159.

17. Interviews, September 2007.

18. D. Eickelman, "Identité nationale et discours religieux en Oman", in Gilles Kepel and Yann Richard (eds), Intellectuels et militants de l'Islam contemporain, Paris, Seuil, 1990, p. 117.

19. Interview, 31 August 2005. There is no Shi'i qadi in Oman. As for appointments of imams of Shi'i mosques, it is settled between marja'iyya of Najaf and the Diwan of the Royal Court, independently of the Ministry of Religious Affairs.

20. www.cia.gov/library/publications/the-world-factbook/geos/mu.html.

21. D. Eickelman, "Kings and People: Information and Authority in Oman, Qatar and the Persian Gulf", in J. Kechichian (ed.), Iran, Iraq, and the Arab Gulf States, New York, Palgrave, 2001, p. 202.

22. J. Peterson, "Oman's Diverse Society: Northern Oman", Middle East Journal 58, 1 (2004), p. 32.

23. D. Eickelman, Identité nationale, op. cit., p. 111.

24. M. Zeghal, "S'éloigner, se rapprocher: la gestion et le contrôle de l'islam dans la République de Bourguiba et la monarchie de Hassan II", in R. Leveau and A. Hammoudi (eds), Monarchies arabes; transitions et dérives dynastiques, Paris, La Documentation Française, 2002, p. 69.

25. Le Monde, 29 May 1993.

26. F. Mermier, "De l'invention du patrimoine omanais", in M. Lavergne and B. Dumortier (eds), op. cit., p. 255.

27. See an account of some harsh debates among Ibadi scholars since the 1990s in K. al-Azri, Social and Gender Inequality in Oman: The Power of Religious and Political Tradition, London, Routledge, 2012.

28. Tabligh's Omani development was already noted by Dale Eickelman in the late 1980s (in Identité nationale, op. cit., p. 121).

29. Interview, 7 March 2003.

30. B. Anderson, op. cit., p. 195.

31. Speech on the day of his accession, in The Royal Speeches, op. cit., p. 14.

32. B. Anderson, op. cit., p. 201.

33. Interview, 27 May 2003.

34. J.-F. Bayart, Le gouvernement du monde. Une critique politique de la mondialisation, Paris, Fayard, 2004, p. 85 (personal translation).

35. Speech on the occasion of the fourth National Day, 18 November 1974, in The Royal Speeches, op. cit., p. 24 and 29.

36. Interview, 14 February 2006.

37. Speech on the occasion of Sultan Qaboos' arrival in Muscat, on 27 July 1970, in The Royal Speeches, op. cit., p. 15.

38. Speech on the occasion of the 20th National Day, 18 November 1990, in ibid., p. 138.

39. Speech on the occasion of the second National Day, 18 November 1972, in ibid., p. 18.

40. The Oman Observer, 18 November 2003.

41. Interview, 2 February 2003.

42. F. Clements, Oman. The Reborn Land, London, Longman, 1980.

43. P. Searle, Dawn over Oman, London, Allen and Unwin, 1979.

44. D. Hawley, Oman and its Renaissance, London, Stacey International, 1977. In British and French newspapers, as soon as Qaboos overthrew his father, the tone was similar: "Darkness into light" (The Guardian, 31 July 1970) or "La fin de la nuit" (Le Monde, 29 May 1971).

45. B. Pridham, "Oman: Change or Continuity?", op. cit., p. 136. There is no question here of concealing the despotic and paranoid nature of Sa'id bin Taimur's rule; but it is necessary to qualify the Manichaean perception we have of both reigns, propagated for political ends since 1970, and to highlight some undeniable elements of continuity, from the point of view of political practice.

46. J. Townsend, Oman, op. cit., pp. 196 and 198.

47. Speech on the occasion of the first National Day, 23 July 1971, in The Royal Speeches, op. cit., pp. 16–17.

48. For an overall perspective of projects undertaken before 1970, see B. Wace, "Master Plan for Muscat and Oman", The Geographical Magazine 41 (1969).

49. Le Monde, 27–8 May 1971.

50. Le Monde, 22 May 1973.

51. J. Miller, "Creating Modern Oman: an Interview with Sultan Qaboos", Foreign Affairs 76, 3 (1997) p. 17.

52. This infantilisation of the Omani population by the authorities has been high-

lighted by Dawn Chatty with respect to women's position in the development of the country; see D. Chatty, "Women Working in Oman: Individual Choice and Cultural Constraints", International Journal of Middle East Studies 32, 2 (2000).

53. M. al-Salimi, op. cit.

54. http://www.omanet.om/english/hmsq/hmsq2.asp?cat=hmsq (checked on 13 March 2008).

55. The Financial Times, 27 December 1985.

56. Personal interviews.

57. The Times, 27 July 1970.

58. N. Vatin et G. Veinstein, op. cit., p. 259.

59. The official historiography (see The Royal Speeches, op. cit., p. 14) establishes that this speech was given on 23 July (the actual day of the coup), while it was actually given four days later. In fact, the coup, which happened on a Thursday, was publicised on the next Sunday only, giving time to make sure that Sa'id bin Taimur was rendered harmless, far from Muscat (see J. Townsend, Oman, op. cit., p. 77).

60. The Guardian, 31 July 1970.

61. J. Townsend, Oman, op. cit., pp. 168–9.

62. Sultan Qaboos' words, quoted in the 2002 edition booklet of the Omani costumes festival.

63. G. Lenclud, "La tradition n'est plus ce qu'elle était…", Terrain 9 (1987), p. 121.

64. Interview, 19 May 2003.

65. F. Mermier, De l'invention du patrimoine omanais, op. cit., pp. 256 ff.

66. The International Symposium on Magan: Through Ages and the Trade Relations with Mesopotamia and Indus Valley (bilingual English-Arabic), Muscat, Ministry of Heritage and Culture, 2004, p. 5.

67. M. Zubayr and V. McBrierty, Oman-Ancient Civilisation: Modern Nation; Towards a Knowledge and Service Economy, Muscat/Dublin, Bait Zubair Foundation/ Trinity College Dublin Press, 2004.

68. E. Hobsbawm and T. O. Ranger, The Invention of Tradition, Cambridge University Press, 1996, p. 1.

69. This boat lies now in the middle of one of Muscat's roundabouts, near the al-Bustan hotel.

70. M. Stegath Dorr and N. Richardson, The Craft Heritage of Oman, Dubai, Motivate Publishing, 2004.

71. Omani dessert prepared with sugar and cardamom.

72. Oman: Years of Achievements, Muscat, Ministry of Information, 2001, p. 114.

73. The World Heritage Committee removed the site from the list in June 2007 because of Oman's decision to reduce the size of the protected area by 90% and plans to proceed with oil and gas exploration, in contravention of the Operational Guidelines of the Convention. See http://whc.unesco.org/en/news/362 (checked on 14 March 2008).

74. This term has been used by Linda Layne to describe Jordan's tribal culture: see "The Dialogics of Tribal Self-representation in Jordan", American Ethnologist 16, 1 (1989), p. 35.

75. B. Anderson, op. cit., p. 182.

76. It is interesting to note the symbolic role of roundabouts in Oman. These wide grassy areas with flower beds command the entrances to towns or mark the boundaries between urban districts, but above all serve as landmarks. The monuments adorning the central knoll usually mix an old-inspired architectural style with modern iconography and represent symbiosis between historical heritage and technical modernity; as expressions of the country's past heritage and the Sultan Qaboos-led renaissance, they embody the Omani nation's repositories of memory, for lack of battlefields or war memorials.

6. THE REINVENTED POLITICAL TRADITION

1. C. Geertz, "The Integrative Revolution. Primordial Sentiments and Civil Politics in the New States", in C. Geertz (ed.), Old Societies and New States. The Quest for Modernity in Asia and Africa, London, Free Press of Glencoe, 1963, p. 128.

2. O. Roy, "Groupes de solidarité au Moyen-Orient et en Asie Centrale; États, territoires et réseaux", Cahiers du CERI 16 (1996), pp. 7–9 and 45.

3. J.-F. Médard, "L'Etat patrimonialisé", Politique Africaine 39 (1990), p. 28.

4. F. Bailey, Stratagems and Spoils. A Social Anthropology of Politics, Oxford, Blackwell, 1969.

5. Speech on the occasion of the fourth National Day, 18 November 1974, in The Royal Speeches, op. cit., p. 28.

6. Interview, 26 May 2003.

7. G. Gause, "The Persistence of Monarchy in the Arabian Peninsula: a Comparative Analysis", in J. Kostiner (ed.), Middle East Monarchies. The Challenge of Modernity, Boulder and London, Lynne Rienner, 2000, pp. 174–5.

8. K. al-Naqeeb, op. cit., p. 107.

9. Interview, 1 December, 2002.

10. C. Allen and L. Rigsbee, op. cit., p. 76.

11. Dalil 'am wilayat wa qaba'il 'uman, Muscat, Ministry of the Interior, 1979.

12. Interview, 12 August 2004.

13. Obviously, in the rural zones, the hara usually coincides with a clan's own settlement area, which strengthens the perception by the individuals of a state in continuity with the pre-1970 period.

14. In the case of a child of two individuals who have Omani passports, the rashid's attestation is no more necessary.

15. Interview, 4 May 2004.

16. D. Eickelman, Identité nationale, op. cit., p. 120.

17. Interview, 13 August 2004.
18. Taghyurat al-qaba'il fi 'Uman, Muscat, Diwan of the Royal Court, n.d.
19. Speech to Senior State Officials, 15 May 1978, in The Royal Speeches, op. cit., pp. 58–9.
20. Speech on the occasion of the opening of the State Consultative Council, 3 November 1981, in The Royal Speeches, op. cit., p. 73.
21. D. Eickelman, "Kings and People: Oman's State Consultative Council", Middle East Journal 31, 1 (1984), pp. 59ff.
22. Ibid., p. 69.
23. The number of terms has later been limited to two, but since 2003 that clause has been cancelled once again.
24. For a detailed study of the 2003 elections, see M. Valeri, Le sultanat d'Oman: une révolution en trompe-l'oeil, Paris, Karthala, 2007, pp. 257 ff.
25. Any individual over 21, of good morals and mental health, with no criminal record, who does not belong to any military or security structure and is on the electoral register within the time defined by the law is allowed to vote.
26. A. Rouquié, "Conclusion", in G. Hermet, A. Rouquié and J. Linz, Des élections pas comme les autres, Paris, Presses de la FNSP, 1978, p. 173 (author's translation).
27. Interviews, April 2004 and September 2007.
28. Gulf News, 26 October 2007.
29. See for instance the series of articles entitled "The criteria of the successful candidate" in al-Watan on 10, 15 and 20 September 2003.
30. The only exception is Lujaina al-Za'abi, elected in Muscat in 2000 and 2003; but she did not stand in 2007.
31. Interviews, September and October 2003, and September 2007.
32. See the various pamphlets issued by the Ministry of Interior before the 2007 elections to press individuals, and particularly women, to register and vote. Moreover an "election awareness team" sponsored by the ministry toured the country during the first half of 2007.
33. Interview, 8 September 2003.
34. Interview, 25 April 2004.
35. Gulf News, 29 October 2007.
36. See also al-Watan, 7 October 2003.
37. Interview, 4 October 2003.
38. Interviews, 11 and 20 September 2007. As one Sohar citizen explained on 11 September: "Today this candidate offers 40 OR for a vote, but it is like stock exchange! The price will increase until the last day…"
39. Interview, 4 May 2004.
40. Interview, 31 August 2003.
41. Interview, 3 May 2004.

42. Speech on the occasion of the Opening of the Council of Oman on 27 December 1997, in The Royal Speeches, op. cit., pp. 202.

43. State Council. Royal Decrees of the State Council, Muscat, State Council, 2001, p. 22.

44. Ibid., pp. 23–4.

45. In al-Sharq al-Awsat (London), 4 March 1998.

46. M. Weber, op. cit., p. 231.

47. Ibid., p. 232.

48. H. Chehabi and J. Linz, "A Theory of Sultanism I", in H. Chehabi and J. Linz (eds), Sultanistic Regimes, Baltimore, Johns Hopkins University Press, 1998, p. 7.

49. The Guardian, 17 October 1970.

50. In Kings and People, op. cit., p. 70.

51. J. Miller, op. cit., p. 17.

52. A. Hammoudi, Master and Disciple. The Cultural Foundations of Moroccan Authoritarianism, University of Chicago Press, 1997, p. 63.

53. L. Layne, Home and Homeland; the Dialogics of Tribal and National Identities of Jordan, Princeton University Press, 1994, p. 146.

54. The Times of Oman, 18 March 2007.

55. al-Watan, 28 January 2003.

56. Le Monde, 22 June 1973; Political Prisoners in the Oil States: Oman, Bahrein, Saudi Arabia, Iran, London, Gulf Committee, 1974, pp. 10–11 and interview, 6 March 2003.

57. The Guardian, 8 August 1984.

58. Political Prisoners, op. cit., pp. 11–14. See also J. Townsend, Oman, op. cit., p. 135; B. Pridham, "Oman: Change or Continuity?", op. cit., p. 149.

59. http://www.wikileaks.org/plusd/cables/04MUSCAT2180_a.html (checked on 7 August 2014).

60. Interview, 4 May 2004.

61. Interview, 10 May 2003.

62. http://www.sipri.org/research/armaments/milex/milex_database.

63. International Herald Tribune, 21 November 1985 and Le Monde, 5–6 January 1986.

64. J. Beasant, op. cit., 2002, pp. 174–8; C. Jones and J. Stone, "Britain and the Arabian Gulf: New Perspectives on Strategic Influence", International Relations 13, 4 (1997), p. 10.

65. C. Jones and J. Stone, op. cit., p. 10; J. Beasant, op. cit., pp. 153–66.

66. Interview, 21 January 2003.

67. The Guardian, 28 August 2007.

68. J. Townsend, Le sultanat d'Oman, op. cit., p. 46; The Guardian, 16 August 1984.

69. C. Allen and L. Rigsbee, op. cit., pp. 76–8 and 91.

70. H. Eilts, "Foreign Policy Perspectives of the Gulf States" in R. Sindelar and

J. Peterson (eds), Crosscurrents in the Gulf: Arab, Regional and Global Interests, London/New York, Routledge, 1988, p. 32.

71. D. Eickelman, M. Dennison, "Arabizing the Omani Intelligence Services: Clash of Cultures?" International Journal of Intelligence and Counter-Intelligence 7 (1994), pp. 1–2.

72. A. Cordesman, Bahrain, Oman, Qatar and the UAE: Challenges of Security, Boulder, CO, Westview Press, 1997, p. 205.

73. Interview, 25 April 2004.

74. Statistical Yearbook 2016, op. cit.

7. LABORIOUS RENEWAL OF THE BASIS OF THE REGIME

1. The country's total production increased again after 2007, given that some fields, temporarily unexploited, are becoming profitable again.

2. Statistical Yearbook 2016, op. cit.

3. C. Allen and L. Rigsbee, Oman under Qaboos, op. cit., p. 119.

4. Besides information collected in Oman, this paragraph relies on Salem Abdullah's study: Omani Islamism: an Unexpected Confrontation with the Government, Washington, United Association for Studies and Research, Occasional Papers Series no. 8 (1995).

5. D. Eickelman, Identité nationale, op. cit., p. 127.

6. Interview, 23 February 2003. This approach is defended by Salem Abdullah (op. cit., p. 13).

7. S. Abdullah, op. cit., p. 15.

8. al-Hayat, August 30, 1994 and al-Sharq al-Awsat, August 30, 1994. At the same time, about thirty Shi'a from Muscat, accused of belong to the al-Da'wa political-religious movement, originating in Iraq, were arrested. Some of them were condemned to five years' imprisonment, but they were all released on the occasion of the Sultan's clemency measures in November 1995 (source: interview, 18 March 2007).

9. Speech on the occasion of the 24th National Day, 18 November 1994, in The Royal Speeches, op. cit., pp. 167–8.

10. S. Abdullah, op. cit., pp. 17 and 23.

11. Ibid., p. 24.

12. Detailed data for 83 of them, partial data for the others (in ibid.).

13. Interviews, 19 May 2003 and 19 April 2004.

14. Speech on the occasion of the 26th National Day, in The Royal Speeches, op. cit., p. 197.

15. N. Siegfried, "Legislation and Legitimation in Oman: the Basic Law", Islamic Law and Society, 7, 3 (2000), pp. 370–1.

16. In April 2003, Royal decree no. 35 authorised for the first time the establishment

of representative committees of employees, whether Omani or expatriate, at the level of the company, in the private sector alone. The Ministry of Manpower has the final decision on every committee registration and requires prior notification and agendas for committee meetings. To supervise all these committees, the government created in May 2005 a Main Representative Committee, at the national level, composed of elected members. In July 2006, Royal decree no. 74 granted to private-sector workers in Oman, for the first time, the right to form independent trade unions. It also stipulated the establishment of the General Federation of Oman Trade Unions (GFOTU) to be the formal body representing the workers of the Sultanate. This effort followed United States pressure, in connection with the bilateral Free Trade Agreement (FTA), which was signed in January 2006 and ratified by the US Congress on 20 July 2006. In November 2006, a ministerial decision outlined provisions for collective bargaining in the private sector but also stated the right of private-sector workers to stage peaceful strikes, and of owners to order lockouts. In February 2010, the GFOTU elected its chairman and its board, composed of 11 members for four years.

17. Interviews, 12 August 2004 and 10 and 21 February 2006.
18. Information collected in Oman in 2002.
19. AFP, 23 July 2002. See also Le Monde, 24 October 2002.
20. al-Sharq al-Awsat, 25 August 2002.
21. AFP, 25 August 2002.
22. Interviews since 2003.
23. In March 2005, there was a second wave of arrests in the military and police; at least 40 officers, including prominent members of the Royal Flight, were accused of "involvement in a conspiracy to overthrow the government" and tried before a military court in June. While they received prison sentences ranging from three to 25 years, they were granted royal pardon one month later (interviews, September 2007; see also the Amnesty International Report 2007, on http://thereport. amnesty.org/eng/Regions/Middle-East-and-North-Africa/Oman).
24. al-Hayat, 26 January 2005.
25. 'Uman, 31 January 2005.
26. The Times of Oman, 3 May 2005.
27. al-Hayat, 19 April 2005.
28. al-Hayat, 21 April 2005.
29. www.aljazeera.net (1 May 2005).
30. www.7days.ae/20050415/Special/At.Omans.heart.asp (checked on 19 April 2005).
31. See www.hrw.org (checked on 19 July 2005) and Reuters, 19 July 2005.
32. Interview, 20 March 2007 and www.omania2.net (checked on 10 April 2007).
33. J. Miller, op. cit., p. 17.
34. Interview, 13 August 2004.

35. On 15 May 2017, these posts were respectively occupied by the Gen. Sultan bin Muhammad al-Na'amani (both director of the office of the Supreme Commander and minister of the Palace Office), Lt-Gen. Hassan bin Muhsin al-Shuraiqi, Lt-Gen. Ahmad bin Harith al-Nabhani, Major-Gen. Matar bin Salim al-Balushi, Air Vice Marshal Matar bin 'Ali al-'Ubaidani, Major-Gen. Khalifa bin 'Abd Allah al-Junaibi, Rear Admiral 'Abd Allah bin Khamis al-Ra'isi, and Lt-Gen. Sa'id bin 'Ali al-Hilali.
36. Interview, 4 May 2004.
37. Interview, 19 May 2003.
38. Interview, 11 September 2003.
39. Interview, 31 January 2003.
40. Meeting place where men of a same district gather regularly, around the sheikh, to discuss the problems in a community. It gave its name in the mid-2000s to the first Omani Internet discussion websites, Sabla 'Uman (www.omania.net).
41. Interview, 25 April 2004.
42. AFP, 13 April 2002; see also AFP, 15 March, 30 March and 6 April 2002.
43. Such popularity has been already noticed by Fariba Adelkhah, in "Qui a peur du mollah Omar? L'économie morale du «talebanisme» dans le Golfe", Critique Internationale, 12 (2001).
44. Interview, 21 February 2003.
45. Personal observations, 23 February and 22 March 2003.
46. Interview, 17 March 2003.
47. O. Winckler, "Gulf Monarchies as Rentier States: the Nationalization Policies of the Labor Force", in J. Kostiner (ed.), op. cit.; A. Kapiszewski, Nationals and Expatriates. Population and Labour Dilemmas of the Gulf Cooperation Council States, Reading, Ithaca Press, 2001.
48. D. Eickelman, "Oman's Next Generation: Challenges and Prospects", in R. Sindelar and J. Peterson (eds), op. cit., p. 170.
49. O. Winckler, Gulf Monarchies, op. cit., p. 246.
50. Speech on the occasion of the opening of the Fourth State Consultative Council session on 9 January 1988, in The Royal Speeches, op. cit., p. 112.
51. Financial Times, 4 April 1990.
52. AFP, 19 January 1994.
53. Speech on the occasion of the conclusion of the annual tour on 31 January 1995, in The Royal Speeches, op. cit., p. 176.
54. Speech on the occasion of the 28th National Day, 18 November 1998, in ibid., p. 208.
55. MEED, 4 May 2001, p. 24.
56. The Times of Oman, 20 January 2003.
57. The Intilaqa programme had been started in 1995, while Sanad was totally new.
58. The Oman Daily Observer, 7 August 2004.

59. The Times of Oman, 19 May 2003.

60. al-Watan, 9 and 21 February 2005.

61. "Back Cover: Letter from Muscat" available at http://meionline.com/backcover/print256.shtml (11 February 2005).

62. Interview, 30 May 2003.

63. The Times of Oman, 30 January 2007.

64. Except when otherwise stated, figures are drawn from the National Centre for Statistics and Information website (www.ncsi.gov.om).

65. The Daily Oman Observer, 21 November 2005.

66. Interview, 6 September 2005.

67. The Times of Oman, 28 March 2005.

68. It consists of OR 225 as a basic salary plus OR 100 as transport and housing allowance.

69. Interview, 16 September 2003.

70. Interview, 26 January 2003. OR 120 was the basic minimum wage at the time of the interview.

71. Interview, 29 August 2005.

72. http://meionline.com/backcover/print256.shtml (checked on 11 February 2005).

73. Khalil al-Khonji, Secretary of the Businessmen' Council, in Times of Oman, 2 February 2003.

74. Interview, 21 January 2003.

75. Interview, 30 August 2005.

76. Interview, 11 May 2003.

77. O. Winckler, Gulf Monarchies, op. cit., p. 41.

78. Middle East Economist Digest, 2 May 2003, p. 23. When we directly tackled this issue with a senior official of the Ministry of National Economy in charge of this issue, his answer expressed the shared embarrassment: "I do not have figures. But I think it is not too low..." (Interview, 31 August 2005).

79. Economist Intelligence Unit. Country Report Oman (March 2004), p. 17.

80. Interview, 30 August 2005.

81. For 2003, see www.moneoman.gov.om/123/population/14–2.htm (checked on 18 October 2004); for 1995, see Oman Family Health Survey 1995: Principal Reports. Muscat, Ministry of Health, 2000, p. 88.

82. Interview, 7 March 2003.

83. 'Uman, 20 December 2006.

84. For instance, costs of residential plots in al-Mawaleh quarter of Muscat have risen from OR 8,000 to 35,000 between 2005 and 2007; houses sold in August 2006 for OR 100,000 in al-'Azaiba quarter were evaluated at OR 400,000 in early 2008 (personal interview).

85. Interview, 10 May 2003.

86. Interview, 30 August 2005.

87. Interview, 30 August 2003.

88. Interview, 4 September 2005.

89. Interview, 30 August 2005.

90. International Herald Tribune, 9 April 2004.

91. MEED, 2 May 2003, p. 26.

92. Muscat Daily, 8 February 2014.

93. MEED, 14–20 January 2005, p. 43.

94. 1.usa.gov/1ub7Bwh (checked on 8 August 2014).

95. www.soharportandfreezone.com.

96. MEED, 10–16 June 2005, pp. 47–8.

97. Statistical Yearbook 2016, op. cit.

98. MEED, 10–16 June 2005, p. 48.

99. Interview, 24 March 2006.

100. 'Uman, 9 February 2005.

101. The Middle East and North Africa 2007, London, Routledge, 2007, p. 862.

102. C. Allen and L. Rigsbee, op. cit., p. 141.

103. The Middle East and North Africa 2005, London, Europa Publications, 2004, pp. 908 and 917.

104. The Times of Oman, 17 September 2003. In 2010, the new tax system cancelled the distinction between local and foreign companies by establishing a fixed tax rate on profits of 12% for all companies after an initial tax-free exemption of profits of OR 30,000.

105. The Times of Oman, 16 October 2006.

106. Maqbul al-Sultan, in The Times of Oman, 17 August 2004.

107. 'Uman, 27 October 2005.

108. The Times of Oman, 17 July 2005.

109. "Oman: Resolving a Taxing Issue," Oxford Business Group, 17 June 2009.

110. The Financial Times, 12 June 2001.

8. NATIONAL IDENTITY CHALLENGED?

1. Le Monde, 4 September 1971; The Economist, 8 January 1972.

2. F. Halliday, Arabia Without Sultans, op. cit., pp. 295–6.

3. Gulf News, 17 August 2004.

4. The Times of Oman, 5 February 2003.

5. Interview, 3 September 2005.

6. D. Eickelman, Identité nationale, op. cit., p. 114.

7. Ibid., pp. 105 ff.

8. M. Limbert, Of Ties and Time, op. cit., pp. 186–7.

9. Interview, 17 September 2003.

10. Interview, 31 August 2003.

11. A. al-Riyami, National Genetic Blood Disorders Survey, Muscat, Ministry of Health, 2000, p. 51.

12. K. al-Azri, op. cit.

13. M. Limbert, Of Ties and Time, op. cit, p. 266.

14. Interview, 8 February 2003.

15. Interview, 10 March 2003.

16. Interview, 23 January 2003.

17. T. Jeapes, SAS: Operation Oman, London, William Kimber, 1980, p. 47.

18. Interview, 1 May 2004.

19. Interview, 17 April 2004.

20. Interview, 8 January 2003.

21. Interview, 31 August 2003.

22. Interview, 26 May 2003.

23. Translation of the Arabic "'arab mukassar"; Omanis laugh at the Arabic speech of Indian immigrants and some Baluchi-native citizens.

24. C. Geertz, The Integrative Revolution, op.cit., p. 155.

25. Interview, 21 January 2003.

26. Interviews, 11 and 18 March 2003.

27. Interview, 4 March 2003.

28. O. Roy, op. cit., p. 42 (author's translation).

29. Interview, 19 February 2006.

30. Interview, 15 February 2006.

31. This same quest for origins is currently pursued by Khodjas in Zanzibar. See B. Scarcia Amoretti, "Controcorrente? Il caso della comunità khogia di Zanzibar," Oriente Moderno 1–6 (1995).

32. Interview, 13 February 2006. Many specialists, relying on the widely-accepted idea that Lawatiyya are Hindus converted to Islam, adopt this lexical distinction between "Indian Shi'a" and "Arab Shi'a". See for example C. Allen, "The Indian Merchant Community of Masqat," Bulletin of the School of Oriental and African Studies 44, 1 (1981); W. Madelung, "Khodja," in Encyclopaedia of Islam, vol. V, Leiden, Brill, 1986, pp. 25–6; J. Peterson, Oman's Diverse Society: Northern Oman, op. cit., p. 41.

33. Interview, 7 March 2003.

34. The use of this term does not have any moral connotation, but only designates the process of "re-studying history in order to correct it", pursued by some Lawatiyya scholars as an answer to historical interpretations which consider them as originally Hindu people converted to Islam.

35. C. Allen, The Indian Merchant, op. cit., p. 49.

36. J. al-Khaburi, Al-adwar al-'umaniyya fi al-qara al-hindiyya. Dur Bani Sama bin Lu'ay—Ahl Lawatiyya (The Omani role on the Indian continent. Role of the Bani Sama bin Lu'ay—the Lawatiyya), Beirut, Dar al-nubala', 2001, pp. 47 ff.

37. Interviews, 25 March and 16 September 2003, 20 February 2006.

38. Interview, 16 September 2003; see also C. Allen, The Indian Merchant, op. cit., p. 49.

39. Interview, 20 February 2006.

40. Interview, 22 March 2003.

41. Interview, 11 May 2003.

42. Interview, 22 March 2003.

43. Interview, 2 October 2003.

44. Ibid.

45. O. Roy, "Patronage and Solidarity Groups: Survival or Reformation?" in G. Salamé (ed.) Democracy without Democrats? The Renewal of Politics in the Muslim World, London, I.B. Tauris, 1994, p. 270.

46. Interview, 23 May 2003.

47. Interview, 29 January 2003.

48. Interview, 27 May 2003.

49. Interview, 9 June 2003.

50. Interview, 2 June 2003.

51. Interview, 2 June 2003.

52. For more details, see M. Valeri, "Nation-Building and Communities in Oman since 1970: the Swahili-speaking Omani in Search for Identity", African Affairs 106, 424 (2007).

53. Interview, 31 August 2003.

54. F. Scholz, "La différenciation socio-spatiale de la ville arabo-musulmane. Le cas de Mascate", in M. Lavergne and B. Dumortier (eds), op. cit., p. 203.

55. Interview, 1 May 2004.

56. Interview, 4 May 2004.

57. Statistical Yearbook 2016, op. cit.

58. J. Peterson, "The Emergence of Post-traditional Oman", Durham Middle East Papers, 78 (2004), p. 10.

9. THE OMANI SPRING: TESTING THE QABOOS STATE

1. S. al-Hashimi, 'Uman: al-insan wa-l-sulta (Oman. Man and Power), Beirut: Markaz darasat al-wahda al-'arabiyya, 2013, p. 182.

2. Sultanate of Oman, Oman Statistical Yearbook 2016 (Muscat: National Center for Statistics and Information, 2016), tables 6–14 (p. 307) and 2–15 (p. 335).

3. S. al-Hashimi, op. cit., p. 182.

4. Sultanate of Oman, Monthly Statistical Bulletin March 2011 (Muscat: National Center for Statistics and Information, 2011).

5. "We want to see the benefit of our oil wealth distributed evenly to the population," chanted protesters in Sohar in March 2011.

6. "We will not be silenced; we beg the Sultan to look into our two-month-old demand to sack people who have been embezzling government funds for years" (poster in Salalah protests, May 2011).

7. Interview, Muscat, 11 November 2012.

8. K. al-'Azri, op. cit., pp. xvi and 110.

9. This was reversed by the UAE government after 2003, out of the perception that such a presence could have adverse effects in case of UAE-Oman political tensions.

10. By comparison total population in Oman grew by 18.5% only during the same period.

11. Calculations based on figures of 2003 and 2010 national censuses available on Oman's National Centre for Statistics and Information website (http://www.ncsi.gov.om)

12. Sayyid Haitham set himself up as a businessman in 1991 when he became one of the main shareholders, in partnership with the Special Adviser to the Sultan 'Umar al-Zawawi and the former Minister of National Economy Ahmad Makki, of the newly-privatised Sun Farms agricultural company, one of the biggest owners of lands in Batina and top vegetables producer in Oman (see C. Allen and L. Rigsbee, op. cit., p. 141).

13. "Oman Now Owns Blue City Project," The National, 1 April 2011; Camilla Hall, "Oman Fund Seeks to Buy Blue City Bonds," The Financial Times, 7 November 2012.

14. Interview, Muscat, 10 October 2011.

15. In January 2011 the Omani security forces claimed that they had uncovered a UAE spy ring within the Omani government and military. The UAE denied the allegations (Oman News Agency, 30 January 2011).

16. Interview with a coordinator of Sohar protests, 11 October 2011.

17. Interview with a businessman from Sohar, 13 November 2012.

18. Interviews, October and November 2012.

19. In preparation for the 34th GCC summit in December 2013, the Minister responsible for Foreign Affairs Yusef bin 'Alawi declared that Oman would not prevent the upgrading of the GCC into a union of six countries, but would "not be part of it" if it happens. However in January 2014 Sultan Qaboos ratified the GCC security pact signed in November 2012, which strengthens cooperation and mutual assistance in security matters. It allows the hunting down of those who are outside the law or the system, or who are wanted by party states, regardless of their nationalities, and the taking of necessary measures against them. It also allows the integration of signatories' security apparatuses to provide support during times of security disturbances and unrest in a signatory state.

20. See for instance the US Department of State Country Reports for Oman on Human Rights Practices 2012 (1.usa.gov/URP0Gp), and 2013 (1.usa.

gov/1s8ym3S); Gulf Center for Human Rights, "Torture in Oman," 29 January 2014 (http://gc4hr.org/report/view/20); "Oman: Rights Routinely Trampled," Human Rights Watch, 19 December 2014.

21. Stockholm Institute for Peace Research Institute (SIPRI), "Military Expenditure Database" (available here: https://www.sipri.org/databases/milex).

22. SIPRI, "Trends in World Military Expenditure 2012", April 2013 (available here: http://books.sipri.org/product_info?c_product_id=458).

23. Quoted in H. Eakin, "In the Heart of Mysterious Oman," The New York Review of Books 61(13), 14 August 2014, p. 59.

24. "Sohar Protesters Given Five-Year Jail Term", Gulf News, 28 June 2011; "Court Jails 12 in Sohar Terrorism Case", Gulf News, 7 July 2011. These sentences were upheld by Oman's Supreme Court in April 2012.

25. Talib al-Ma'amari, in Liwa (Batina), Salim al-'Aufi, in Izki (Dakhliyya) and Salim al-Ma'ashani, in Taqa (Dhofar).

26. "Oman Editors Jailed for 'Insulting' Justice Minister", BBC, 21 September 2011 (http://www.bbc.co.uk/news/world-middle-east-15009766). On 31 December 2011, the court of appeal upheld the verdict.

27. In addition the ruler can issue royal decrees that have the same power of law between the terms of the Council of Oman and during the adjourned period of the Consultative Council and the holding of the State Council sessions (article 58 bis 39).

28. On 29 October 2011, Wadi al-Ma'awil (Batina) representative Khalid bin Hilal al-Ma'awali was elected chairman of the Majlis al-Shura by its members. A former Director General for Investment of the Ministry of Tourism (2005–8) and member of the Muscat Municipality Council (2005–8), Khalid al-Ma'awali was a member of the USA-Oman Free Trade Agreement negotiation team. Member of the board of trustees of the first Omani private university (Sohar University) since 2001, he has been active in business, as chairman and member of the board of a number of hospitality and finance companies listed on the Muscat Securities Market. One of his brothers Nasir has been chairman of the State Audit Institution (with a rank of minister) since 2011, and his cousin Lieutenant-General (Rtd.) Hilal bin Khalid al-Ma'awali is a former Inspector General for Police and Customs and Minister of Civil Service (2004–7).

29. Previously only Muscat governorate had a (fully-appointed) municipal council.

30. "50 Candidates Rejected," Gulf News, 21 December 2012. In December 2016, only 39.9 percent of the 623,224 registered voters cast their ballots in the municipal elections ("Women Win New Seats on Oman Municipal Councils," AFP, 26 December 2016).

31. "Omani CEO Jailed for 23 Years in Graft Case: Court," Reuters, 27 February 2014; "Ahkam wa qadaya jadida fi muhakamat al-fasad" (New Verdicts and Cases in Corruption Trials), al-Zaman, 3 March 2014.

32. Interview, 13 November 2012.
33. C. A. Ennis and R. Z. al-Jamali, "Elusive Employment. Development Planning and Labor Market Trends in Oman," Chatham House Research Paper, September 2014, p. 14.
34. "Oman Producing All-Out on Oil As Price Rout Seen Over," Bloomberg, 22 February 2015.
35. "Oman 2017 State Budget Projects Smaller Deficit, Continued Austerity," Reuters, 1 January 2017.
36. Oman News Agency, 13 June 2012.
37. Interview, Sohar, 13 November 2012.
38. "Oman: Rights Routinely Trampled," Human Rights Watch, 19 December 2014.
39. "Idana Udu Majlis al-Shura Talib al-Ma'amari Bi 3 Sanawat Sijn" (Majlis al-Shura Member Talib al-Ma'amari Sentenced to Three Years of Jail), al-Balad, 30 October 2014.
40. Interview, Sohar, 13 November 2012.
41. "Al-sultat tufrij an al-katib 'Ali al-Rawahi bad ayyam min al-tahqiq" (Authorities Free Writer 'Ali al-Rawahi After Days of Interrogations), al-Balad, 2 January 2015.
42. "Mowaten Online Magazine Ceases Publication Due to Harassment of the Internal Security Services," Gulf Center for Human Rights, 20 January 2016.
43. "Oman Court Reverses Ban on Al Zaman Daily," Gulf News, 26 December 2016.
44. The law prohibits members of the armed forces, other public security institutions, government employees, and domestic workers from forming or joining unions.
45. "Oman Bans Strikes at Facilities Providing Essential Services," Muscat Daily, 11 November 2013.
46. "Lack of Coordination Blamed for Octal Strike," Gulf News, 9 March 2014.
47. The full text (in Arabic) of the law is available of the ministry of Legal Affairs website: http://mola.gov.om/royals.aspx?Gzy=14.
48. D. Eickelman, From Theocracy to Monarchy, op. cit., p. 18.
49. Interview, Muscat, 14 November 2012.
50. Ibid.
51. United National Development Programme, "Human Development Report 2010. The Real Wealth of Nations: Pathways to Human Development," New York, 2010, p. 29.
52. Personal electronical communication, 16 June 2012.
53. Poster during a protest in Salalah, 30 April 2011.
54. Ibid.
55. Interview, Muscat, 15 November 2012.
56. Interview, Muscat, 11 October 2011.
57. Interview, Muscat, 14 November 2012.
58. Interview, Muscat, 16 October 2011.
59. "Statement by the United Nations Special Rapporteur on the rights to freedom

of peaceful assembly and of association at the conclusion of his visit to the Sultanate of Oman," Muscat, 13 September 2014, www.ohchr.org/EN/NewsEvents/Pages/DisplayNews.aspx?NewsID=15028&LangID=E.

60. Interview, Sohar, 12 October 2011.

SELECT BIBLIOGRAPHY

Books

Calvin H. Allen and W. Lynn Rigsbee, *Oman under Qaboos: From Coup to Constitution, 1970–1996*, London, Frank Cass, 2000.

Khalid al-Azri, *Social and Gender Inequality in Oman: The Power of Religious and Political Tradition*, London, Routledge, 2012.

Fredrik Barth, *Sohar: Culture and Society in an Omani Town*, Baltimore, Johns Hopkins University Press, 1983.

John Beasant, *Oman: The True-Life Drama and Intrigue of an Arab State*, Edinburgh, Mainstream, 2002.

Hazem Beblawi and Giacomo Luciani (eds), *The Rentier State*, London, Croom Helm, 1987.

Mohammed Reda Bhacker, *Trade and Empire in Muscat and Zanzibar: Roots of British Domination*, London, Routledge, 1992.

Hugh Boustead, *The Wind of Morning*, London, Chatto and Windus, 1974.

John R. L. Carter, *Tribes in Oman*, London, Peninsular Publishing, 1982.

Dawn Chatty, *Mobile Pastoralists: Development Planning and Social Change in Oman*, New York, Columbia University Press, 1996.

Jill Crystal, *Oil and Politics in the Gulf: Rulers and Merchants in Kuwait and Qatar*, Cambridge, Cambridge University Press, 1995.

Christopher Davidson (ed.), *Power and Politics in the Persian Gulf Monarchies*, London, Hurst, 2011.

Paul Dresch and James Piscatori (eds), *Monarchies and Nations: Globalisation and Identity in the Arab States of the Gulf*, London, I. B. Tauris, 2005.

Christine Eickelman, *Women and Community in Oman*, New York, New York University Press, 1984.

Dale F. Eickelman, *The Middle East and Central Asia: an Anthropological Approach*, 4th ed., Upper Saddle River, Prentice Hall, 2002.

F. Gregory Gause, *Oil Monarchies: Domestic and Security Challenges in the Arab Gulf States*, New York, Council on Foreign Relations Press, 1994.

Hussein Ghubash, *Oman: The Islamic Democratic Tradition*, New York, Routledge, 2006.

Fred Halliday, *Arabia without Sultans*, London, Penguin Books, 1974.

Adam Hanieh, *Capitalism and Class in the Gulf Arab States*, New York, Palgrave McMillan, 2011.

Sa'id al-Hashimi (ed.), *Al-rabi' al-'umani. Qara'a fi-l-siyaqat wa-l-dalalat* (The Omani Spring. A Reading of its Context and Implications), Beirut, Dar al-Farabi, 2013.

———, *'Uman: al-insan wa-l-sulta* (Oman: Man and Power), Beirut, Markaz dirasat al-wahda al-'arabiyya, 2013.

Abdulmalik al-Hinai, *State Formation in Oman, 1861–1970* (University of London, unpublished PhD, 1991).

Valerie J. Hoffman, *The Essentials of Ibâdî Islam*, Syracuse, Syracuse University Press, 2012.

Derek Hopwood (ed.), *The Arabian Peninsula: Society and Politics*, London, Georges Allen and Unwin, 1972.

Ibn Ruzaiq, *Al-fath al-mubin fi-sirat al-sada al-Bu Sa'idiyyin* (The Glorious Conquest in the al-Busa'idi History), 5th ed., Muscat, Ministry of National Heritage and Culture, 2001 [1st ed. 1858].

Sonallah Ibrahim, *Warda*, Arles, Actes Sud, 2002.

Jorg Janzen, *Nomads in the Sultanate of Oman: Tradition and Development in Dhofar*, Boulder, Westview Press, 1986.

Jeremy Jones and Nicholas Ridout, *Oman, Culture and Diplomacy*, Edinburgh, Edinburgh University Press, 2012.

Andrzej Kapiszewski, *Nationals and Expatriates: Population and Labour Dilemmas of the Gulf Cooperation Council States*, Reading, Ithaca Press, 2001.

Joseph A. Kechichian, *Oman and the World: the Emergence of an Independent Foreign Policy*, Santa Monica, Rand, 1995.

Abdulhadi Khalaf and Giacomo Luciani (eds), *Constitutional Reform and Political Participation in the Gulf*, Dubai, Gulf Research Center, 2006.

Sulaiman al-Kharussi, *Malamah min al-tarikh al-'umani* (Outline of the Omani history), 3rd ed., Seeb: Maktab al-damri li-nashr wa-l-tawzi', 2002.

Philip S. Khoury and Joseph Kostiner (eds), *Tribes and State Formation in the Middle East*, London, I. B. Tauris, 1991.

Joseph Kostiner, *Middle East Monarchies: the Challenge of Modernity*, London, Lynne Rienner, 2000.

Robert G. Landen, *Oman since 1856: Disruptive Modernization in a Traditional Arab Society*, Princeton, Princeton University Press, 1967.

Marc Lavergne and Brigitte Dumortier (eds), *L'Oman contemporain: Etat, territoire, identité*, Paris, Karthala, 2003.

Mandana E. Limbert, *In the Time of Oil: Piety, Memory, and Social Life in an Omani Town*, Stanford, Stanford University Press, 2010.

John G. Lorimer, *Gazetteer of the Persian Gulf, ʿOman, and Central Arabia*, Gerrards Cross, Archives Editions, 1986 [1ˢᵗ ed.: 1915].

Laurence Louër, *Transnational Shia Politics: Religious and Political Networks in the Gulf*, London, Hurst, 2008.

Khaldun al-Naqeeb, *Society and State in the Gulf and Arab Peninsula: a Different Perspective*, London, Center for Arab Unity Studies, 1990 [1ˢᵗ ed. 1987].

Francis Owtram, *A Modern History of Oman: Formation of the State since 1920*, London, I. B. Tauris, 2004.

John E. Peterson, *Oman in the Twentieth Century: Political Foundations of an Emerging Arab State*, London, Croom Helm, 1978.

——, *Oman's Insurgencies: The Sultanate's Struggle for Supremacy*, London, Saqi Books, 2007.

——, *Historical Muscat: An Illustrated Guide and Gazetteer*, Leiden, Brill, 2007.

Sergey Plekhanov, *A Reformer on the Throne: Sultan Qaboos bin Said Al Said*, London, Trident Press, 2004.

Lawrence G. Potter (ed.), *Sectarian Politics in the Persian Gulf*, London, Hurst, 2013.

Brian R. Pridham (ed.), *Oman: Economic, Social and Strategic Developments*, London, Croom Helm, 1987.

Uzi Rabi, *The Emergence of States in a Tribal Society: Oman under Saʿid bin Taymur, 1932–1970*, Portland, Sussex Academic Press, 2006.

Riad al-Rayyes, *Dhufar: Al-siraʿ al-siyassi wa-l-ʿaskari fi al-khalij al-ʿarabi 1970–1976* (Dhofar. Political and Military Conflicts in the Arabian Gulf, 1970–1976), London, Riad el-Rayyes Books, 1997.

Carol J. Riphenburg, *Oman: Political Development in a Changing World*, Westport, Praeger, 1998.

Basma Mubarak Saʿid, *al-Tajruba al-Dusturiyya fi ʿUman* (Constitutional Experience in Oman), Beirut, Markaz dirasat al-wahda al-ʿarabiyya, 2013.

Muhammad al-Salimi, *Nahdat al-aʿyan bi-hurriyat ʿUman* (The Renaissance of the Notables Through the History of Oman), Cairo, n.d.

Nur al-Din al-Salimi, *Tuhfat al-aʿyan bi-sirat ahl ʿUman* (The Work of the Notables in the History of the People of Oman), Seeb, Maktabiyya Nur al-Din al-Salimi, 2000 [1ˢᵗ ed.: 1913].

Oliver Schlumberger (ed.), *Debating Arab Authoritarianism: Dynamics and Durability in Nondemocratic Regimes*, Stanford, Stanford University Press, 2007.

Salim al-Siyabi, *ʿUman abr al-tarikh* (Oman throughout History), 4th ed., Muscat, Ministry of National Heritage and Culture, 2001 [1ˢᵗ ed. 1982].

Ian Skeet, *Oman before 1970: the End of an Era*, London, Faber and Faber, 1985.

——, *Oman: Politics and Development*, London, McMillan, 1992.

Abdel Razzaq Takriti, *Monsoon Revolution: Republicans, Sultans, and Empires in Oman, 1965–1976*, Oxford, Oxford University Press, 2013.

Wilfred Thesiger, *Arabian Sands*, London, Penguin, 1985 [1ˢᵗ ed. 1959].

John Townsend, *Oman: The Making of a Modern State*, London, Croom Helm, 1977.

Fawwaz Trabulsi, *Dhufar. Shihada min zaman al-thawra* (Dhofar: Account from the Time of Revolution), London, Riad el-Rayyes Books, 1998.

Marc Valeri, *Le sultanat d'Oman: une révolution en trompe-l'œil*, Paris, Karthala, 2007.

Unni Wikan, *Behind the Veil in Arabia: Women in Oman*, Baltimore, Johns Hopkins University Press, 1982.

John C. Wilkinson, *The Imamate Tradition of Oman*, Cambridge, Cambridge University Press, 1987.

———, *Ibâḍism: Origins and Early Development in Oman*, London, Oxford University Press, 2010.

Steffen Wippel (ed.), *Regionalizing Oman: Political, Economic and Social Dynamics*, London, Springer, 2013.

Journal Articles and Chapters in books

Salem Abdullah, 'Omani Islamism: an Unexpected Confrontation with the Government', Washington DC, *United Association for Studies and Research* (September 1995, Occasional Papers Series no. 8).

Abdulla Juma Alhaj, 'The Political Elite and the Introduction of Political Participation in Oman', *Middle East Policy*, 7 (3), 2000, pp. 97–110.

Calvin H. Allen, 'The Indian Merchant Community of Masqat', *Bulletin of the School of Oriental and African Studies*, 44, 1981, pp. 39–53.

Lisa Anderson, 'Absolutism and the Resilience of Monarchy in the Middle East', *Political Science Quarterly*, 106 (1), 1991, pp. 1–15.

Claire Beaudevin, 'Souks féminins en Oman: séparatisme commercial ou renforcement d'une culture de genre?', *Chroniques Yéménites*, 12, 2004, pp. 141–73.

———, 'Old Diseases and Contemporary Crisis. Inherited Blood Disorders in Oman', *Anthropology & Medicine*, 20 (2), 2013, pp. 175–189.

Dawn Chatty, 'Women Working in Oman: Individual Choice and Cultural Constraints', *International Journal of Middle East Studies*, 32 (2), 2000, pp. 241–54.

———, 'Rituals of Royalty and the Elaboration of Ceremony in Oman: View from the Edge', *International Journal of Middle East Studies*, 41 (1), 2009, pp. 39–58.

Dale F. Eickelman, 'Religious Tradition, Economic Domination and Political Legitimacy: Morocco and Oman', *Revue de l'Occident Musulman et de la Méditerranée*, 29, 1980, pp. 17–30.

———, 'Kings and People: Oman's State Consultative Council', *Middle East Journal*, 38 (1), 1984, pp. 51–71.

———, 'From Theocracy to Monarchy: Authority and Legitimacy in Inner Oman, 1935–1957', *International Journal of Middle East Studies*, 17, 1985, pp. 3–24.

———, 'Identité nationale et discours religieux en Oman', in Gilles Kepel and Yann Richard (eds), *Intellectuels et militants de l'Islam contemporain*, Paris, le Seuil, 1990, pp. 103–28.

———, 'Mass Higher Education and the Religious Imagination in Contemporary Arab Societies', *American Ethnologist*, 19 (4), 1992, pp. 643–55.

Abdullah Juma al-Haj, 'The Politics of Participation in the Gulf Cooperation Council States: the Omani Consultative Council', *Middle East Journal*, 50 (4), 1996, pp. 559–71.

Valerie Hoffman, 'The Articulation of Ibadi Identity in Modern Oman and Zanzibar', *The Muslim World*, 94, 2004, pp. 201–16.

Jeremy Jones and Nicholas Ridout, 'Democratic Development in Oman', *Middle East Journal*, 59 (3), 2005, pp. 376–92.

Anne Joyce, 'Interview with Sultan Qaboos bin Said Al Said', *Middle East Policy*, 3 (4), 1995, pp. 1–6.

Mark Katz, 'Assessing the Political Stability of Oman', *Middle East Review of International Affairs*, 8 (3), 2004, pp. 1–9.

Colette Le Cour Grandmaison, 'Rich Cousins, Poor Cousins: Hidden Stratification among the Omani Arabs in Eastern Africa', *Africa*, 59 (2), 1989, pp. 176–84.

Judith Miller, 'Creating Modern Oman: An Interview with Sultan Qabus', *Foreign Affairs*, 76 (3), 1997, pp. 13–8.

John E. Peterson, 'Britain and 'the Oman War': An Arabian Entanglement', *Asian Affairs*, 63 (3), 1976, pp. 285–98.

———, 'Guerilla Warfare and Ideological Confrontation in the Arabian Peninsula: the Rebellion in Dhufar', *World Affairs*, 139 (4), 1977, pp. 278–95.

———, 'Legitimacy and Political Change in Yemen and Oman', *Orbis*, 27 (4), 1984, pp. 971–98.

———, 'Oman's Diverse Society: Northern Oman', *Middle East Journal*, 58 (1), 2004, pp. 32–51.

———, 'Oman's Diverse Society: Southern Oman', *Middle East Journal*, 58 (2), 2004, pp. 254–69.

———, 'The Emergence of Post-Traditional Oman', *Durham Middle East Papers*, 78, 2004, pp. 1–21.

———, 'Three and Half Decades of Change and Development', *Middle East Policy*, 11 (2), 2004, pp. 125–37.

Uzi Rabi, 'Majlis al-Shura and Majlis al-Dawla: Weaving Old Practices and New Realities in the Process of State Formation in Oman', *Middle Eastern Studies*, 38 (4), 2002, pp. 41–50.

———, 'Oman's Foreign Policy: the Art of Keeping all Channels of Communication Open', *Orient*, 46 (4), 2005, pp. 549–64.

Nikolaus Siegfried, 'Legislation and Legitimation in Oman: the Basic Law', *Islamic Law and Society*, 7 (2), 2000, pp. 358–97.

SELECT BIBLIOGRAPHY

Abdel Razzaq Takriti, 'The 1970 Coup in Oman Reconsidered', *Journal of Arabian Studies*, 3 (2), 2013, pp. 155–173.

Marc Valeri, 'Nation-Building and Communities in Oman since 1970: the Swahili-Speaking Omani in Search for Identity', *African Affairs*, 106 (424), 2007, pp. 479–96.

———, 'High Visibility, Low Profile: The Shia in Oman under Sultan Qaboos', *International Journal of Middle East Studies*, 42 (2), 2010, pp. 251–268.

———, '"J'ai respiré l'air de la liberté". La légitimation autoritaire au Bahreïn et en Oman à l'épreuve du "printemps arabe"', Critique Internationale, 61, 2013, pp. 107–126.

Unni Wikan, 'Man Becomes Woman: Transsexualism in Oman as a Key to Gender Roles', *Man* (New Series), 13 (2), 1977, pp. 304–19.

Onn Winckler, 'Demographic Developments and Policies in the Arabian Gulf: the Case of Oman under Sultan Qaboos', *Journal of South Asian and Middle Eastern Studies*, 24 (3), 2001, pp. 34–60.

———, 'The Challenge of Foreign Workers in the Persian/Arabian Gulf: the Case of Oman', *Immigrants and Minorities*, 19 (2), 2000, pp. 23–52.

INDEX